Summary of Contents

CSS MASTER

BY TIFFANY B. BROWN

CSS Master

by Tiffany B. Brown

Copyright © 2015 SitePoint Pty. Ltd.

Product Manager: Simon Mackie   **English Editor**: Ralph Mason
Technical Reviewer: Rachel Andrew   **Cover Designer**: Alex Walker

Notice of Rights

All rights reserved. No part of this book may be reproduced, stored in a retrieval system or transmitted in any form or by any means, without the prior written permission of the publisher, except in the case of brief quotations embodied in critical articles or reviews.

Notice of Liability

The author and publisher have made every effort to ensure the accuracy of the information herein. However, the information contained in this book is sold without warranty, either express or implied. Neither the authors and SitePoint Pty. Ltd., nor its dealers or distributors will be held liable for any damages to be caused either directly or indirectly by the instructions contained in this book, or by the software or hardware products described herein.

Trademark Notice

Rather than indicating every occurrence of a trademarked name as such, this book uses the names only in an editorial fashion and to the benefit of the trademark owner with no intention of infringement of the trademark.

Published by SitePoint Pty. Ltd.

48 Cambridge Street Collingwood
VIC Australia 3066
Web: www.sitepoint.com
Email: business@sitepoint.com

ISBN 978-0-9941826-2-3 (print)

ISBN 978-0-9943469-4-0 (ebook)
Printed and bound in the United States of America

About Tiffany B. Brown

Tiffany B. Brown is a freelance web developer and writer based in Los Angeles, California. She has worked on the web for more than a decade, for a mix of media companies and agencies. Brown is also a co-author of SitePoint's "Jump Start: HTML5." Before founding her consultancy, Webinista, Inc, she was part of the Opera Software Developer Relations & Tools team. Now she offers web development and consulting services to agencies and small design teams.

About SitePoint

SitePoint specializes in publishing fun, practical, and easy-to-understand content for web professionals. Visit http://www.sitepoint.com/ to access our blogs, books, newsletters, articles, and community forums. You'll find a stack of information on JavaScript, PHP, Ruby, mobile development, design, and more.

To Molly H.

Table of Contents

Chapter 2   CSS Architecture and Organization

Chapter 3   Debugging and Optimization

Chapter 7   Applying CSS Conditionally

Chapter 8   Using CSS with SVG

Chapter 9   Preprocessors

Preface

CSS has grown from a language for formatting documents into a robust language for designing web applications. Its syntax is easy to learn, making CSS a great entry point for those new to programming. Indeed, it's often the second language that developers learn, right behind HTML.

The simplicity of CSS is deceptive, however. It belies the complexity of the box model, stacking contexts, specificity, and the cascade. It's tough to develop interfaces that work across a variety of screen sizes and with an assortment of input mechanisms. CSS mastery lies in understanding these concepts and how to mitigate them.

Mastering CSS development also means learning how to work with new tools such as linters, optimizers, and preprocessors. Linters inspect your code for potential trouble spots. Preprocessors make writing and organizing CSS easier. Optimizers improve CSS quality, and reduce the number of bytes delivered to the browser. And of course, there's the question of CSS architecture: which selectors to use, how to modularize files, and how to prevent selector creep.

CSS is also growing in its capabilities. Until now, we've had to use clunky methods such as float, or weighty JavaScript libraries to create the kinds of layouts made possible with the flexbox and multi-column layout modules. Three-dimensional effects were impossible—or required images—before the rise of CSS transforms. What's on the horizon is even more exciting.

It's really a fascinating time to be a front-end developer. My hope is that you'll come away from this book with a better sense of how CSS works and how to write it well.

Who Should Read This Book

This book is for intermediate-level CSS developers, as it assumes a fair amount of experience with HTML and CSS. No time is spent covering the basics of CSS syntax. Coverage of CSS concepts such as the box model and positioning are included to illuminate tricky concepts for the experienced developer. They're not meant as an introduction for beginners. Experience with JavaScript/DOM Scripting is helpful, but not necessary.

Conventions Used

You'll notice that we've used certain typographic and layout styles throughout this book to signify different types of information. Look out for the following items.

Code Samples

Code in this book is displayed using a fixed-width font, like so:

```html
<h1>A Perfect Summer's Day</h1>
<p>It was a lovely day for a walk in the park. The birds
were singing and the kids were all back at school.</p>
```

If the code is to be found in the book's code archive, the name of the file will appear at the top of the program listing, like this:

example.css

```css
.footer {
  background-color: #CCC;
  border-top: 1px solid #333;
}
```

If only part of the file is displayed, this is indicated by the word *excerpt*:

example.css (excerpt)

```css
  border-top: 1px solid #333;
```

If additional code is to be inserted into an existing example, the new code will be displayed in bold:

```
function animate() {
  new_variable = "Hello";
}
```

Where existing code is required for context, rather than repeat all of it, ⋮ will be displayed:

```
function animate() {
  ⋮
  return new_variable;
}
```

Some lines of code should be entered on one line, but we've had to wrap them because of page constraints. An ➥ indicates a line break that exists for formatting purposes only, and should be ignored:

```
URL.open("http://www.sitepoint.com/responsive-web-design-real-user-
➥testing/?responsive1");
```

Tips, Notes, and Warnings

 Hey, You!

Tips provide helpful little pointers.

 Ahem, Excuse Me ...

Notes are useful asides that are related—but not critical—to the topic at hand. Think of them as extra tidbits of information.

 Make Sure You Always ...

... pay attention to these important points.

 Watch Out!

Warnings highlight any gotchas that are likely to trip you up along the way.

Supplementary Materials

https://www.sitepoint.com/premium/books/csspro1
The book's website, containing links, updates, resources, and more.

https://github.com/spbooks/csspro1/
The downloadable code archive for this book.

http://community.sitepoint.com/

SitePoint's forums, for help on any tricky web problems.

books@sitepoint.com

Our email address, should you need to contact us for support, to report a problem, or for any other reason.

Want to take your learning further?

Thanks for choosing to buy a SitePoint book. Would you like to continue learning? You can now gain unlimited access to ALL SitePoint books and courses plus high-quality books from our selected partners at SitePoint Premium[1]. Enroll now and start learning today!

---

[1] https://www.sitepoint.com/premium/home

Selectors

CSS rules are matched to elements with **selectors**. There are a number of ways to do this, and you're probably familiar with most of them. Element type, class name, ID, and attribute selectors are all well-supported and widely used.

The Selectors Level 3[1] and Level 4[2] specifications introduced several new selectors. In some cases, these are new variations of existing types. In other cases, they are new features of the language.

In this chapter, we'll look at the current browser landscape for CSS selectors, with a focus on newer selectors. This includes new attribute selectors and combinators, and a range of new pseudo-classes. In the section *Choosing Selectors Wisely*, we look at the concept of specificity.

This chapter stops short of being a comprehensive look at all selectors—that could be a book unto itself. Instead, we'll focus on selectors with good browser support that are likely to be useful in your current work. Some material may be old hat, but it's included for context.

---

[1] http://dev.w3.org/csswg/selectors-3/

[2] http://dev.w3.org/csswg/selectors-4/

Browser Coverage for Selectors

A comprehensive look at the current state of browser support for selectors can be found at CSS4-Selectors.[3]

Combinators

Combinators are character sequences that express a relationship between the selectors on either side of it. Using a combinator creates what's known as a complex selector. **Complex selectors** can, in some cases, be the most concise way to define styles.

You should be familiar with most of these combinators:

- descendant combinator, or whitespace character
- child combinator, or >
- adjacent sibling combinator, or +
- general sibling combinator, or ~

Let's illustrate each of these combinators. We'll use them to add styles to the HTML form shown in Figure 1.1.

---

[3] http://css4-selectors.com/

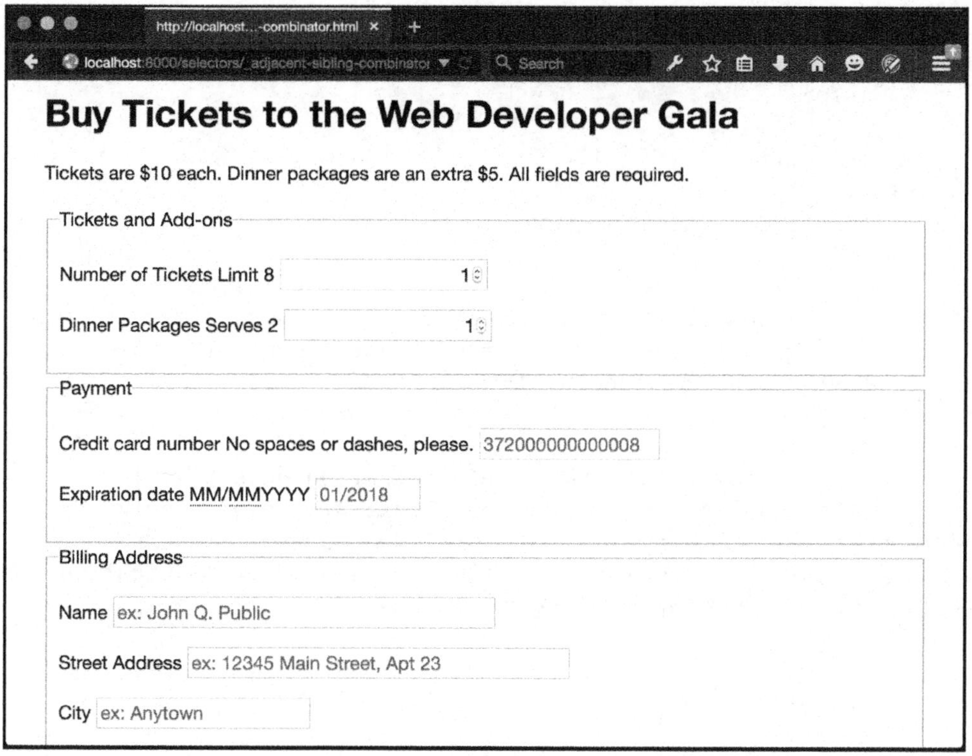

Figure 1.1. Our HTML form that we'll style using combinators

This form was created using the following chunk of HTML:

```
<form method="GET" action="/processor">
    <h1>Buy Tickets to the Web Developer Gala</h1>
    <p>Tickets are $10 each. Dinner packages are an extra $5. All
➥ fields are required.</p>
    <fieldset>
        <legend>Tickets and Add-ons</legend>

        <p>
            <label for="quantity">Number of Tickets</label>
            <span class="help">Limit 8</span>
            <input type="number" value="1" name="quantity"
➥ id="quantity" step="1" min="1" max="8">
    </p>

        <p>
            <label for="quantity">Dinner Packages</label>
            <span class="help">Serves 2</span>
```

```
                <input type="number" value="1" name="quantity"
➡ id="quantity" step="1" min="1" max="8">
        </p>

    </fieldset>
    <fieldset>
        <legend>Payment</legend>
        <p>
            <label for="ccn">Credit card number</label>
            <span class="help">No spaces or dashes, please.</span>
            <input type="text" id="ccn" name="ccn" placeholder=
➡"372000000000008" maxlength="16" size="16">
        </p>
        <p>
            <label for="expiration">Expiration date</label>
            <span class="help"><abbr title="Two-digit month">MM
➡</abbr>/<abbr title="Four-digit Year">MM</abbr>YYYY</span>
            <input type="text" id="expiration" name="expiration"
➡placeholder="01/2018" maxlength="7" size="7">
        </p>

    </fieldset>
    <fieldset>
        <legend>Billing Address</legend>
        <p>
            <label for="name">Name</label>
            <input type="text" id="name" name="name" placeholder=
➡"ex: John Q. Public" size="40">
        </p>
        <p>
            <label for="street_address">Street Address</label>
            <input type="text" id="name" name="name" placeholder=
➡"ex: 12345 Main Street, Apt 23" size="40">
        </p>

        <p>
            <label for="city">City</label>
            <input type="text" id="city" name="city" placeholder=
➡"ex: Anytown">
        </p>

        <p>
            <label for="state">State</label>
            <input type="text" id="state" name="state" placeholder=
➡"CA" maxlength="2" pattern="[A-W]{2}" size="2">
```

```
        </p>

        <p>
            <label for="zip">ZIP</label>
            <input type="text" id="zip" name="zip" placeholder=
➥"12345" maxlength="5" pattern="0-9{5}" size="5">
        </p>
    </fieldset>

    <button type="submit">Buy Tickets!</button>
</form>
```

The Descendant Combinator

You're probably quite familiar with the descendant combinator. It's been around since the early days of CSS (though it was without a type name until CSS2.1). It's widely used and widely supported.

The **descendant combinator** is just a whitespace character. It separates the parent selector from its descendant, following the pattern *A B*, where *B* is an element contained by *A*. Let's add some CSS to our markup from above and see how this works:

01-selectors/descendent-combinator.html *(excerpt)*

```
form h1 {
    color: #009;
}
```

We've just changed the color of our form title, the result of which can be seen in Figure 1.2.

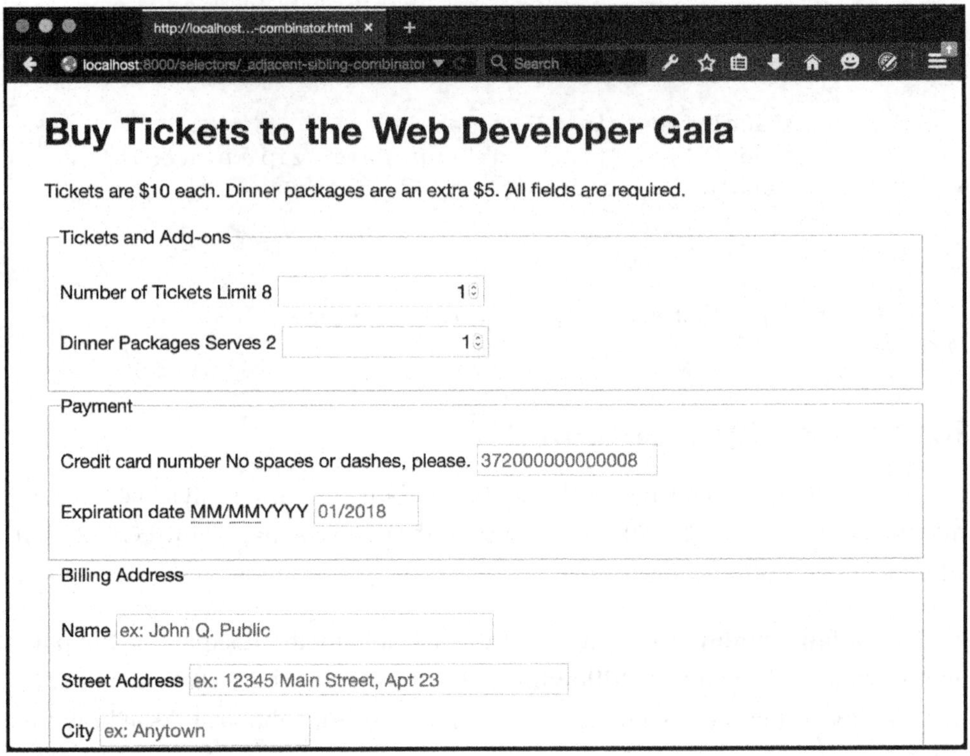

Figure 1.2. The effect of a descendant combinator

Let's add some more CSS, this time to increase the size of our pricing message ("Tickets are $10 each"):

01-selectors/descendent-combinator.html *(excerpt)*

```
form p {
    font-size: 22px;
}
```

There's a problem with this selector, however, as you can see in Figure 1.3. We've actually increased the size of the text in *all* of our form's paragraphs, which isn't what we want. How can we fix this? Let's try the child combinator.

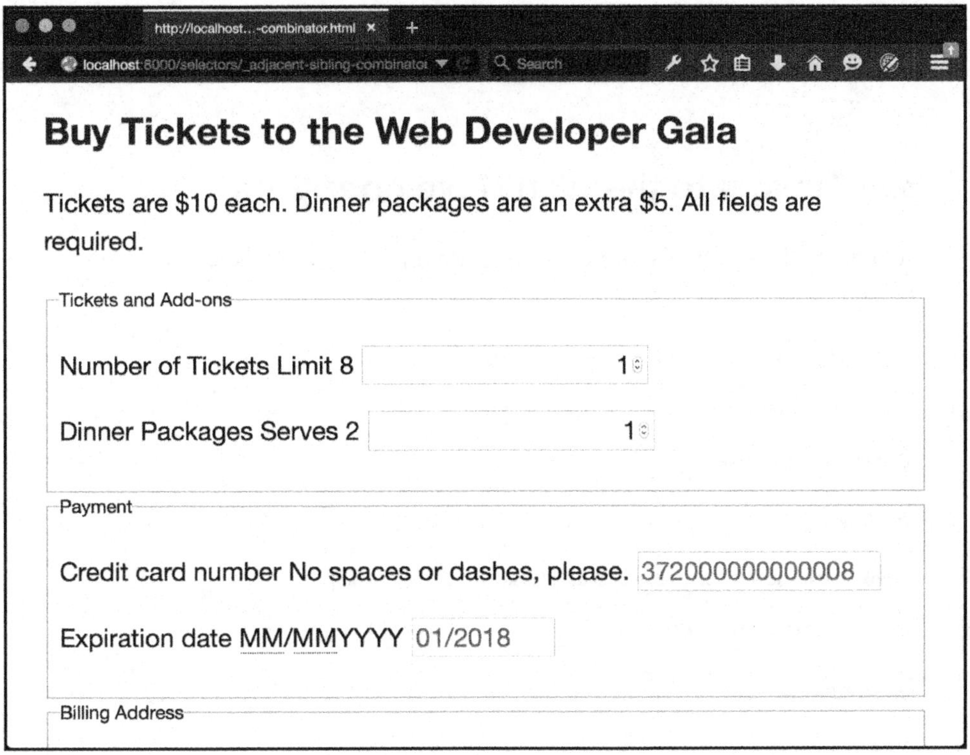

Figure 1.3. Oops! Our selector is too broad

The Child Combinator

In contrast to the descendant combinator, the **child combinator** (>) selects only the *immediate children* of an element. It follows the pattern $A > B$, matching any element B where A is the immediate ancestor.

If elements were people, to use an analogy, the child combinator would match the child of the mother element. But the descendant combinator would also match her grandchildren, and great-grandchildren. Let's modify our previous selector to use the child combinator:

```
01-selectors/child-combinator.html (excerpt)
form > p {
    font-size: 22px;
}
```

Now only the direct children of `article` are affected, as shown in Figure 1.4.

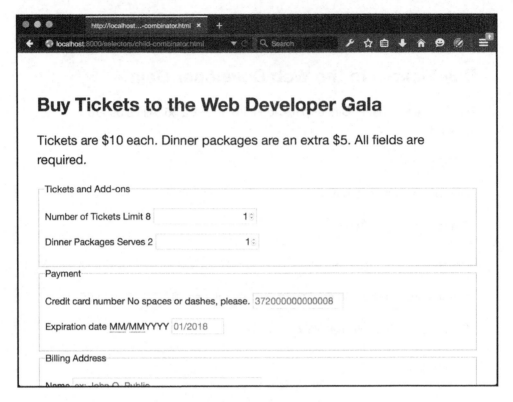

Figure 1.4. The effect of the child combinator

The Adjacent Sibling Combinator

With the **adjacent sibling combinator** (+), we can select elements that follow each other and have the same parent. It follows the pattern *A + B*. Styles will be applied to *B* elements that are *immediately* preceded by *A* elements.

Let's go back to our example. Notice that our labels and inputs sit next to each other. That means we can use the adjacent sibling combinator to make them sit on separate lines:

```
label + input {
    display: block;
    clear: both;
}
```

You can see the results in Figure 1.5.

Figure 1.5. Adjacent combinator to the rescue

Let's look at another example that combines the universal selector (*) with a type selector:

```
                                01-selectors/adjacent-sibling-combinator.html (excerpt)

* + fieldset {
    margin: 5em 0;
}
```

This example adds a 5em margin to the top and bottom of every `fieldset` element, shown in Figure 1.6. Since we're using the universal selector, there's no need to worry about whether the previous element is another `fieldset` or `p` element.

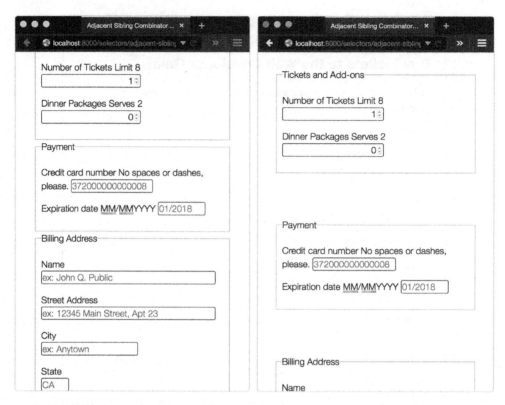

Figure 1.6. Using the adjacent sibling combinator to adjust the bottom margin for our `fieldset` elements

More Uses of the Adjacent Sibling Selector

Heydon Pickering explores more clever uses of the adjacent sibling selector in his article "Axiomatic CSS and Lobotomized Owls."[4]

What if we want to style a sibling element that *isn't* adjacent to another, as with our **Number of Tickets** field? In this case, we can use the general sibling combinator.

The General Sibling Combinator

With the **general sibling combinator**—a tilde—we can select elements that share the same parent without considering whether they're adjacent. Given the pattern $A \sim B$, this selector matches all B elements that are preceded by an A element, whether or not they're adjacent.

---

[4] http://alistapart.com/article/axiomatic-css-and-lobotomized-owls

Let's look at the **Number of Tickets** field again. Its markup looks like this:

```
<p>
    <label for="quantity">Number of Tickets</label>
    <span class="help">Limit 8</span>
    <input type="number" value="1" name="quantity" id="quantity"
 ➥ step="1" min="1" max="8">
</p>
```

Our `input` element follows the `label` element, but there is a `span` element in between. Since a `span` element sits between `input` and `label`, the adjacent sibling combinator will fail to work here. Let's change our adjacent sibling combinator to a general sibling combinator:

01-selectors/general-sibling-combinator.html *(excerpt)*

```
label ~ input {
    display: block;
}
```

Now all of our `input` elements sit on a separate line from their `label` elements, as seen in Figure 1.7.

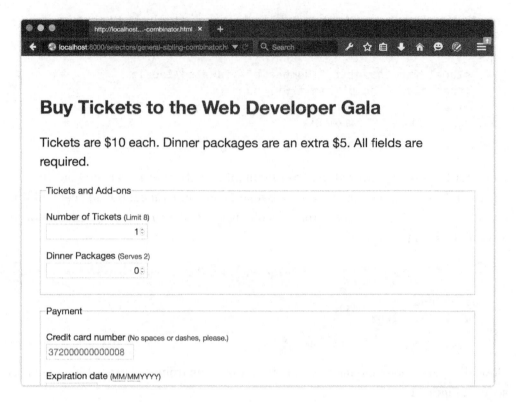

Figure 1.7. The ~ combinator targets sibling elements, regardless of whether they're adjacent

Using the general sibling combinator is the most handy when you lack full control over the markup. Otherwise, you'd be better off adjusting your markup to add a class name. Keep in mind that the general sibling combinator may create some unintended side effects in a large code base, so use with care.

Attribute Selectors

Attribute selectors match elements based on their attributes. This can be an attribute alone, such as `[type]`, or it can be an attribute and value combination, such as `[type=checkbox]` or `[for="email"]`.

We can also do attribute presence and substring matching with attribute selectors. For example, we can match attribute values in a space-separated list, or we can match attribute values that start with `tel:`. We can even match hyphenated attribute values such as `en-US`.

Some of the attribute selectors we'll cover here are old hat. Both the hyphenated attribute value selector and the space-separated attribute value selector were defined in CSS2. Selectors Level 3, on the other hand, adds a few powerful selectors that let us match partial attribute values.

We'll focus on the new and lesser-known attribute selectors in this section. Let's take a look.

Matching Attribute Presence

It's common to match elements based on the exact value of their attributes. Reset style sheets commonly use selectors selector such as `[type=text]` and `[type=email]`. But we can also match attributes when there are multiple space-separated values. We need to use our space-separated attribute value selector: `[att~=val]`.

The space-separated attribute value selector matches elements with the attribute `att` and a list of values, one of which is `val`. This can be any attribute that accepts space-separated values, including `class` or `data-*`.

Space-separated lists of attributes are admittedly uncommon. They are sometimes used with the `rel` attribute and microformats[5] to describe relationships between people and documents. We might mark up an external link like so:

```
<a href="http://example.com/" rel="external friend">Bob</a>
```

We can then use this presence-based attribute selector to match this link and links like it:

```
                              01-selectors/attribute-space-separated.html (excerpt)

[rel~=friend] {
    font-size: 2em;
    background: #eee;
    padding: 4px;
    text-decoration: none;
    border-bottom: 3px solid #ccc;
}
[rel~=friend]:link,
[rel~=friend]:visited {
```

---

[5] http://microformats.org/wiki/existing-rel-values

```
    color: #34444C;
}
[rel~=friend]:hover{
    background: #ffeb3b;
    border-color: #ffc107;
}
```

This gives us the image in Figure 1.8.

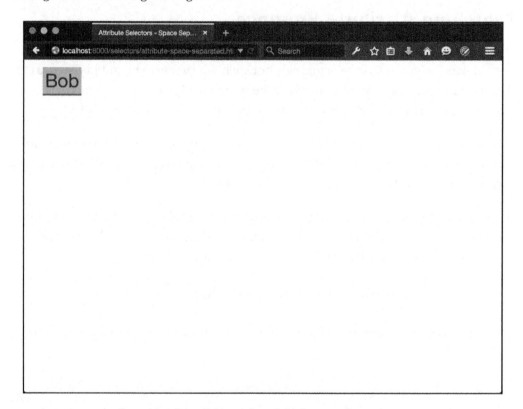

Figure 1.8. A link to Bob's website styled using an attribute selector

Matching Hyphenated Attribute Values

One of the more interesting tasks we can do with attribute selectors is match elements with hyphenated attribute values by using [attr|=val]. This selector matches elements by attribute when its value is hyphenated and its prefix equals val.

At first glance, this may seem like a useless selector; however, it's quite practical for working with languages and language codes—such as en-US or es-MX—which is its intended use.

Let's say we have a site targeting English speakers. Our site also supports two regional variations in English: United Kingdom and United States. The language codes for these languages are en-GB and en-US respectively. We've also set the language on our html tag; for example, <html lang="en-US">.

Our site teaches English speakers to be conversant in French, Spanish, and Portuguese. It contains lots of markup similar to this example:

```
<p lang="fr-FR"><q>Tout le monde.</q></p>
<p><q>All the world.</q>, or <q>Everyone</q></p>
```

Let's italicize our French text and add language-appropriate angle quotes (« and ») to either side of it:

```
[lang|="fr"] {
    font-style: italic;
}
[lang|="fr"] q:before{
    content: '\00AB'; /* Left angle quote */
}
[lang|="fr"] q:after{
    content: '\00BB';  /* Right angle quote */
}
```

What's cool about this selector is that it will also match if the attribute equals the prefix. These styles would also apply to <p lang="fr">. We could further limit the scope of these selectors, for example, by adding a p element to the lang attribute: p[lang|="fr"].

Though intended to be used with language codes, this selector isn't limited to them. We can use it with any hyphenated attribute value. Consider the following markup:

```
<article class="articlepromo">
    <h3>U.S. ratifies Kyoto Protocol</h3>
    <p>Lorem ipsum dolor sit amet, consectetur adipisicing ....</p>
</article>
```

```
<article class="articlepromo-entertainment">
    <h3>Kardashian-Wests welcome South to the world</h3>
    <p>Lorem ipsum dolor sit amet, consectetur adipisicing ....</p>
</article>

<article class="articlepromo-sports">
    <h3>New York Knicks win NBA title</h3>
    <p>Lorem ipsum dolor sit amet, consectetur adipisicing ....</p>
</article>

<article class="articlepromo-business">
    <h3>Google Buys EverythingOnTheInternet.com</h3>
    <p>Lorem ipsum dolor sit amet, consectetur adipisicing ....</p>
</article>
```

These are all article promos or teasers. They share some of the same visual characteristics and behavior, along with an `articlepromo` prefix. Here, too, we can use the hyphenated attribute selector to match these class names:

01-selectors/attribute-hyphenated.html *(excerpt)*

```
[class|="articlepromo"] {
    border-top: 5px solid #4caf50;
    color: #555;
    line-height: 1.3;
    padding-top: .5em;
}

[class|="articlepromo"] h3 {
    color: #000;
    font-size: 1.2em;
    margin:0;
}

[class|="articlepromo"] p {
    margin: 0 0 1em;
}
```

Follow this up with specific border colors for each section type, and you'll achieve something along the lines of the layout you see in Figure 1.9.

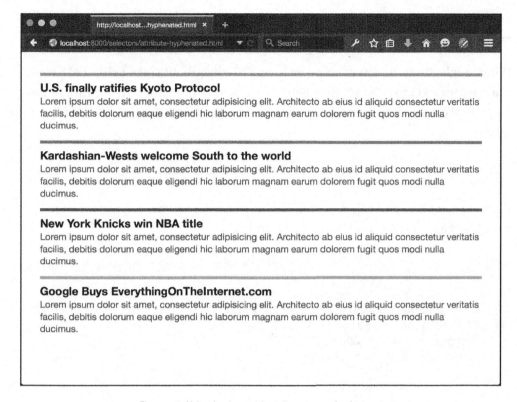

Figure 1.9. Using hyphenated attributes to style elements

We can also use it with id names; for example, [id|=global] would match #global-footer, #global-menu, and so on.

Now, just because you *can* do something doesn't necessarily mean you *should*. The hyphenated attribute value selector is ideal for styling differences in language. For any other usage, though, you'd do just as well to use a class name selector. Class names provide a lower risk of unintended effects in a large project. They're also a must if your project still requires Internet Explorer 8 support, since IE8 does not support this selector.

Matching Attribute Values by Substring

We can also select elements when the attribute values match a particular substring. Three character sequences let us match elements depending on whether this substring sits at the beginning, end, or elsewhere in the attribute value:

^=   matches when the substring sits at the beginning of the string.

$=   matches when the substring sits at the end of the string.

*=   matches when the substring is present at any position within the string.

When might these selectors come in handy? Think about links using `tel:` (non-standard) or `mailto:`. "Since they behave differently from other hyperlinks, it makes sense to style them differently just as a hint to the user. Take the *Call this business* link:

```
<a href="tel:+14045555555">Call this business</a>
```

We can select this and other `tel:` links by using the `^=` character sequence: `[href^="tel:"]`. Let's add some declarations:

01-selectors/attribute-substring-combinator.html *(excerpt)*

```
[href^="tel:"] {
    background: #2196f3 url(../images/phone-icon.svg) 10px center /
➥ 20px auto no-repeat;
    border-radius: 100px;
    padding: .5em 1em .5em 2em;
}
```

You can see the result in Figure 1.10.

Figure 1.10. Our new **Call this business** button

To match elements when the attribute value *ends* with a substring, change `^` to `$`. If, for some odd reason—and let me emphasize that it would be odd—we wanted to match the last four digits of our phone number (5555), we might use the following:

```
[href$="5555"] {
    background: #e91e63;
}
```

It's more useful, obviously, to match elements that end with the same suffix. For example, you could match both `<aside class="sports-sidebar">` and `<aside class="arts-sidebar">` with `[class$=sidebar]`.

Using `$=` won't, however, match an element with the class name `sports-sidebar-a`. For that we'd need to use the `*=` sequence. Changing our selector to `[class*=sidebar]` does the job.

Most of the new selectors added in CSS3 and CSS4 are not attribute selectors at all. They're pseudo-classes or pseudo-elements. We'll discuss these over the next few sections.

Pseudo-classes versus Pseudo-elements

Though you've probably used pseudo-classes and pseudo-elements in your code, you may not have thought about what they are or the difference between them.

Pseudo-classes let us style objects based on information distinct from the document tree, or that's unable to be expressed using simple selectors. For example, an element can only have a hover or focus state once the user interacts with it. With the `:hover` and `:focus` pseudo-classes, we can define styles for those states. Otherwise, we'd have to rely on scripting to add and remove class names.

Pseudo-elements, on the other hand, let us style elements that aren't directly present in the document tree. There's no `firstletter` element in HTML, so we need another way to select it. The `::first-letter` pseudo-element gives us that capability.

Pseudo-elements

The CSS Pseudo-elements Module Level 4 specification [6]clarifies behavior for existing pseudo-elements and defines several new ones. Only a few, however, have any degree of support in current browsers. Those are the ones we'll focus on here:

---

[6] http://dev.w3.org/csswg/css-pseudo-4/

`::before`	inserts additional generated content before the content of an element
`::after`	inserts additional generated content after the content of an element
`::first-letter`	selects the first letter of an element
`::first-line`	selects the first line of an element
`::selection`	styles text selected by the cursor

Of these, `::first-letter`, `::first-line`, and `::selection` affect content that's part of the document source. The `::before` and `::after` pseudo-elements, on the other hand, inject content into a document without it existing in the document source. Let's look at each of these pseudo-elements more closely.

 Single-colon Syntax

You may come across single-colon versions of `::first-letter`, `::first-line`, `::before`, and `::after` in old CSS. These pseudo-elements were defined in CSS2 with a single `:`. Though Internet Explorer 8 requires single-colon syntax, most other browsers support both versions. It is recommeded to use the double-colon syntax.

`::before` and `::after`

Most pseudo-elements allow us to select content that's already part of the document source—in other words, the HTML you authored—but not specified by the language. With `::before` and `::after`, however, matters work differently. These pseudo-elements add generated content to the document tree. This content does not exist in the HTML source, but it is available visually.

Why would you want to use generated content? You might, for example, want to indicate which form fields are required by adding content after its label:

```
/* Apply to the label element associated with a required field */
.required::after {
    content: ' (Required) ';
```

```
    color: #c00;
    font-size: .8em;
}
```

Required form fields use the `required` HTML property. Since that information is already available to the DOM, using `::before` or `::after` to add helper text is supplemental. It isn't critical content, so it's okay that it's not part of the document source.

 Generated Content and Accessibility

Some screen-reader and browser combinations recognize and read generated content, but most do not. Avoid relying on content generated using `::before` or `::after` being available to assistive technology users. More on this is available in Leonie Watson's piece "Accessibility support for CSS generated content."[7]

Another use case for `::before` or `::after` is adding a prefix or suffix to content. Perhaps the aforementioned form includes helper text, as shown here:

```
<form method="post" action="/save">
    <fieldset>
        <legend>Change Your Password</legend>
        <p>
            <label for="password">Enter a new password</label>
            <input type="password" id="password" name="password">
        </p>
        <p>
            <label for="password2">Retype your password</label>
            <input type="password" id="password2" name="password2">
        </p>
        <p class="helptext">Longer passwords are stronger.</p>
        <p><button type="submit">Save changes</button></p>
    </fieldset>
</form>
```

Let's enclose our helper text in parentheses using `::before` and `::after`:

---

[7] http://tink.uk/accessibility-support-for-css-generated-content/

```
.helptext::before {
    content: '( ';
}
.helptext::after {
    content: ')';
}
```

The result is shown in Figure 1.11.

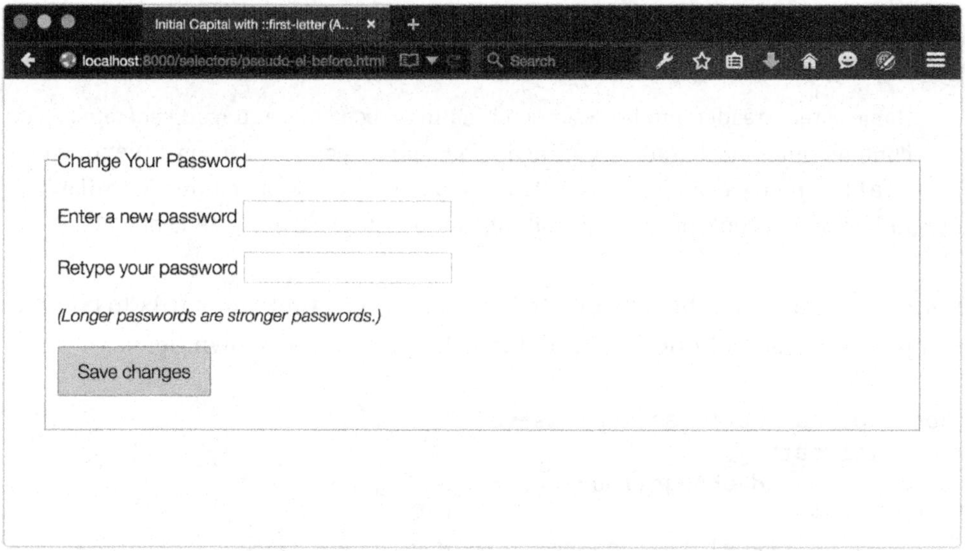

Figure 1.11. Using `::before` and `::after` to add supplemental content

Perhaps the most useful way to use `::before` and `::after` is to clear floated elements. Nicolas Gallagher introduced this technique (which builds on the work of Thierry Koblentz) in his post "A new micro clearfix hack":[8]

```
/* Use :before and :after if you need to support IE <= 8 */

.clearfix::before,
.clearfix::after {
    content: " "; /* Note the space between the quotes. */
    display: table;
}
```

---

[8] http://nicolasgallagher.com/micro-clearfix-hack/

```
.clearfix::after {
    clear: both;
}
```

Add the `clearfix` class to any element that needs to be cleared after a floated element.

Both `::before` and `::after` behave just like regular descendants of the element to which they're attached. They inherit all inheritable properties of their parent, and sit within the box created by their parent. But they also interact with other element boxes as though they were true elements. Adding `display: block` or `display: table` to `::before` or `::after` works the same way as it does for other elements.

One Pseudo-element per Selector

Currently, only one pseudo-element is allowed per selector. This means that a selector such as `p::first-line::before` is invalid.

Creating Typographic Effects with `::first-letter`

While the `::before` and `::after` pseudo-elements inject content, `::first-letter` works with content that exists as part of the document source. With it, we can create initial or drop-capital letter effects, as you might see in a magazine or book layout.

Initial and Drop Capitals

An **initial capital** is an uppercase letter at the start of a text set in a larger font size than the rest of the body copy. A **drop capital** is similar to an initial capital, but is inset into the first paragraph by at least two lines.

This CSS snippet adds an initial capital letter to every p element in our document:

```
p::first-letter {
    font-family: serif;
    font-weight: bold;
    font-size: 3em;
```

```
    font-style: italic;
    color: #3f51b5;
}
```

The result can be viewed in Figure 1.12.

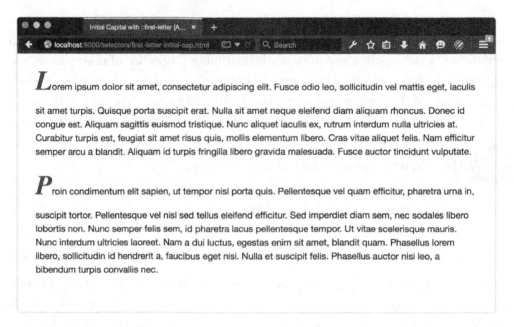

Figure 1.12. Creating initial caps with the ::first-letter pseudo-element

As you may have noticed from this screenshot, ::first—letter will affect the line-height of the first line if you've set a unitless line-height for the element. In this case, each p element inherits a line-height value of 1.5 from the body element.

There are three ways to mitigate this:

1. Decrease the value of line-height for the ::first—letter pseudo-element. A value of .5 seems to work most of the time.

2. Set a line-height with units on the ::first—letter pseudo-element.

3. Set a line-height with units on either the body or the ::first—letter parent.

The first option preserves the vertical rhythm that comes with using unitless `line-heights`.[9] The second option limits the side effects of using fixed `line-heights` just to those pseudo-elements. Option three is the worst of these options because there's a high likelihood that you'll create a side effect that requires more CSS to override it.

In this case, let's decrease the `line-height` value for `p::first-letter` to `.5` (and rewrite our file properties to use the `font` shorthand):

01-selectors/pseudo-el-first-letter-init.html *(excerpt)*

```
p::first-letter {
    font: bold italic 3em / .5 serif;
    color: #3f51b5;
}
```

This change produces the result shown in Figure 1.13. Notice here that we also had to adjust the bottom margin of each p element to compensate for the reduced `line-height` of `p::first-letter`.

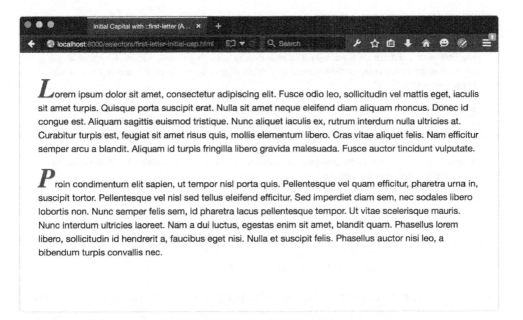

Figure 1.13. Mitigating the effect of `::first-letter` on `line-height`

---

[9] The Mozilla Developer Network entry for `line-height` explains why unitless values [https://developer.mozilla.org/en-US/docs/Web/CSS/line-height] are the way to go.

Creating a drop capital requires a few more lines of CSS. Unlike an initial capital, the adjacent text to the drop capital letter wraps around it. This means that we need to add `float: left;` to our rule set. We'll also add top, right, and bottom margins:

01-selectors/pseudo-el-first-letter-drop.html (excerpt)

```
p::first-letter {
    font: bold italic 3em / .5 serif;
    font-style: italic;
    color: #607d8b;
    float: left;
    margin: 0.2em 0.25em .01em 0;
}
```

Floating an element, or in this case a pseudo-element, causes the remaining text to flow around it, as illustrated in Figure 1.14.

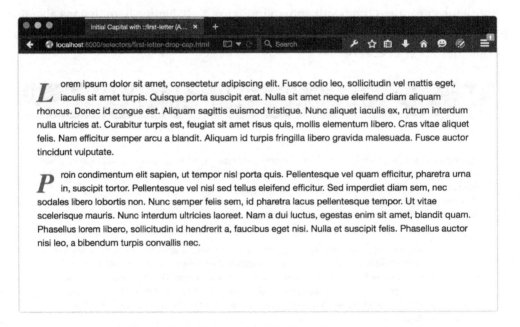

Figure 1.14. Creating a drop capital with `::first-letter`

Be aware that `::first-letter` can be difficult to style with pixel-perfect accuracy across browsers, unless you use `px` or `rem` units for size, margin, and line height.

Sometimes the first letter of a text element is actually punctuation; for example, a news story that begins with a quote:

```
<p>&#8220;Lorem ipsum dolor sit amet, consectetur adipiscing elit.
➥&#8221; Fusce odio leo, sollicitudin vel mattis eget, ...</p>
```

In this case, the styles defined for `::first-letter` will affect both the opening punctuation mark and the first letter, as presented in Figure 1.15. All browsers handle this in the same way.

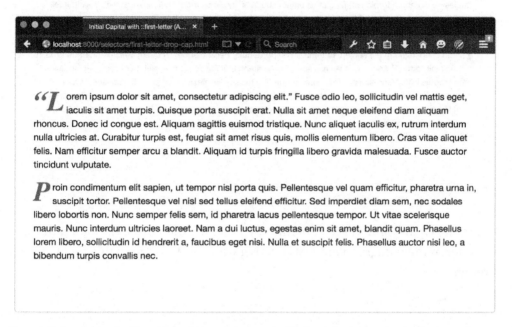

Figure 1.15. Punctuation is affected by `::first-letter` styles if it immediately precedes the first letter character

However, this isn't necessarily how it works when the punctuation mark is generated by an element. Consider the following markup:

```
<p><q>Lorem ipsum dolor sit amet, consectetur adipiscing elit.</q>
➥ Fusce odio leo, sollicitudin vel mattis eget, iaculis sit ...</p>
```

Current browsers typically render the q element with language-appropriate quotation marks before and after the enclosed text; however, not all browsers treat those quotation marks the same way. In Firefox 42 (Figure 1.16), Safari 8, and earlier versions, `::first-letter` only affects the opening quotation mark.

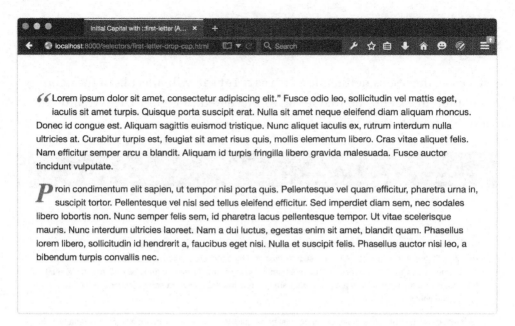

Figure 1.16. ::first-letter only affects the opening quotation mark in Firefox 40

In Chrome, Opera, and Yandex, neither the opening quotation mark for q nor the first letter of the paragraph are restyled. Figure 1.17 shows how this looks like in Chrome.

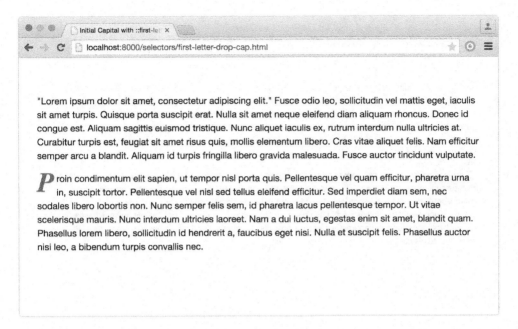

Figure 1.17. Chrome ignores the opening quotation mark and first letter when using q

Internet Explorer, however, applies first-letter styles to both the opening quotation mark *and* the first letter of the paragraph, as shown in Figure 1.18.

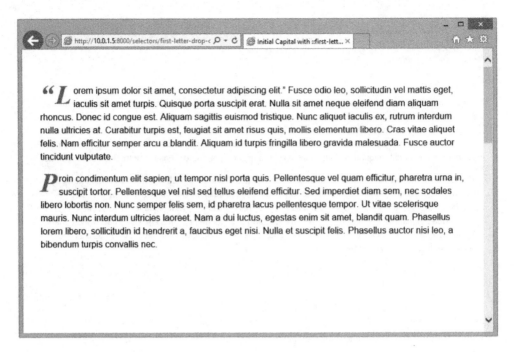

Figure 1.18. Internet Explorer includes punctuation in first-letter styles

According to the CSS Pseudo-elements Module Level 4 specification,[10] punctuation that immediately precedes or succeeds the first letter or character should be included; however, the specification is unclear about whether this also applies to generated punctuation.[11]

Browser Bugs When Using `::first-letter`

For the most part, `::first-letter` works as expected across browsers. As with any CSS feature, there are some edge cases and browser bugs of which to be aware.

In Firefox 39 and earlier, some punctuation characters cause Firefox to ignore a `::first-letter` rule set altogether:

- - (dash)
- \$ (dollar sign)
- ^ (caret)

---

[10] http://dev.w3.org/csswg/css-pseudo-4/#first-letter-pseudo

[11] The specification actually uses the phrase "typographic letter unit." This includes Unicode letters and numbers, but also characters used in East Asian and Middle Eastern writing systems.

- _   (underscore)
- +   (plus sign)
- `   (back tick)
- ~   (tilde)
- >   (greater than sign)
- <   (less than sign)

This is true whether the first character is set using `::before` and the `content` property, or included in the document source. There is no fix for this. You'll need to avoid using these characters as the first character if you're also using `::first-letter`.

 Bugs in Blink-based Browsers

Some versions of Blink-based browsers will not apply `::first—letter` rules if the parent element has a `display` value of `inline` or `table`. This bug exists in Chrome 42, Opera 29, and Yandex 15. It's fixed in Chrome 44, however, which should be released by the time this book reaches your hands. If you need to work around this bug, the easiest fix is to add `display: inline-block`, `display: block`, or `display: table-cell` to the parent element.

Creating Typographic Effects with `::first-line`

The `::first-line` pseudo-class works similarly to `::first-letter`, but affects the entire first line of an element. We could, for example, make the first line of every paragraph element be a larger text size and different color than the rest of each paragraph:

01-selectors/pseudo-el-first-line.html (excerpt)

```
p::first-line {
    font: bold 1.5em serif;
    font-style: italic;
    color: #673ab7;
}
```

You can see the result in Figure 1.19. Notice that the first line of each paragraph is affected, rather than the first sentence. How many characters fit on this first line is determined by font size and element width.

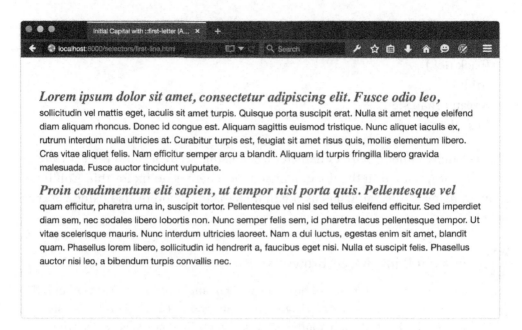

Figure 1.19. Using the ::first-line pseudo-element

It is possible to force the end of a first line by using a br or hr element, as shown in Figure 1.20. Unfortunately, this is far from perfect. If your element is only wide enough to accommodate 72 characters, adding a <br> tag after the 80th character won't affect the ::first-line pseudo-element. You'll end up with an oddly placed line break.

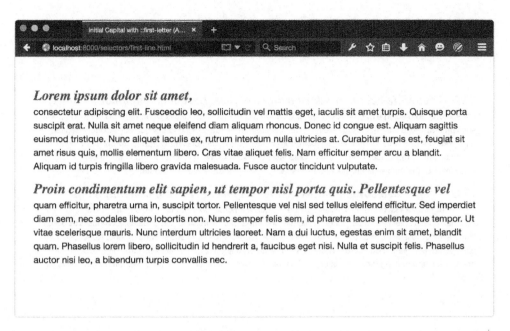

Figure 1.20. Forcing the end of a line with a br element

Similarly, using a non-breaking space ( ) to prevent a line-break between words won't affect ::first-line. Instead, the word that sits before   will be forced on to the same line as the text that comes after it.

Generated content that's added using ::before will become part of the first line, as shown in Figure 1.21.

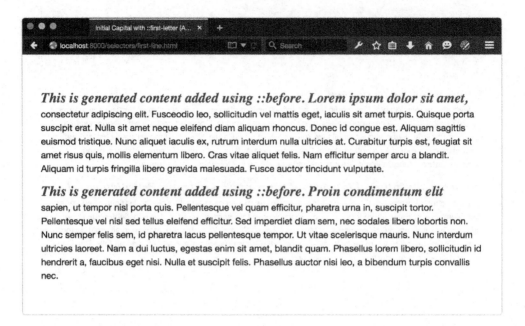

Figure 1.21. Generated content becomes part of the first line

If the generated text is long enough, it will fill the entire first line. However, if we add a `display: block` declaration—for example, `p::before {content: '!!!'; display: block;}`—that content will become the entire first line Figure 1.22.

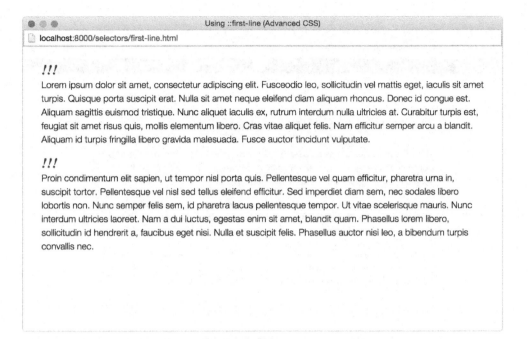

Figure 1.22. Adding `display: block` to content added with `::before` means that styles defined for `p::first-line` will affect that content

Unfortunately, this is yet to work in Firefox version 40 or earlier. Firefox ignores the rule set completely.

User Interface Fun with `::selection`

The `::selection` pseudo-element is one of the so-called "highlight pseudo-elements" defined by CSS Pseudo-Elements Module Level 4.[12] Formerly part of the Selectors Level 3 specification, it's the only highlight pseudo-element implemented by browsers.[13]

With `::selection`, we can apply CSS styles to content that users have highlighted with their mouse. By default, the background and text color of highlighted content is determined by system settings; however, developers can change what that highlight looks like, as indicated in Figure 1.23.

---

[12] http://dev.w3.org/csswg/css-pseudo-4/

[13] In Firefox, this pseudo-element requires a `-moz-` prefix, like so `::-moz-selection`.

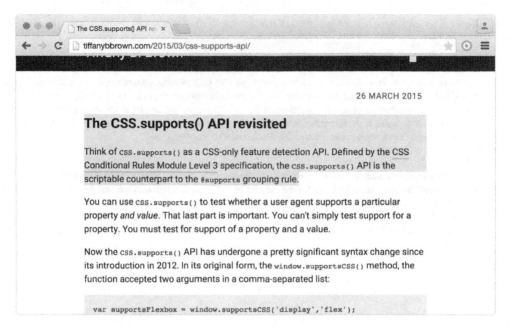

Figure 1.23. An example of a highlight set using `::selection`

Not every CSS property can be used with `::selection`. As outlined in the specification, only these properties will work:

- `color`
- `background-color`
- `cursor`
- `outline` and its expanded properties
- `text-decoration` and related properties (such as `text-decoration-style`)
- `text-emphasis-color`
- `text-shadow`

In practical terms, only `color` and `background-color` have been implemented in multiple browsers. Let's look at an example:

01-selectors/pseudo-el-selection.html *(excerpt)*

```
::selection {
    background: #9f0;
    color: #600;
}
```

This CSS adds a lime green background to any element the user highlights, and changes the text color to a deep red. The example works in every browser that supports `::selection`, and you can see the effect in Figure 1.24.

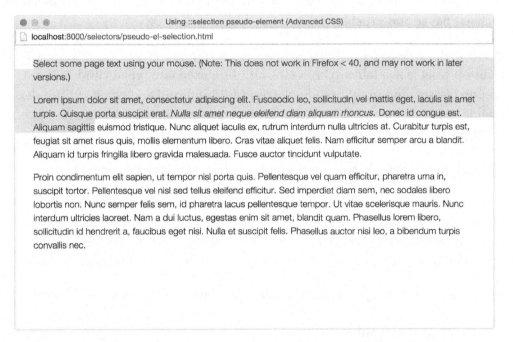

Figure 1.24. Deep red text on a lime green background set using the `::selection` pseudo-element

 Color Combinations

When selecting foreground and background colors to use with `::selection`, keep accessibility in mind. Some color combinations fail to generate enough contrast to be read by low-vision users. Other color combinations may be illegible for color-blind users. Be sure to use a contrast checker and color-blindness simulator before selecting your final colors.

The ::spelling-error and ::grammar-error pseudo-classes are also defined by the Pseudo-Elements Module. When implemented, these pseudo-classes will let us style text that is misspelled or ungrammatical according to the browser's dictionary.

Pseudo-classes

As mentioned earlier in this chapter, pseudo-classes help us define styles for documents based on information that is unable to be gleaned from the document tree or can't be targeted using simple selectors. These include logical and linguistic pseudo-classes such as :not() and :lang(). It also includes user-triggered pseudo-classes such as :hover and :focus.

In this section, we'll cover some esoteric and lesser-known pseudo-classes with a focus on what is available in browsers: child-indexed and typed child-indexed pseudo-classes, and input pseudo-classes. Child-indexed and typed child-indexed pseudo-classes let us select elements by their position in the document subtree. Input pseudo-classes target form fields based on their input values and states.

Highlighting Page Fragments with :target

A fragment identifier is the part of a URL that follows the #; for example, #top or #footnote1. You've probably used them to create in-page navigation: a so-called "jump link." With the :target pseudo-class, we can highlight the portion of the document that corresponds to that fragment, and we can do it without JavaScript.

Say, for example, that you have series of comments or a discussion board thread:

```
<section id="comments">
    <h2>Comments on this post</h2>
    <article class="comment" id="comment-1146937891">...</article>
    <article class="comment" id="comment-1146937892">...</article>
    <article class="comment" id="comment-1146937893">...</article>
</section>
```

With some CSS and other fancy bits, it looks a little like what you see in Figure 1.25.

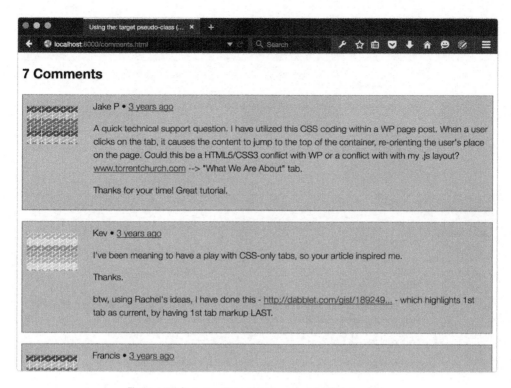

Figure 1.25. A comments section as you might find on a blog

Each comment in the aforementioned code has a fragment identifier, which means we can link directly to it. For example, `<a href="#comment-1146937891">`. Then all we need to do is specify a style for this comment using the `:target` pseudo-class:

```
.comment:target {
    background: #ffeb3b;
    border-color: #ffc107
}
```

When the fragment identifier part of the URL matches that of a comment (for example, `http://example.com/post/#comment-1146937891`), that comment will have a yellow background, seen in Figure 1.26.

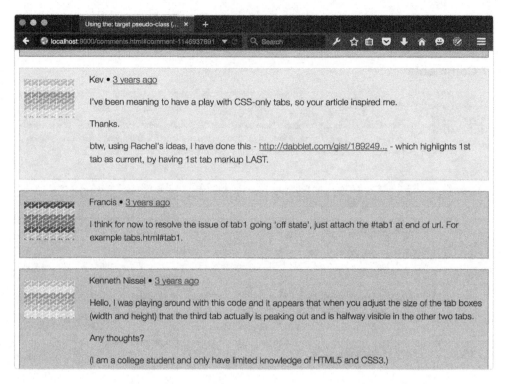

Figure 1.26. A comments section with a yellow background

You can use any combination of CSS with :target, which opens up some fun possibilities such as JavaScript-less tabs. Craig Buckler details this technique in his tutorial "How to Create a CSS3-only Tab Control Using the :target Selector."[14] We'll update it a bit to use more CSS3 features. First, let's look at our HTML:

```
                                        01-selectors/pseudo-class-target.html (excerpt)
<div class="tabbed-widget">
    <div class="tab-wrap">
        <a href="#tab1">Tab 1</a>
        <a href="#tab2">Tab 2</a>
        <a href="#tab3">Tab 3</a>
    </div>

    <ul class="tab-body">
        <li id="tab1">
            <p>This is tab 1.</p>
```

---

[14] http://www.sitepoint.com/css3-tabs-using-target-selector/

```
        </li>
        <li id="tab2">
            <p>This is tab 2</p>
        </li>
        <li id="tab3">
            <p>This is tab 3.</p>
        </li>
    </ul>
</div>
```

It's fairly straightforward, consisting of tabs and associated tab content. Let's add some CSS:

css/chapter1/selectors-target.css *(excerpt)*

```
[id^=tab] {
    position: absolute;
}
[id^=tab]:first-child {
    z-index: 1;
}
[id^=tab]:target {
    z-index: 2;
}
```

Here's where the magic happens. First, we've absolutely positioned all of our tabs. Next, we've made our first tab the topmost layer by adding z-index: 1. This is only important if you want the first tab in the source order to be the first tab users see. Lastly, we've added z-index: 1 to our target tab. This ensures that the targeted layer will always be the topmost one. You can see the result in Figure 1.27.

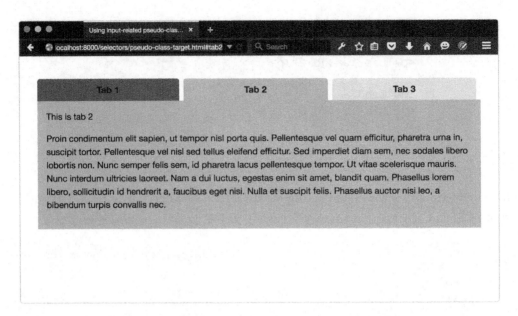

Figure 1.27. Using the `:target` selector to create tabs sans JavaScript

Improving Accessibility

A more accessible version might also use JavaScript to toggle the `hidden` or `aria-hidden=true` attributes based on the visibility of each tab body.

Clicking a tab updates the URL with the new document fragment identifier. This in turn, triggers the `:target` state.

Negating Selectors with `:not()`

Perhaps the most powerful of this new crop of pseudo-classes is `:not()`. It returns all elements except for those that match the selector argument. For example, `p:not(.message)` selects every p element that lacks a `message` class.

The `:not()` pseudo-class is what's known as a **functional pseudo–class**. It accepts a single argument, much like functions in other programming languages do. Any argument passed to `:not()` must be a simple selector such as an element type, a class name, an ID, or another pseudo-class. Pseudo-elements will fail, as will compound selectors such as `label.checkbox` or complex selectors such as `p img`.

Here's an example of a form that uses textual input types and radio buttons:

01-selectors/pseudo-class-target.html *(excerpt)*

```
<form method="post" action="#">
    <h1>Join the Cool Kids Club</h1>
    <p>
        <label for="name">Name:</label>
        <input type="text" id="name" name="name" required>
    </p>

    <p>
        <label for="email">Email:</label>
        <input type="email" id="email" name="email" required>
    </p>
    <fieldset>
      <legend>Receive a digest?</legend>
      <p>
        <input type="radio" id="daily" name="digest">
        <label for="daily" class="label-radio">Daily</label>
        <input type="radio" id="weekly" name="digest">
        <label for="weekly" class="label-radio">Weekly</label>
      </p>
    </fieldset>
    <button type="submit">Buy Tickets!</button>
</form>
```

In the HTML, labels associated with a `radio` type have a `.label-radio` class. We can use the `:not()` pseudo-class: to target those elements without a `label-radio` class, as shown in Figure 1.28:

```
label:not(.label-radio) {
    font-weight: bold;
    display:block;
}
```

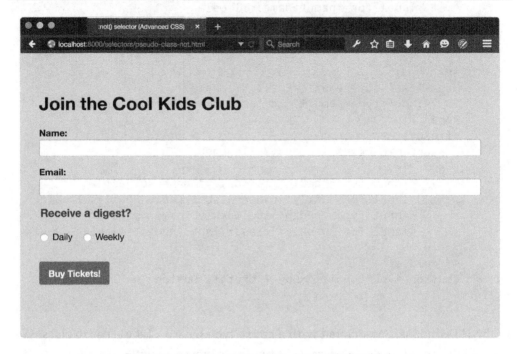

Figure 1.28. Using the :not() pseudo class to style form labels

Here's a trickier example. Let's create styles for textual inputs. These include input types such as number, email, and text along with password and url. But let's do this by excluding radio button, check box, and range inputs. Your first instinct might be to use the following selector list:

```
input:not([type=radio]),
input:not([type=checkbox]),
input:not([type=range]) {
    ...
}
```

Unfortunately, this won't work, as each selector overrides the previous one. It's the equivalent of typing:

```
input:not([type=radio]){ ... }
input:not([type=checkbox]) { ... }
input:not([type=range]) {... }
```

Instead, we need to chain our :not() pseudo-classes, so that they all filter the input element:[15]

```
input:not([type=radio]):not([type=checkbox]):not([type=range]) {
    ...
}
```

Using pseudo-classes (and pseudo-elements) without a simple selector is the equivalent of using it with the universal selector. In other words, :not([type=radio]) is the same as *:not([type=radio]). In this case, every element that lacks a type attribute and value of radio will match—including html and body. To prevent this, use :not() with a selector such as a class name, ID, or attribute selector. By the way, this also holds true true for class name, ID, and attribute selectors: .warning and [type=radio] are the same as *.warning and *[type=radio].

CSS Selectors Level 4 refines the way :not() works, so that it can accept a list as an argument, and not just simple selectors. Rather than chaining pseudo-classes as previously, we'll be able to use a comma-separated argument:

```
input:not([type=radio], [type=checkbox], [type=range]) {
    ...
}
```

Unfortunately, no major browser supports this yet, so use chaining in the meantime.

Selecting Elements by Their Index

CSS also provide selectors for matching elements based on their position in the document subtree. These are known as **child–indexed pseudo-classes**, because they rely on the position or order of the element rather than its type, attributes, or ID. There are five:

---

[15] The selector chain below will also match [type=image], [type=reset], [type=color], and [type=submit] elements.

- :first-child
- :last-child
- :only-child
- :nth-child()
- :nth-last-child()

:first-child and :last-child

As you've probably guessed from the names, the :first-child and :last-child pseudo-classes make it possible to select elements that are the first child or last child of a node (element). As with other pseudo-classes, :first-child and :last-child have the fewest side effects when qualified by a simple selector.

Let's take a look at the HTML and CSS below:

```
<!DOCTYPE html>
    <html lang="en-US">
    <head>
    <meta charset="utf-8">
    <title>:first-child and :last-child</title>
    <style type="text/css">
    body {
       font: 16px / 1.5 sans-serif;
    }
    :first-child {
          color: #e91e63;
    }
    :last-child {
    color: #4caf50;
}
    </style>
</head>
<body>
        <h2>List of fruits</h2>
          <ul>
             <li>Apples</li>
             <li>Bananas</li>
             <li>Blueberries</li>
             <li>Oranges</li>
             <li>Strawberries</li>
```

```
        </ul>
      </body>
  </html>
```

You can see what this looks like in Figure 1.29.

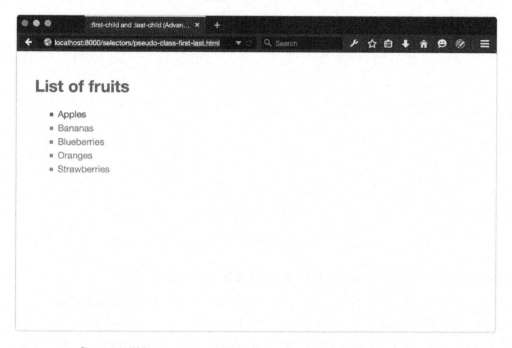

Figure 1.29. Using `:first-child` by itself matches more elements than we want

Because `:first-child` is unqualified, both the h2 element and first li element are hot pink. After all, h2 is the first child of body, and li is the first child of the ul element. But why are the remaining li elements green? Well, that's because `:last-child` is also unqualified, and ul is the last child of body. We've essentially typed `*:first-child` and `*:last-child`.

If we qualify `:first-child` and `:last-child` by adding a simple selector, it all makes more sense. Let's limit our selection to list items. Change `:first-child` to `li:first-child` and `:last-child` to `li:last-child`. Figure 1.30 shows the result.

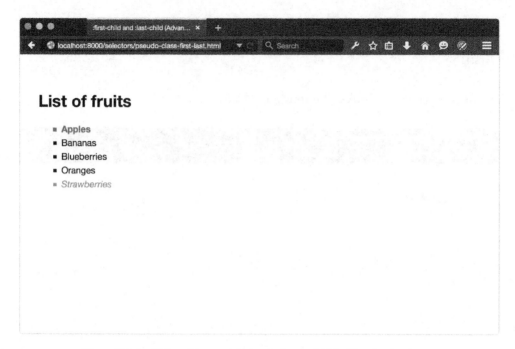

Figure 1.30. Qualifying `:first-child` and `:last-child` with a simple selector

`:nth-child()` and `:nth-last-child()`

The ability to select the first and last children of a document is fine. But what if we want to select odd or even elements instead? Perhaps we'd like to pick the sixth element in a document subtree, or apply styles to every third element. This is where the `:nth-child()` and the `:nth-last-child()` pseudo-classes come into play.

Like `:not()`, `:nth-child()` and `:nth-last-child()` are also functional pseudo-classes. They accept a single argument, which should be either:

- the `odd` keyword

- the `even` keyword

- an integer such as 2 or 8, or

- an argument in the form $An+B$[16] where A is a step interval, B is the offset, and n is a variable representing a positive integer.

---

[16] This $An+B$ syntax is described in CSS Syntax Module Level 3. [http://www.w3.org/TR/css-syntax-3/#anb]

That last item has a degree of complexity. We'll come back to it in a moment.

What's the difference between `:nth-child()` and `:nth-last-child()`? The starting point: `:nth-child()` counts forwards and `:nth-last-child()` counts backwards. CSS indexes use counting numbers and start with one rather than zero.

Both `:nth-child()` and `:nth-last-child()` are useful for alternating patterns. Creating zebra-striped table row colors is the perfect use case. The CSS that follows gives even-numbered table rows a light bluish-gray background, the result of which can be seen in Figure 1.31:

css/chapter1/selectors-nth-child.css (excerpt)

```css
tr:nth-child(even) {
    background: rgba(96, 125, 139, 0.1);
}
```

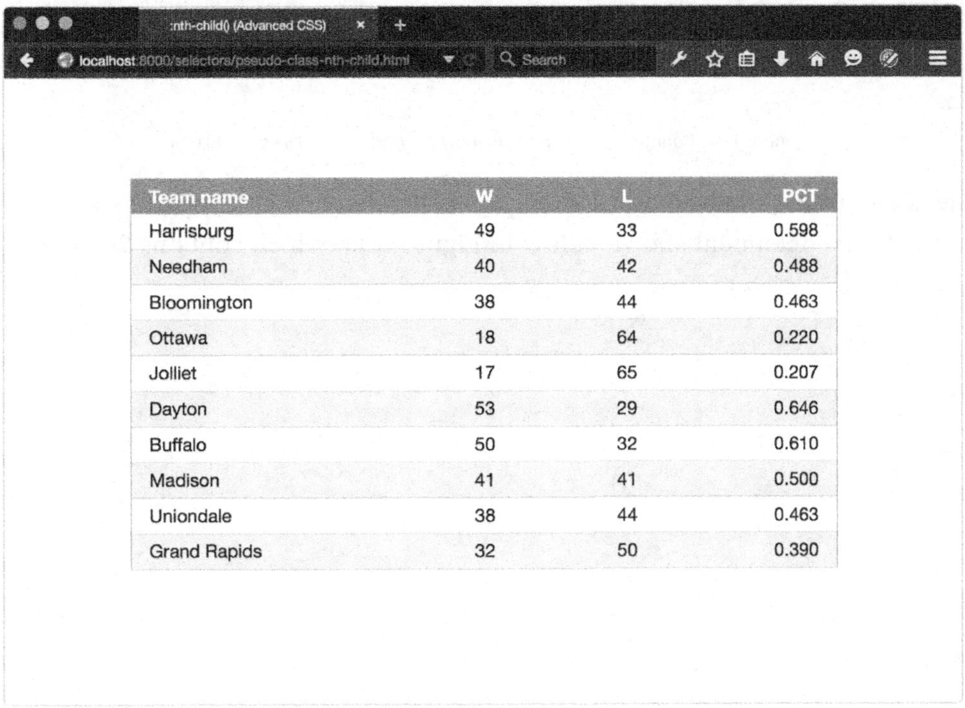

Team name	W	L	PCT
Harrisburg	49	33	0.598
Needham	40	42	0.488
Bloomington	38	44	0.463
Ottawa	18	64	0.220
Jolliet	17	65	0.207
Dayton	53	29	0.646
Buffalo	50	32	0.610
Madison	41	41	0.500
Uniondale	38	44	0.463
Grand Rapids	32	50	0.390

Figure 1.31. Using `:nth-child(even)` to style table rows

Switching `:nth-child` to `:nth-last-child` inverts this banding, since the counting begins from the bottom, shown in Figure 1.32.

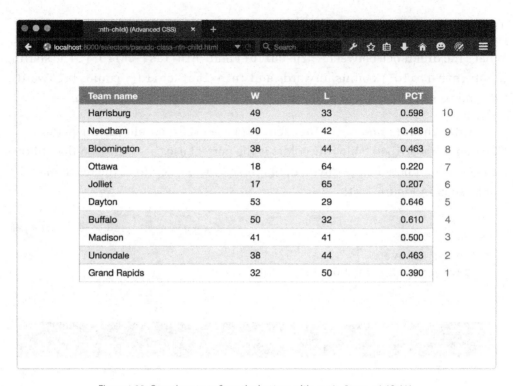

Figure 1.32. Counting starts from the bottom with `:nth-last-child()`

How about trying some complex examples using more complex arguments? We'll start with the document shown below in Figure 1.33, which contains 20 items.

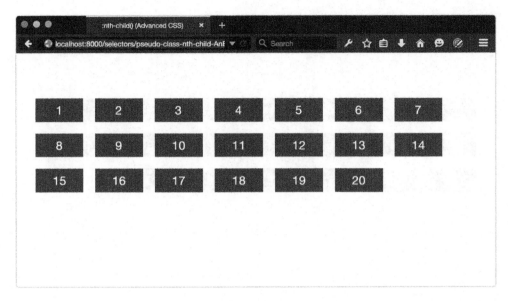

Figure 1.33. A document of 20 div elements

With :nth-child() and :nth-last-child(), we can select a single child at a particular position. We can select all of the children *after* a particular position, or we can select elements by multiples, with an offset. Let's change the background color of the sixth item:

```
.item:nth-child(6) {
    background: #e91e63;
}
```

This gives us the result in Figure 1.34.

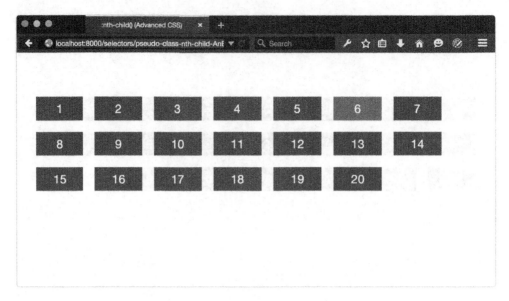

Figure 1.34. Using `:nth-child()` to select a single item by its index

But what if we want to select every third element? Here's where the *An+B* syntax comes in:

```
.item:nth-child(3n) {
    background: #e91e63;
}
```

Again, *A* is a step interval. It's almost like a multiplier for *n*, which starts at 1. So if *A* = 3, then *3n* would match the 3rd, 6th, 9th, and so on elements. That's exactly what happens, as you can see in Figure 1.35.

Figure 1.35. Using *An+B* syntax to select every third element

Here's where matters become a little more interesting. We can use `:nth-child()`
and `:nth-last-child()` to select all elements after a certain point. Let's try selecting
all but the first seven elements:

```
.item:nth-child(n+8) {
    background: #e91e63;
}
```

Here, there is no step value. As a result, n+8 matches every element *n* beginning
with the eighth element, as shown in Figure 1.36.

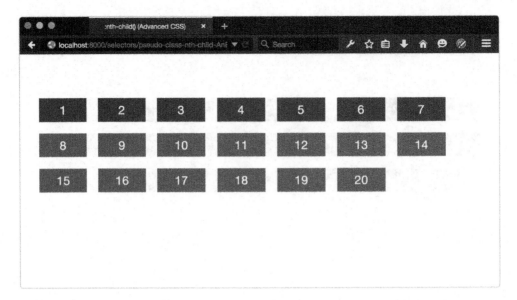

Figure 1.36. Using the step *An+B* microsyntax to select items 8 through 20

Negative Offsets

Negative offset and range values are also valid. Using `:nth-child(-n+8)` would invert our selection, and match the first eight elements.

We can also use the offset and step values to select every third element, starting with the fifth:

```css
.item:nth-child(3n+5) {
    background: #e91e63;
}
```

You can see the results of this selector in Figure 1.37.

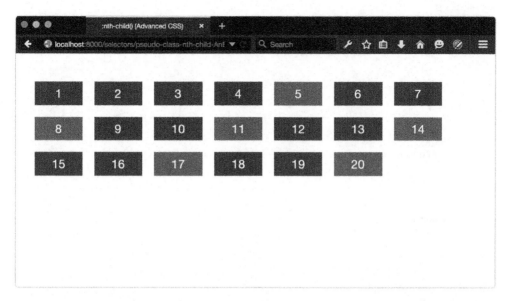

Figure 1.37. Selecting every third element, starting with the fifth

:only-child

The :only-child pseudo-class matches elements if they are the *only* child of another element. Below are two unordered lists. The first has one item while the second contains three:

```
                                           01-selectors/pseudo-class-only-child.html (excerpt)
<ul>
    <li>Apple</li>
</ul>

<ul>
    <li>Orange</li>
    <li>Banana</li>
    <li>Raspberry</li>
</ul>
```

Using li:only-child{color: #9c27b0;} will select <li>Apple</li>, since it's the only child of our first list. None of the items in the second list match, however, because there are three siblings. You can see what this looks like in Figure 1.38.

Figure 1.38. Matching elements with `li:only-child`

:empty

It's also possible to select elements that have *no* children using the `:empty` pseudo-class. Now when we say `:empty`, we mean *empty*. In order for an element to match the `:empty` pseudo-class, it can't contain anything else—not even whitespace. In other words, `<p></p>` will match, but `<p> </p>` will not.

Sometimes WYSIWYG (What You See Is What You Get) editors insert empty p elements to your content. You could use `:empty` in combination with the `:not()` pseudo-class to avoid applying styles to these elements; for example `p:not(:empty)`.

Selecting Elements of a Particular Type by their Index

The pseudo-classes discussed in the previous section match elements if they occupy the given position in a document subtree. For instance, `p:nth-last-child(2)` selects every p element that is the next-to-last element of its parent.

In this section, we'll discuss **typed child-indexed pseudo-classes**. These pseudo-classes also match elements based on the value of their indexes; however, matches are limited to elements of a particular type. Selecting the fifth p element, or even-indexed h2 elements, for example.

There are five such pseudo-classes with names that mirror those of their untyped counterparts:

- `:first-of-type`
- `:last-of-type`
- `:only-of-type`
- `:nth-of-type()`
- `:nth-last-of-type()`

The difference between these and child-indexed pseudo-classes is a subtle one. Where `p:nth-child(5)` matches the fifth item only if it is a p element, `p:nth-of-type(5)` matches all p elements, then finds the fifth p element among those.

Let's start with a slightly different document. It still has 20 items, but some of them are p elements and some of them are div elements. The p elements have rounded corners, as can be seen in Figure 1.39.

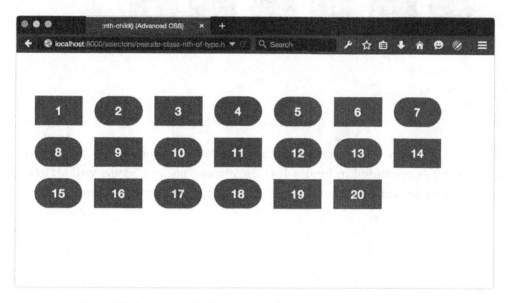

Figure 1.39. A document of 20 items, with p elements indicating rounded corners

Using `:first-of-type`, `:last-of-type`, and `:only-type`

With `:first-of-type`, we can select the first element that matches a selector. How about we give our first p element a lime green background:

```
p:first-of-type {
    background: #cddc39;
}
```

This will match every p element that's the first p element of its parent, shown in Figure 1.40.

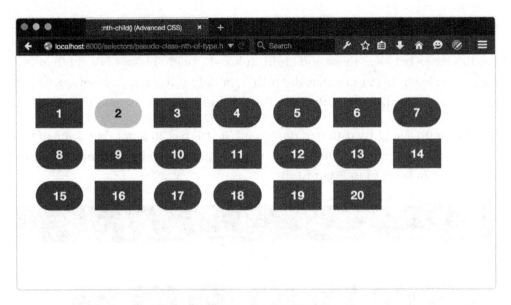

Figure 1.40. Matching the first child p element

The :last-of-type pseudo-class works similarly, matching the last such element of its parent as presented in Figure 1.41. However, :only-of-type will match an element if it's the *only* child element of that type of its parent, illustrated in Figure 1.42.

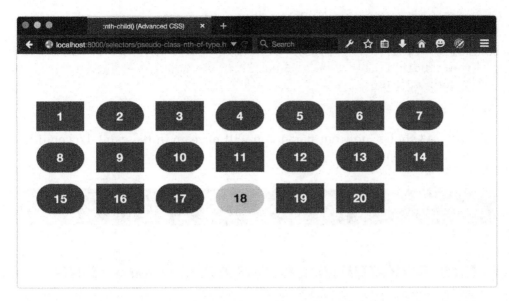

Figure 1.41. The :last-of-type pseudo-class matches the last element of a type

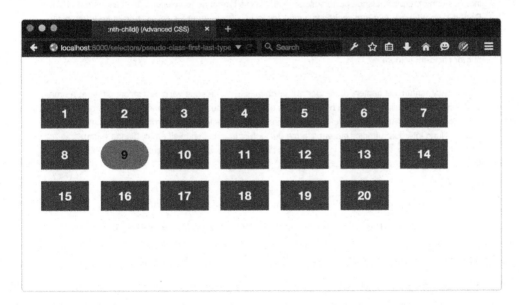

Figure 1.42. Using p:only-of-type to match the only child that's a paragraph element

Let's look at another example of using :first-of-type, but this time with a pseudo-element. Remember the ::first-letter pseudo-element from earlier in this chapter? Well, as you saw, it created an initial capital for every element to which it was applied. How about we go one step further, and limit this initial capital to the first paragraph instead:

01-selectors/pseudo-class-first-of-type-first-letter.html *(excerpt)*

```
p:first-of-type::first-letter {
    font: bold italic 3em / .5 serif;
    color: #3f51b5;
}
```

As Figure 1.43 shows, now our paragraph will have an initial capital, even if it's preceded by a headline.

Figure 1.43. Using `:first-of-type` with the `::first-letter` pseudo-element

Using `:nth-of-type` and `:nth-last-of-type`

The `:nth-of-type()` and `:nth-last-of-type()` are also functional pseudo-classes. They accept the same arguments as `:nth-child()` and `:nth-last-child()`. But like `:first-of-type` and `:last-of-type`, the indexes resolve to elements of the same type. For example, to select the first p element and every other subsequent p element, we can use the odd keyword with `:nth-of-type()`:

```
p:nth-of-type(odd) {
    background: #cddc39;
    color: #121212;
}
```

As you can see from Figure 1.44, this only matches odd-numbered p elements, rather than odd-numbered children.

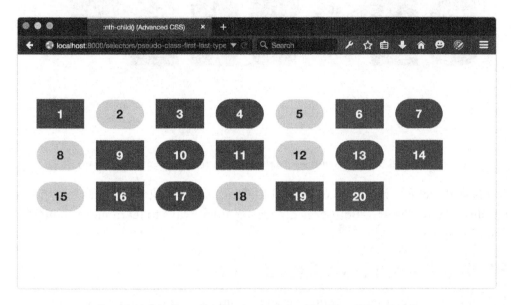

Figure 1.44. Selecting odd-indexed p elements with :nth-of-type(odd)

Similarly, using :nth-last-of-type(even) selects even-numbered p elements, but the count begins from the last p element in the document—in this case, item 18 (Figure 1.45).

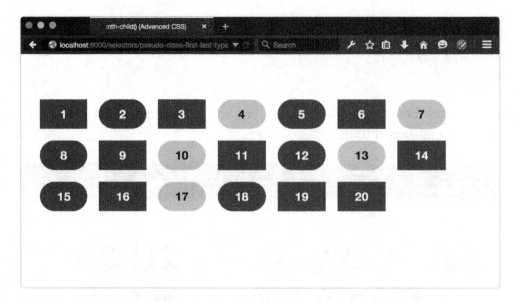

Figure 1.45. Selecting even-indexed p elements with `:nth-last-of-type(even)`

If this still seems fuzzy, play with Paul Maloney's Nth-Test tool,[17] or view the examples at Nth Master.[18] Both projects are excellent ways to learn more about these pseudo-classes.

Styling Form Fields Based on Input

Let's take a look at some pseudo-classes that are specific to form fields and form field input. These pseudo-classes can be used to style fields based on the validity of user input, whether the field is required or currently enabled.

All of the pseudo-classes that follow are specific to forms. As a result, there's less of a need to limit the scope with a selector. Using `:enabled` won't introduce side effects for span elements. Limiting the scope is helpful, however, when you want to syle various types of form controls differently.

`:enabled` and `:disabled`

As their name suggests, these pseudo-classes match elements that have (or lack) the `disabled` HTML5 attribute. This can be an input control such as input, select, or button element (seen shortly), or it can be a `fieldset` element:

---

[17] http://nth-test.com/
[18] http://nthmaster.com/

```
<button type="submit" disabled>Save draft</button>
```

Form elements are enabled by default; that is, they only become disabled if the `disabled` attribute is set. Using `input:enabled` will match every `input` element that is without a `disabled` attribute set. Conversely, `button:disabled` would match all button elements with a `disabled` attribute:

css/chapter1/selectors-nth-child.css (excerpt)

```
button:disabled {
    opacity: .5;
}
```

Figure 1.46 shows the `:enabled` and `:disabled` states for our `button` element.

Figure 1.46. A button in `:enabled` (left) and `:disabled` (right) states

`:required` and `:optional`

Required and optional states are determined by the presence or absence of the `required` attribute on the field.[19] For example:

01-selectors/input-pseudo-class.html (excerpt)

```
<p>
    <label for="email">E-mail:</label>
    <input type="email" id="email" name="email" placeholder=
➥"example: jane.doe@example.com" required>
</p>
```

Most browsers only indicate whether a field is required once the form is submitted. With the `:required` pseudo-class, we can indicate to the user that the field is re-

---

[19] Remember that in HTML5, the presence or absence of the attribute determines its value. In other words, `required="false"` has the same effect as `required="true"`, `required="required"` and `required`.

quired before submission. For example, the following CSS will add a yellow border to our email field from above, and is shown in Figure 1.47:

css/chapter1/selectors-input.css *(excerpt)*

```
input:required {
    border: 1px solid #ffc107;
}
```

E-mail:

example: jane.doe@example.com

Figure 1.47. Indicating that a field is required with `:required`

The `:optional` class works similarly, by matching elements that *do not* have a re-quired attribute. For example, the CSS that follows gives us the results seen in Figure 1.48.

css/chapter1/selectors-input.css *(excerpt)*

```
select:optional {
    border: 1px solid #ccc;
}
```

I am:

— Select —

Figure 1.48. An optional `select` element styled with the `:optional` pseudo-class rendered in Firefox 40

:checked

Unlike the other pseudo-classes that we've covered, `:checked` only applies to radio and checkbox form controls. As the name indicates, this pseudo-class lets us define separate styles for selected inputs.

Unfortunately, styling radio controls and checkboxes in most browsers is about as pleasant as a trip to the dentist for a filling. CSS Basic User Interface Module Level 4[20] attempts to address this with the appearance property, but this property is not

---

[20] http://dev.w3.org/csswg/css-ui-4/#appearance-switching

yet supported. WebKit/Blink-based browsers and Firefox do, however, support nonstandard, vendor-prefixed versions of it.

In order to create custom radio button and checkbox inputs that work well across browsers, we need to become clever with our selectors. We'll use a sibling combinator, a pseudo-element, and `:checked` to create custom radio button and checkbox controls. For example, to change the style of a label when its associated radio button is checked, we could use the following CSS:

```
[type=radio]:checked + label {
    font-weight: bold;
    font-size: 1.1rem;
}
```

This makes the label bold and increases its size when its associated control is checked. We can improve this, though, by using the `::before` pseudo-element with our `label` element to inject a custom control:

css/chapter1/selectors-input.css (excerpt)

```
[type=radio] { opacity: 0; }

[type=radio] + label::before {
    background: #fff;
    content: '';
    display: inline-block;
    border: 1px solid #444;
    height: 1.2rem;
    margin-right: 1em;
    vertical-align: middle;
    width: 1.2rem;
}

[type=radio]:checked + label::before {
    background: #4caf50;
}
```

This gives us the customized controls you see in Figure 1.49.

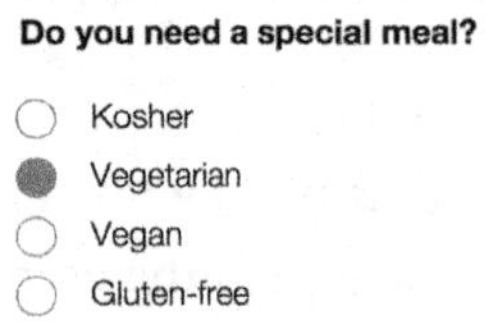

Do you need a special meal?

○ Kosher
● Vegetarian
○ Vegan
○ Gluten-free

Figure 1.49. Using the adjacent sibling combinator and `::before` pseudo-class to create custom radio controls

In order for this technique to work, of course, our HTML needs to be structured appropriately:

▣ The `label` element must be immediately adjacent to its input control.

▣ The form control must have an `id` attribute in addition to the `name` attribute (for example, `<input type="radio" id="chocolate" name="flavor">`).

▣ The `label` must have a `for` attribute, and its value must match the `id` of the form control (for example, `<label for="chocolate">Chocolate</label>`).

Associating the label using `for` with the input ensures that the form input will be selected when the user clicks or taps the label or its child pseudo-element (`::before`).

`:in-range` and `:out-of-range`

The `:in-range` and `:out-of-range` pseudo-classes can be used with `range`, `number`, and `date` input controls. Using `:in-range` and `:out-of-range` requires setting `min` and/or `max` attribute values for the control. Here's an example using the `number` input type:

```
<p>
    <label for="picknum">Enter a number from 1-100</label>
    <input type="number" min="1" max="100" id="picknum" name=
➥"picknum" step="1">
</p>
```

Let's add a little bit of CSS to change styles if the values are within or outside of our range of one to 100:

css/chapter1/selectors-input.css *(excerpt)*

```
:out-of-range {
    background: #ffeb3b;
}

:in-range {
    background: #fff;
}
```

Should the user enter -3 or 101, the background color of `#picknum` will change to yellow as defined in our `:out-of-range` rule set (see Figure 1.50). Otherwise, it will remain white as defined in our `:in-range` rule set.

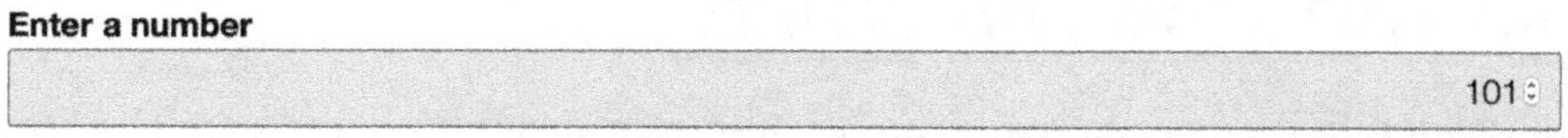

Enter a number

| 101 |

Figure 1.50. Styling `:out-of-range` values

`:valid` and `:invalid`

With the `:valid` and `:invalid` pseudo-classes, we can set styles based on whether or not the form input meets our requirements. This will depend on the validation constraints imposed by the `type` or `pattern` attribute value. For example, an input with `type="email"` will be invalid if the user input is "foo 123," as represented in Figure 1.51.

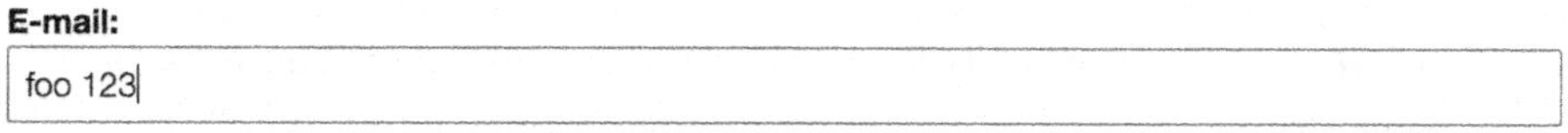

E-mail:

| foo 123 |

Figure 1.51. An email field in the `:invalid` state

A form control will have an invalid state under the following conditions:

- when a required field is an empty field

- when the user's input does not match the `type` or `pattern` constraints

- when the field's input falls outside of the range of its `min` and `max` attribute values

Optional fields with empty values are valid by default. Obviously, if user input satisfies the constraints of the field, it exists in a valid state.

Form controls can have multiple states at once. So you may find yourself managing specificity (discussed in the next section) and cascade conflicts. A way to mitigate this is by limiting which pseudo-classes you use in your projects. For example, don't bother defining an `:optional` rule set if you'll also define a `:valid` rule set.

It's also possible, however, to *chain* pseudo-classes. For example, we can mix the `:focus` and `:invalid` pseudo-classes to style an element only while it has focus: `input:focus:invalid`. By chaining pseudo-classes, we can style an element that has more than one state.

Selectors and Specificity

Think of **specificity** as a score or rank that determines which style declarations are ultimately applied to an element. The universal selector (`*`) has low specificity. ID selectors are highly specific. Descendant selectors such as `p img` and child selectors such as `.panel > h2` are more specific than type selectors such as `p`, `img`, or `h1`.

Calculating exact specificity values seems tricky at first. As explained in Selectors Level 3,[21] you need to:

- count the number of ID selectors in the selector (= A)

- count the number of class selectors, attribute selectors, and pseudo-classes in the selector (= B)

- count the number of type selectors and pseudo-elements in the selector (= C)

- ignore the universal selector

These A, B, and C values are then combined to form a final specificity value. An ID selector such as `#foo` has a specificity of 1,0,0. Attribute selectors, such as `[type=email]` and class selectors such as `.chart` have a specificity of 0,1,0. Adding a pseudo-class such as `:first-child` (for example, `.chart:first-child`) gives us

---

[21] http://dev.w3.org/csswg/selectors-3/#specificity

a specificity of 0,2,0. But using a simple type or element selector such as h1 or p only gives us a specificity of 0,0,1.

Calculating Specificity

Keegan Street's Specificity Calculator[22] and Joshua Peek's CSS Explain[23] are helpful for learning about and calculating selector specificity.

Complex and combinator selectors, of course, give us higher specificity values. Let's look at an example. Consider the following CSS:

```css
ul#story-list > .book-review {
    color: #0c0;
}

#story-list > .book-review {
    color: #f60;
}
```

These two rule sets are similar, but they are not the same. The first selector, ul#story-list > .bookreview, contains a type selector (ul), an ID selector, (#story-list), and a class selector (.bookreview). It has a specificity value of 1,1,1. The second selector, #story-list > .book-review only contains an ID and a class selector. Its specificity value is 1,1,0. Even though our #story-list > .book-review rule succeeds ul#story-list > .bookreview, the higher specificity of the former means that those elements with a .book-review class will be green rather than orange.

Pseudo-classes such as :link or :invalid have the same level of specificity as class selectors. Both a:link and a.external have a specificity value of 0,1,1. Similarly, pseudo-elements such as ::before and ::after are as specific as type or element selectors. In cases where two selectors are equally specific, the cascade kicks in. Here's an example:

[22] http://specificity.keegan.st/
[23] http://josh.github.io/css-explain/

```
a:link {
    color: #369;
}
a.external {
    color: #f60;
}
```

If we applied this CSS, every link would be slate blue except for those with
class="external" applied. Those links would be orange instead.

Keeping specificity low helps prevent **selector creep**, or the tendency for selector
specificity and length to increase over time. This often happens as you add new
developers to a team, or new forms of content to a website. Selector creep also
contributes to long-term maintenance headaches. You either end up using more
specific selectors to override other rule sets, or needing to refactor your code. Longer
selectors also increase the weight of your CSS files.

We discuss strategies for keeping specificity low in Chapter 2.

Conclusion

After reading this chapter, you should have a good understanding of CSS selectors.
Specifically, you should now know how to:

- use selectors to apply CSS to particular elements, pseudo-elements, and pseudo-
  classes

- understand the difference between pseudo-elements and pseudo-classes

- employ newer pseudo-classes introduced by the Selectors Level 3 and 4 specifications

- calculate specificity

In the next chapter, we'll address some golden rules for writing maintainable,
scalable CSS.

Chapter 2

CSS Architecture and Organization

If you've ever worked on a CSS code base of any size—or even a small code base with multiple developers—you quickly realize how difficult it is to create CSS that is predictable, reusable, and maintainable without being bloated. With added developers often comes added complexity: longer selectors, colliding selectors, and heavier CSS.

In this chapter, we'll explore CSS architecture and organization. First up is file structure. We'll take a look at how to manage CSS across large sites, or as part of your own CSS framework. We'll also address how to manage CSS for older browsers.

Next we'll discuss some guidelines for writing CSS. Even if you disavow the CSS architecture methodologies we cover later, you should adhere to these golden guidelines. These rules make it easier to avoid selector-naming collisions and overly long selectors—the kinds of issues that come up within teams.

Finally, we'll take a look at two CSS architecture methodologies: Block-Element-Modifier (BEM) and Atomic CSS. They're radically different to each other, but each approach has its advantages. In both cases, the goal is to create highly reusable, lightweight CSS.

CSS File Organization

Part of a good CSS architecture is file organization. A monolithic file is fine for solo developers or very small projects. For large projects—sites with multiple layouts and content types, or multiple brands under the same design umbrella—it's smarter to use a modular approach and split your CSS across multiple files.

Splitting your CSS across files makes it easier to parcel tasks out to teams. One developer can work on typography-related styles, while another can focus on developing grid components. Teams can split work sensibly and increase overall productivity.

So what might a good file structure that splits the CSS across files look like? Here's a structure similar to ones I've used in recent projects:

- **reset.css**: reset and normalization styles; minimal color, border, or font-related declarations

- **typography.css**: font faces, weights, line heights, sizes, and styles for headings and body text

- **layouts.css**: styles that manage page layouts and segments, including grids

- **forms.css**: styles for form controls and labels

- **lists.css**: list-specific styles

- **tables.css**: table-specific styles

- **carousel.css**: styles required for carousel components

- **accordion.css**: styles for accordion components

If you're using a preprocessor, such as Sass or Less, you may also want to include a **_config.scss** or **_config.less** file that contains color variables and the like.

In this structure, each CSS file has a specific and narrow scope. How many files you'll ultimately end up with depends on how many visual patterns or components are called for by your site's design.

CSS frameworks such as Foundation[1] and Bootstrap[2] use this approach. Both become quite granular with separate files for progress bars, range inputs, close buttons, and tooltips. This allows developers to include only the components that they need for a project.

 Pattern Libraries

A closely related concept to splitting CSS across files like this is the **pattern library**. A great primer on the subject is Anna Debenham's "Getting Started with Pattern Libraries."[3]

How many files?

Even though we're using several CSS files for development, we're not going to serve all of them to the browser in this form. The number of HTTP requests that we'd require would make our site take lonegr to load. Instead, we'll *concatenate* our smaller CSS files into a few larger ones for production.

Concatenation, in this context, means combining multiple files into a single CSS payload. It eliminates the need for @import statements or multiple link elements. Current browsers have limits on how many files they can download at once. We can use concatenation to reduce the number of network requests, getting your content to users in less time.

Often your web development framework will handle concatenation as part of its asset management features, such as Ruby on Rails. Some content management systems do the same, whether as a core feature or an add-on. Preprocessors—introduced in Chapter 9—also make concatenation easy. If neither preprocessors nor development frameworks are part of your workflow, chances are that your operating system has a concatenation utility that you can use instead.

For Mac OS X or Linux, concatenate files using the cat utility:

---

[1] http://foundation.zurb.com

[2] http://getbootstrap.com/

[3] http://alistapart.com/blog/post/getting-started-with-pattern-libraries/

```
cat file1.css file2.css > combined-output-file.css
```

Using Windows? Try the `type` utility:

```
type file1.css file2.css > combined-output-file.css
```

You can also write your own concatenation script using Bash, PHP, Python, or another scripting language of your choice.

 CSS Optimization

> Concatenation is one aspect of CSS optimization. It's just as important to minify your files to remove excess characters and whitespace. Minification tools are covered in ???.

So how many files should you use? That's where it gets tricky. The current best practice is to identify your **critical path** CSS—the minimum amount of CSS your page needs to render—and embed it in your pages using the `style` element. Additional CSS files should be loaded using JavaScript. Addy Osmani's presentation "CSS Performance Tooling"[4] provides an excellent overview of this technique and some tools you can use to implement it. Also see the Filament Group's loadCSS.[5]

If your content will be served using the SPDY or HTTP/2 protocols, concatenation may be unnecessary. With HTTP/1.1, browsers download assets sequentially; the next request begins when the previous one ends. Under that model, reducing the number of network requests improves site performance; however, SPDY and HTTP/2, can download multiple assets at once. As a result, there is no real benefit to reducing the number of requests. There is, however, a cost to sending more bytes than necessary to render the page. William Chan's "HTTP/2 Considerations and Tradeoffs"[6] explains this in greater detail. The best approach would be to identify if your server is serving HTTP/2 and, if so, check whether more of you users will benefit from actually splitting your assets down and only loading that which the page needs, or continuing to work in the old way. If you're interested in learning more about per-

---

[4] https://www.youtube.com/watch?v=FEs2jgZBaQA
[5] https://github.com/filamentgroup/loadCSS
[6] https://insouciant.org/tech/http-slash-2-considerations-and-tradeoffs/

formance optimization methods, the SitePoint book *Lean Websites*[7] is a useful resource.

Managing Styles for Legacy Browsers

Cross-browser compatibility is the best it's ever been. The speed with which users upgrade their browsers is also the best it's ever been. Unfortunately, not all web users are using the latest and greatest version of their browser, so we'll still need to manage CSS for those browsers. There are a couple of ways to do this.

Using Conditional Comments (IE9 and Earlier)

Internet Explorer 9 and earlier versions support conditional comments, which enable us to serve CSS, JavaScript, or portions of HTML only to IE users:

```
<!--[if IE]>
CSS, JavaScript, or HTML goes here.
<![endif]-->
```

Conditional comments use a collection of operators to specify the condition under which the code contained within it should be applied, as shown in Table 2.1.[8]

Table 2.1. Commonly used conditional comments operators

Operator	Purpose
!	NOT operator; negates the condition
lt	Less-than operator
lte	Less-than or equal-to operator
gt	Greater-than operator
gte	Greater-than or equal-to operator

To serve CSS to Internet Explorer 9 alone, you could use the following:

---

[7] https://www.sitepoint.com/premium/books/lean-websites
[8] The Microsoft Developer Network documentation features a complete list of conditional comment operators. [https://msdn.microsoft.com/en-us/library/ms537512%28v%3Dvs.85%29.aspx]

```
<!--[if IE 9]>
<link rel="stylesheet" href="ie9.css" type="text/css">
<![endif]-->
```

A better approach, however—particularly if you still need to support Internet Explorer 8—is to add the less-than or equal-to operator:

```
<!--[if lte IE 9]>
<link rel="stylesheet" href="ie.css" type="text/css">
<![endif]-->
```

Conditional comments are deprecated in Internet Explorer 10+; they aren't available in standards mode. That brings us to our other approach.

Using CSS Parsing to Our Advantage

Another approach to supporting older browsers is inherent to CSS. We can take advantage of CSS error handling and the cascade to define styles for older browsers. This method relies on two rules of CSS parsing:

1. The last declaration parsed is the one that's used.
2. If a browser fails to understand a rule, it will ignore it.

In other words, we can provide a fallback value and an enhanced value for a property. The browser will choose which to implement based on what it supports. Here's an example:

```
.title {
    text-decoration: underline;
    text-decoration: underline wavy #c09;
}
```

In browsers that support CSS 3 `text-decoration` values, users will see a wavy pink line under elements with the `title` class; in browsers without support, they'll see a plain underline. These rules can exist within the same CSS file and declaration block, but you may decide to segregate legacy rules in their own file so that they can be removed as your audience adopts newer browsers.

Now that we've discussed the basics of CSS file structure and legacy browser management, let's look at some CSS architecture techniques.

Golden Guidelines for Writing Clean CSS

As mentioned, there are some rules for writing clean CSS that you should try your best to avoid breaking. They'll help you write CSS that is lightweight and reusable:

- Avoid global and element selectors
- Omit overly specific selectors
- Use semantic class names
- Don't tie CSS too closely to markup structure

Let's look at these one by one.

Avoid Global Selectors

Global selectors include the universal selector (*), element selectors such as p, button, and h1, and attribute selectors such as [type=checkbox]. Style declarations applied to these selectors will be applied to every such element across the site. Here's an example:

```
button {
    background: #FFC107;
    border: 1px outset #FF9800;
    display: block;
    font: bold 16px / 1.5 sans-serif;
    margin: 1rem auto;
    width: 50%;
    padding: .5rem;
}
```

This seems innocuous enough. But what if we want to create a button that's styled differently? Let's style a .close button that will be used to close dialog modules:

```
<section class="dialog">
    <button type="button" class="close">Close</button>
</section>
```

 Why not use dialog?

We're using section here instead of the dialog element because support for dialog is limited to Blink-based browsers such as Chrome/Chromium, Opera, and Yandex.

Now we need to write CSS to override every line that we don't want to inherit from the button rule set:

```
.close {
    background: #e00;
    border: 2px solid #fff;
    color: #fff;
    display: inline-block;
    margin: 0;
    font-size: 12px;
    font-weight: normal;
    line-height: 1;
    padding: 5px;
    border-radius: 100px;
    width: auto;
}
```

We'd still need many of these declarations to override browser defaults. But what if we scope our button styles to a .default class instead? We can then drop the display, font-weight, line-height, margin, padding, and width declarations from our .close rule set. That's a 23% reduction in size:

```
.default {
    background: #FFC107;
    border: 1px outset #FF9800;
    display: block;
    font: bold 16px / 1.5 sans-serif;
    margin: 1rem auto;
    width: 50%;
    padding: .5rem;
}
```

```
.close {
    background: #e00;
    border: 2px solid #fff;
    color: #fff;
    font-size: 12px;
    padding: 5px;
    border-radius: 100px;
}
```

Just as importantly, avoiding global selectors reduces the risk of styling conflicts. A developer working on one module or document won't inadvertently add a rule that creates a side effect in another module or document.

Global styles and selectors are perfectly okay for resetting and normalizing default browser styles. In most other cases, however, they invite bloat.

Avoid Overly Specific Selectors

Maintaining low specificity in your selectors is one of the keys to creating light-weight, reusable, and maintainable CSS. As you may recall from the previous chapter's section on specificity, a type selector has the specificity 0,0,1. Class selectors, on the other hand, have a specificity of 0,1,0:

```
/* Specificity of 0,0,1 */
p {
    color: #222;
    font-size: 12px;
}

/* Specificity of 0,1,0 */
.error {
    color: #a00;
}
```

When you add a class name to an element, the rules for that selector take precedence over more generic-type selector rules. There's no need to further qualify a class selector by combining it with a type selector. Doing so increases the specificity of that selector and increases the overall file size.

Put differently, using p.error is unnecessarily specific because .error achieves the same goal. Another advantage is that .error can be reused with other elements. A p.error selector limits the .error class to p elements.

Don't Chain Classes

Also avoid chaining class selectors. Selectors such as .message.warning have a specificity of 0,2,0. Higher specificity means they're hard to override, plus chaining often causes side effects. Here's an example:

```
.message {
    background: #eee;
    border: 2px solid #333;
    border-radius: 1em;
    padding: 1em;
}
.message.error {
    background: #f30;
    color: #fff;
}
.error {
    background: #ff0;
    border-color: #fc0;
}
```

Using <p class="message"> with this CSS gives us a nice gray box with a dark gray border, as seen in Figure 2.1.

Figure 2.1. The visual effect of our .message selector

Using <p class="message error">, however, gives us the background of .message.error and the border of .error shown in Figure 2.2.

An error occurred.

Figure 2.2. The visual result of using .message.error as a selector

The only way to override a chained class selector would be to use an even more specific selector. To be rid of the yellow border, we'd need to add a class name or type selector to the chain: `.message.warning.exception` or `div.message.warning`. It's more expedient to create a new class instead. If you do find yourself chaining selectors, go back to the drawing board. Either the design has inconsistencies, or you're chaining prematurely in an attempt to prevent problems that you don't have. Fix those problems. The maintenance headaches you'll prevent and the reusability you'll gain are worth it.

Avoid Using `id` Selectors

Because you can only have one element per `id` per document, rule sets that use `id` selectors are hard to repurpose. Doing so typically involves using a list of `id` selectors; for example, `#sidebar-features` and `#sidebar-sports`.

Identifiers also have a high degree of specificity, so we'll need longer selectors to override declarations. In the CSS that follows, we need to use `#sidebar.sports` and `#sidebar.local` to override the background color of `#sidebar`:

```
#sidebar {
    float: right;
    width: 25%;
    background: #eee;
}
#sidebar.sports  {
    background: #d5e3ff;
}
#sidebar.local {
    background: #ffcccc;
}
```

Switching to a class selector, such as `.sidebar`, lets us simplify our selector chain:

```
.sidebar {
    float: right;
    width: 25%;
    background: #eee;
}
.sports  {
    background: #d5e3ff;
}
```

```
.local {
    background: #ffcccc;
}
```

As well as saving us a few bytes, our `.sports`, and `.local` rule sets can now be added to other elements.

Using an attribute selector such as `[id=sidebar]` lets us get around the higher specificity of an identifier. Though it lacks the reusability of a class selector, the low specificity means that we can avoid chaining selectors.

When the High Specificity of `id` Selectors is Useful

In some circumstances, you might *want* the higher specificity of an `id` selector. For example, a network of media sites might wish to use the same navigation bar across all of its web properties. This component must be consistent across sites in the network, and should be hard to restyle. Using an `id` selector reduces the chances of those styles being accidentally overridden.

Finally, let's talk about selectors such as `#main article.sports table#stats tr:nth-child(even) td:last-child`. Not only is it absurdly long, but with a specificity of 2,3,4, it's also not reusable. How many *possible* instances of this selector can there be in your markup? Let's make this better. We can immediately trim our selector to `#stats tr:nth-child(even) td:last-child`. It's specific enough to do the job. Yet the far better approach—for both reusability and to minimize the number of bytes—is to use a class name instead.

A Symptom of Preprocessor Nesting

Overly specific selectors are often the result of too much preprocessor nesting. We'll discuss this more in Chapter 9.

Use Semantic Class Names

When we use the word *semantic*, we mean *meaningful*. Class names should describe what the rule does or the type of content it affects. We also want names that will endure changes in the design requirements. Naming is harder than it looks.

Here are examples of what not to do: `.red-text`, `.blue-button`, `.border-4px`, `.margin10px`. What's wrong with these? They are too tightly coupled to the existing design choices. Using `class="red-text"` to mark up an error message does work. But what happens if the design changes and error messages become black text inside orange boxes? Now your class name is inaccurate, making it tougher for you and your colleagues to understand what's happening in the code.

A better choice in this case is to use a class name such as `.alert`, `.error`, or `.message-error`. These names indicate how the class should be used and the kind of content (error messages) that they affect. For class names that define page layout, add a prefix such as `layout-`, `grid-`, `col-`, or simply `l-` to indicate at a glance what it is they do. The section on BEM methodology later on describes a process for this.

Avoid Tying CSS Closely to Markup

You've probably used child or descendant selectors in your code. Child selectors follow the pattern `E > F` where F is an element, and E is its *immediate* parent. For example, `article > h1` affects the h1 element in `<article><h1>Advanced CSS</h1></article>`, but not the h1 element in `<article><section><h1>Advanced CSS</h1></section></article>`. A descendant selector, on the other hand, follows the pattern `E F` where F is an element, and E is an ancestor. To use our previous example, `article h1` selects the h1 element in both cases.

Neither child nor descendant selectors are inherently bad. In fact, they work well to limit the scope of CSS rules. But they're far from ideal, however, because markup occasionally changes.

Raise your hand if you've ever experienced the following. You've developed some templates for a client and your CSS uses child and descendant selectors in several places. Most of those children and descendants are also element selectors, so selectors such as `.promo > h2` and `.media h3` are all over your code. Your client also hired an SEO consultant, who reviewed your markup and suggested you change your h2 and h3 elements to h1 and h2 elements. The problem is that we also have to change our CSS.

Once again, class selectors reveal their advantage. Using `.promo > .headline` or `.media .title` (or more simply `.promo-headline` and `.media-title`) lets us change our markup without having to change our CSS.

Of course, this rule assumes that you have access to and control over the markup. This may not be true if you're dealing with a legacy CMS. It's appropriate and necessary to use child, descendant, or pseudo-class selectors in such cases.

More Architecturally Sound CSS Rules

Philip Walton discusses these and other these rules in his article "CSS Architecture."[9] I also recommend Harry Roberts' site CSS Guidelines[10] and Nicolas Gallagher's post About HTML Semantics and Front-end Architecture[11] for more thoughts on CSS architecture.

We'll now look at two methodologies for CSS architecture. Both methods were created to improve the development process for large sites and large teams; however, they work just as well for teams of one.

Block–Element–Modifier (BEM)

BEM,[12] or Block-Element-Modifier, is a methodology, a naming system, and a suite of related tools. Created at Yandex,[13] BEM was designed for rapid development by sizable development teams. In this section, we'll focus on the concept and the naming system.

BEM methodology encourages designers and developers to think of a website as a collection of reusable component *blocks* that can be mixed and matched to create interfaces. A block is simply a section of a document, such as a header, footer, or sidebar, illustrated in Figure 2.3. Perhaps confusingly, "block" here refers to the segments of HTML that make up a page or application.

---

[9] http://philipwalton.com/articles/css-architecture/

[10] http://cssguidelin.es/

[11] http://nicolasgallagher.com/about-html-semantics-front-end-architecture/

[12] https://en.bem.info/

[13] https://www.yandex.com/

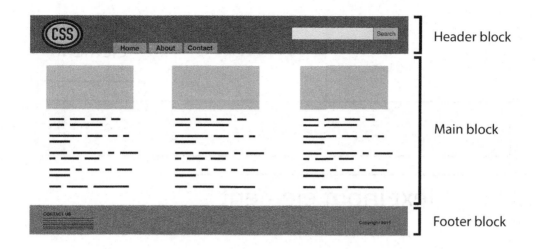

Figure 2.3. A home page might have header, main, and footer blocks

Blocks can contain other blocks. For example, a header block might also contain logo, navigation, and search form blocks as seen in Figure 2.4. A footer block might contain a site map block.

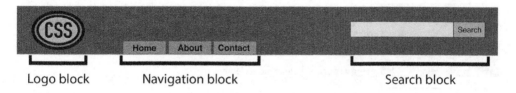

Figure 2.4. A header block that contains logo, navigation, and search blocks

More granular than a block is an **element**. As the BEM documentation explains:[14]

> An element is a part of a block that performs a certain function. Elements are context-dependent: they only make sense in the context of the block they belong to.

A search form block, for example, contains a text input element and a submit button element, as evident in Figure 2.5. To clarify, we're using "element" in the design element sense rather than the HTML element sense.

---

[14] https://en.bem.info/method/definitions/

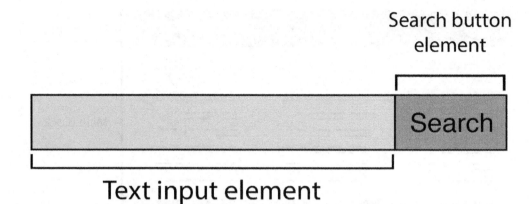

Figure 2.5. A search block with text input and submit button elements

A main content block, on the other hand, might have an article list block. This article list block might contain a series of article promo blocks. And each article promo block might contain image, excerpt, and **Read More** elements, as presented in Figure 2.6.

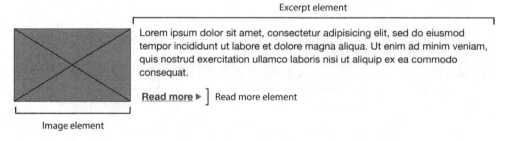

Figure 2.6. A promotional block for a website article

Together, blocks and elements form the basis of the BEM naming convention. According to the rules of BEM:

▥ Block names must be unique within a project.

▥ Element names must be unique within a block.

▥ Variations of a block—say, a search box with a dark background—should add a modifier to the class name.

Block names and element names are usually separated by a double underscore (`.block__element`). Block and element names are typically separated from modifier names by a double hyphen (for example, `.block--modifier` or `.block__element--modifier`).

Here's what BEM looks like using a search form example:

```
<form class="search">
    <div class="search__wrapper">
        <label for="s" class="search__label">Search for: </label>
        <input type="text" id="s" class="search__input">
        <button type="submit" class="search__submit">Search</button>
    </div>
</form>
```

A variation of this form with a dark background might use the following markup:

```
<form class="search search--inverse">
    <div class="search__wrapper search__wrapper--inverse">
        <label for="s" class="search__label search_label--inverse">
➥Search for: </label>
        <input type="text"  id="s" class="search__input search__input
➥--inverse">
        <button type="submit" class="search__submit search__submit--
➥inverse">Search</button>
    </div>
</form>
```

Our CSS might look like this:

```
.search {
    color: #333;
}
.search--inverse {
    color: #fff;
    background: #333;
}
.search__submit {
    background: #333;
    border: 0;
    color: #fff;
    height: 2rem;
    display: inline-block;
}
.search__submit--inverse {
```

```
    color: #333;
    background: #ccc;
}
```

In both our markup and CSS, search--inverse and search__label--inverse are
additional class names. They're not replacements for search and search__label.
Class names are the only type of selector used in a BEM system. Child and descendant selectors may be used, but descendants should also be class names. Element
and ID selectors are verboten. This ensures that selector specificity remains low,
selectors are without side effects, and CSS is independent of markup patterns. En-
forcing block and element name uniqueness also prevents naming collisions, which
can become a problem among teams.

There are several advantages to this approach:

- it's easy for new team members to read the markup and CSS, and understand
  its behavior

- adding more developers increases team productivity

- consistent naming reduces the possibility of class name collisions and side effects

- CSS is independent of markup

- CSS is highly reusable

There's a lot more to BEM than what can comfortably fit in a section of a chapter.
The BEM site describes this methodology in much greater detail, and also features
tools and tutorials to get you started. To learn more about the naming convention
aspect of BEM, another fantastic resource is Get BEM.[15]

Atomic CSS

If BEM is the industry darling, Atomic CSS is its rebellious maverick. Named and
explained by Thierry Koblentz of Yahoo in his 2013 piece, "Challenging CSS Best
Practices,"[16] Atomic CSS uses a tight library of class names. These class names are
often abbreviated and divorced from the content they affect. In an Atomic CSS

[15] http://getbem.com/introduction/
[16] http://www.smashingmagazine.com/2013/10/21/challenging-css-best-practices-atomic-approach/

system, you can tell what the class name does; but there is no relationship between class names—at least, not those used in the stylesheet—and content types.

Let's illustrate with an example. Below is a set of rules in what we might call a conventional CSS architecture. These rule sets use class names that describe the content to which they apply: a global message box, and styles for "success," "warning," and "error" message boxes:

```
.msg {
    background-color: #a6d5fa;
    border: 2px solid #2196f3;
    border-radius: 10px;
    font-family: sans-serif;
    padding: 10px;
}
.msg-success {
    background-color: #aedbaf;
    border: 2px solid #4caf50;
}
.msg-warning {
    background-color: #ffe8a5;
    border-color:  #ffc107;
}
.msg-error {
    background-color: #faaaa4;
    border-color: #f44336;
}
```

To create an error message box, we'd need to add both the msg and msg-error class names to the element's class attribute:

```
<p class="msg msg-error">An error occurred.</p>
```

Let's contrast this with an atomic system, where each declaration becomes its own class:

```
.bg-a {
    background-color: #a6d5fa;
}
.bg-b {
    background-color: #aedbaf;
}
```

```
.bg-c {
    background-color: #ffe8a5;
}
.bg-d {
    background-color: #faaaa4;
}
.bc-a{
    border-color: #2196f3;
}
.bc-b {
    border-color: #4caf50;
}
.bc-c {
    border-color:  #ffc107;
}
.bc-d {
    border-color:  #f44336;
}
.br-1x {
    border-radius: 10px;
}
.bw-2x {
    border-width: 2px;
}
.bss {
    border-style: solid;
}
.sans {
    font-style: sans-serif;
}
.p-1x {
    padding: 10px;
}
```

That's a lot more CSS. Let's now recreate our error message component. Using Atomic CSS, our markup becomes:

```
<p class="bw-2 bss p-1x sans br-1x bg-d bc-d">
    An error occurred.
</p>
```

Our markup is also more verbose. But what happens when we create a warning message component?

```
<p class="bw-2 bss p-1x sans br-1x bg-c bc-c">
    Warning: The price for that item has changed.
</p>
```

Two class names changed: bg-d and bc-d were replaced with bg-c and bc-c. We've reused five rule sets. Now, let's create a button:

```
<button type="button" class="p-1x sans bg-a br-1x">Save</button>
```

Hey now! Here we've reused four rule sets and avoided adding any more rules to our stylesheet. In a robust atomic CSS architecture, adding a new HTML component such as an article sidebar won't require adding more CSS (though, in reality, it might require adding a bit more). Atomic CSS is a bit like using utility classes in your CSS, but taken to the extreme. Specifically, it:

- keeps CSS trim by creating highly granular, highly reusable styles, instead of a rule set for every component

- greatly reduces specificity conflicts by using a system of low-specificity selectors

- allows for rapid HTML component development once the initial rule sets are defined

However, Atomic CSS is not without controversy.

The Case Against Atomic CSS

Atomic CSS runs counter to just about everything we've been taught on writing CSS. It feels almost as wrong as sticking style attributes everywhere. Indeed, this is one of the major criticisms of the Atomic CSS methodology: it blurs the line between content and presentation. If class="fl m-1x" floats an element to the left and adds a ten-pixel margin, what do we do when we no longer want that element to float left?

One answer, of course, is to remove the fl class from our element. But now we're changing HTML. The whole reason behind using CSS is so that markup is unaffected by presentation and vice versa. (We can also solve this problem by removing the .fl {float: left;} rule from our stylesheet, although that would affect every element with a class name of f1). Still, updating the HTML may be a small price to pay for trimmer CSS.

In Koblentz's original post, he used class names such as .M-10 for margin: 10px and .P-10 for padding: 10px. The problem with such a naming convention should be obvious. Changing to a margin of five or 20 pixels means we'd need to update our CSS *and* our HTML, or risk having class names that fail to accurately describe their effect.

Using class names such as p-1x, as done in this section, resolves that issue. The 1x part of the class name indicates a ratio rather than a defined number of pixels. If the base padding is five pixels (that is, .p-1x { padding: 5px; }), then .p-2x would set ten pixels of padding. Yes, that's less descriptive of what the class name does, but it also means that we can change our CSS without updating our HTML, or without creating a misleading class name.

An atomic CSS architecture doesn't prevent us from using class names that describe the content *in our markup*. You can still add .button-close or .accordion-trigger to your code. Such class names are preferable for JavaScript and DOM manipulation.

BEM versus Atomic CSS

BEM works best when you have a large number of developers building CSS and HTML modules in parallel. It helps to prevent the kind of mistakes and bugs that are created by sizable teams. It scales well, in part, because the naming convention is descriptive and predictable. BEM isn't *only* for large teams; but it works *really well* for large teams.

Atomic CSS works better when there is a small team or a single engineer responsible for developing a set of CSS rules, with full HTML components built by a larger team. With Atomic CSS, developers can just look at a style guide—or the CSS source—to determine which set of class names they'll need for a particular module.

Conclusion

After reading this chapter, you should now know:

-   why class selectors are the most flexible selector for writing scalable, maintainable CSS

- how to make your CSS work independently of your markup
- the basics of BEM and Atomic CSS, along with knowing the pros and cons of each

In the next chapter, you'll learn what to do when you find a bug in your CSS. We'll also discuss several tools for making your CSS files smaller.

Debugging and Optimization

On your road to becoming an advanced CSS developer, you'll need to know how to troubleshoot and optimize your CSS. How do you diagnose and fix rendering problems? How do you ensure that your CSS creates no performance lags for end users?

It's also important to ensure code quality. Were you a little too verbose with your comments? Do we have too many unused selectors? Are our selectors overly specific in a way that could affect performance?

Knowing which tools to use will help you ensure that your front end works well. In this chapter, we'll look at tools to help you analyze and troubleshoot your CSS. They fall into three categories:

1. Debugging tools, such as browser-based developer tools and remote debugging services

2. Minification tools

3. Code-quality tools

In this chapter, we'll delve into the browser-based developer tools for Chrome, Safari, Firefox, and Internet Explorer. We'll also explore a few command-line Node.js-based tools to help you streamline the CSS you put into production.

Browser-based Developer Tools

Most modern browsers include an element inspector feature that you can use to troubleshoot your CSS. Start using this feature by right-clicking and selecting **Inspect Element** from the menu. Mac users can also inspect an element by clicking the element while pressing the **Ctrl** key. Figure 3.1 indicates what you should expect to see in Firefox.

Figure 3.1. The developer tools of Firefox Developer edition

In Firefox, Chrome, Opera, and Safari, you can also press **Ctrl** + **Shift** + **I** (Windows / Linux) or **Cmd** + **Option** + **I** (OS X) to open the developer tools panel. Figure 3.2 reveals how Chrome should look.

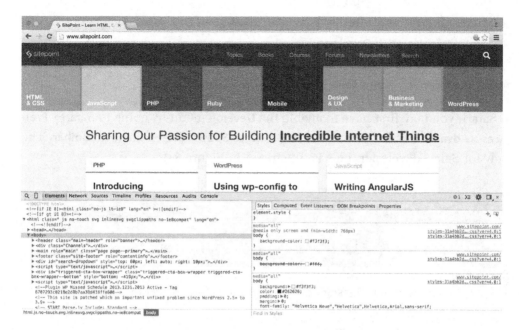

Figure 3.2. Chrome 40 developer

While in Internet Explorer or Microsoft Edge, open developer tools by pressing the **F12** key, as seen in Figure 3.3.

Figure 3.3. Internet Explorer 11 F12 Developer Tools

You can also open each browser's developer tools using the application's menu:

- Microsoft Edge and Internet Explorer: **Tools > F12 Developer Tools**
- Firefox: **Tools > Web Developer**
- Chrome (and Opera 15+): **View > Developer**
- Safari: **Develop > Show Web Inspector**

In Safari, you may first have to enable the **Develop** menu by going to *Safari* > **Preferences** > **Advanced** and checking the box next to **Show Develop menu in toolbar**. The view for Safari developer tools is illustrated in Figure 3.4.

Figure 3.4. Safari 8 developer tools

After opening the developer tools interface, you may then need to select the correct panel:

- Internet Explorer: **DOM Explorer**
- Firefox: **Inspector**
- Chrome (and Opera): **Elements**
- Safari: **Inspect** and **Styles**.

You'll know you're in the right place when you see HTML on one side of the panel, and CSS rules on the other.

Markup in HTML Panel May Differ from Original

The markup you'll see in the HTML panel is a representation of the DOM. It's generated when the browser finishes parsing the document and may differ from your original markup.

Using the Styles Panel

Sometimes an element doesn't behave as expected. Maybe a typographical change failed to take or there's less padding around a paragraph than you wanted. You can determine which rules are affecting an element by using the **Styles** panel of the Web Inspector.

Browsers are fairly consistent in how they organize the **Styles** panel, seen in Figure 3.5. Inline styles, if any, are typically listed first. These are styles set using the `style` attribute of HTML, whether by the CSS author or programmatically via scripting.

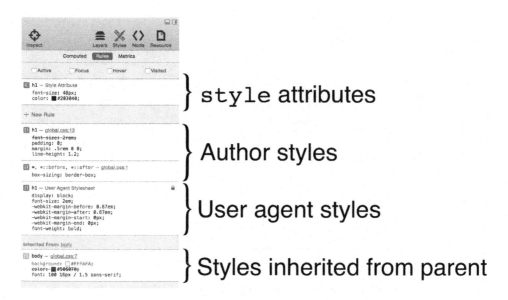

Figure 3.5. Inspecting styles in Safari

Inline styles are followed by a list of style rules applied via author stylesheets—those written by you or your colleagues. Styles in this list may be grouped by media query and/or filename.

Authored style rules precede user agent styles. These are the browser's own default styles that have an impact on your site's look and feel.[1]

Properties and values are grouped by selector. A checkbox sits next to each property, letting you toggle specific rules on and off. Clicking on a property or value allows you to change it, so you can avoid having to edit, save and reload.

Identifying Cascade and Inheritance Problems

As you inspect styles, you may notice that some properties appear crossed out. These properties have been overridden either by a cascading rule, a conflicting rule, or a more specific selector, as depicted in Figure 3.6.

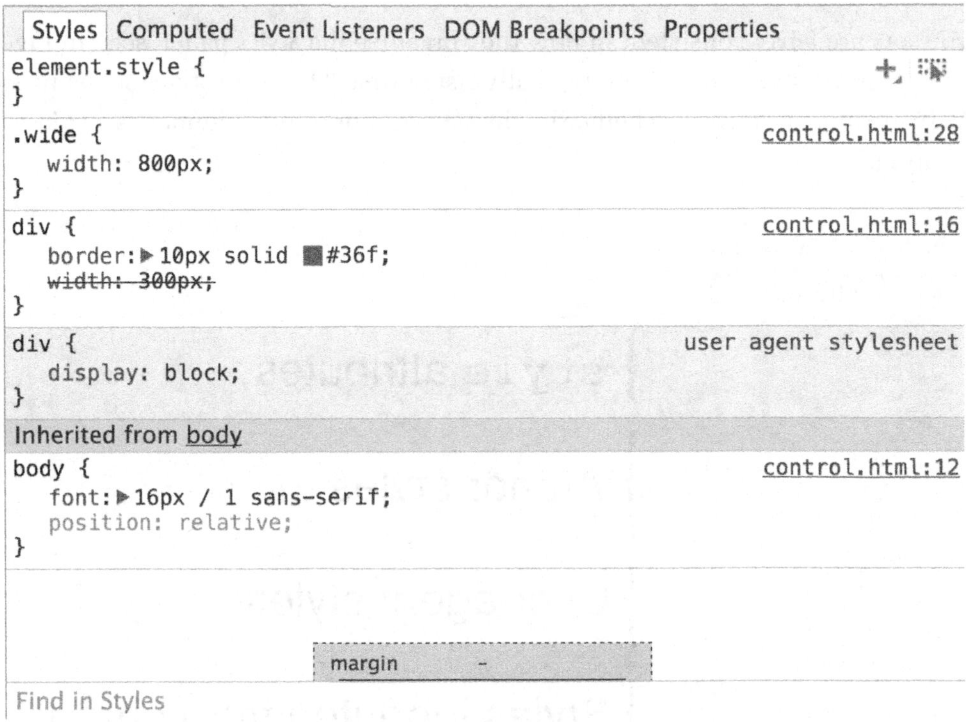

| Styles | Computed | Event Listeners | DOM Breakpoints | Properties |

```
element.style {                                    +, ⌖
}
.wide {                                    control.html:28
    width: 800px;
}
div {                                      control.html:16
    border:▶10px solid ■#36f;
    width: 300px;
}
div {                                 user agent stylesheet
    display: block;
}
Inherited from body
body {                                     control.html:12
    font:▶16px / 1 sans-serif;
    position: relative;
}


            margin        -
```

Find in Styles

Figure 3.6. The width for .wide overrides the width for the div element selector

---

[1] In Firefox, you may have to select the **Show Browser Styles** option in order to view user agent styles. You can find this setting in the **Toolbox Options** panel.

Spotting Invalid Properties and Values

You can also use the element inspector to spot invalid properties or property values. In Chrome and Opera, invalid CSS rules both have a line through them and an adjacent warning icon, which can be seen in Figure 3.7.

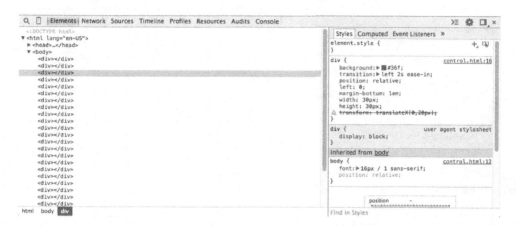

Figure 3.7. Spotting an invalid CSS property value using Chrome

In Figure 3.8, Safari strikes through invalid rules with a red line.

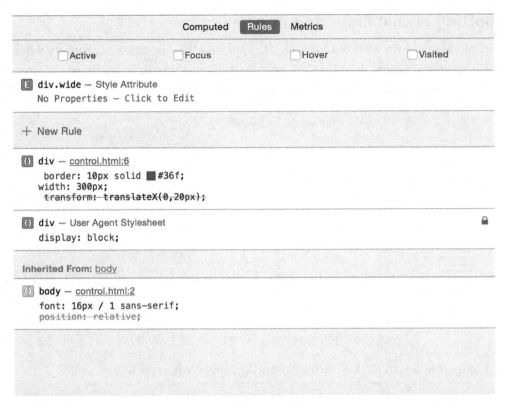

Figure 3.8. An invalid CSS property value in Safari

Microsoft Edge also uses a strike-through to indicate invalid rules. However, Internet Explorer 10 and 11 use a squiggly red underline, seen in Figure 3.9.

Figure 3.9. An unsupported CSS property value in Internet Explorer 11

Earlier versions of Internet Explorer and current versions of Firefox ignore unrecognized properties and values, and don't display them in the styles inspector.

When it comes to basic debugging and inheritance conflicts, whichever browser you use is of no consequence. You should still familiarize yourself with all of them for those occasions when you need to diagnose a browser-specific issue.

Multi-device Tools

On-device testing is always best, but during development, it's often helpful to simulate mobile devices with your desktop browser. All major desktop browsers except for Safari < 9 include a mode for responsive debugging.

Chrome and Opera

Chrome and Opera 19+ offer a **device mode** feature as part of its developer toolkit. To use it, click the device icon (pictured in Figure 3.10) in the upper-left corner, next to the search icon.

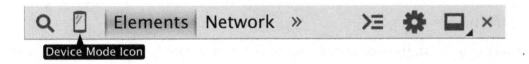

Figure 3.10. The device mode icon in Chrome 40

Device mode lets you emulate several kinds of Android and iOS devices, including the BlackBerry Z10 and iPhone, as shown in Figure 3.11. Device mode also includes a network throttling feature for approximating different network speeds.

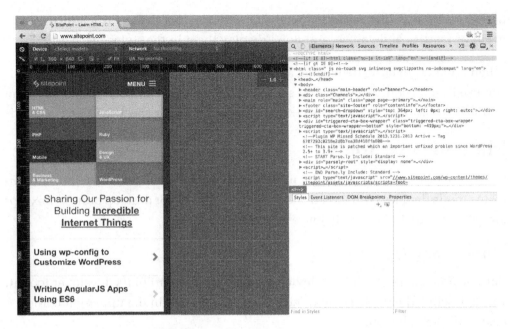

Figure 3.11. Emulating mobile devices and network speeds using your desktop browser

Firefox

In Firefox, the equivalent mode is known as *responsive design mode*. It's the square-within-a-square icon in the developer tools panel seen in Figure 3.12.

Figure 3.12. Look for the square-within-a-square icon to activate Firefox's responsive mode

In responsive mode, you can toggle between portrait and landscape orientations, simulate touch events, and capture screenshots, as shown in Figure 3.13.

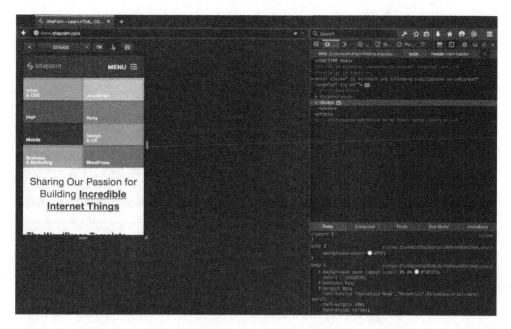

Figure 3.13. Responsive mode in action in Firefox 35

Microsft Edge and Internet Explorer 11

Both Microsoft Edge and Internet Explorer 11 makes it possible to mimic Windows Phone devices with its **Emulation** tab. Select **Windows Phone** from the **Browser profile** menu seen in Figure 3.14.

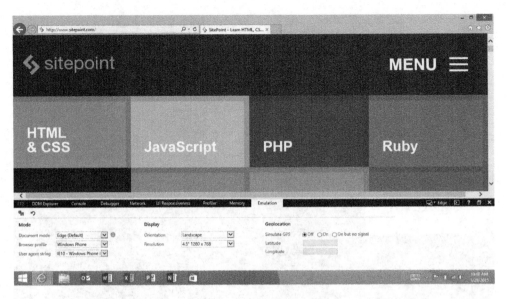

Figure 3.14. SitePoint.com using Internet Explorer 11's device emulation mode

In addition to mimicking orientation and resolution, emulation mode enables you to test geolocation features.

Safari 9+

Safari 9 has a responsive design mode in its developer toolkit; previous versions lacked such a feature. It's similar to the responsive mode in Firefox, but adds the ability to mimic iOS devices as illustrated in Figure 3.15.

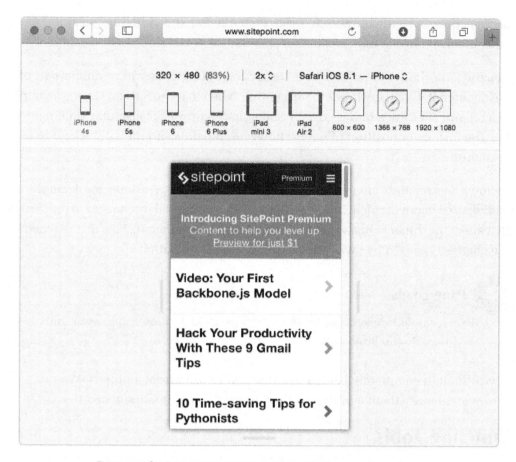

Figure 3.15. SitePoint.com as viewed using Safari 9's responsive design mode

To enter Safari 9's responsive design mode, select **Develop > Responsive Design Mode**, or **Alt + Command + R**.

Debugging for UI Responsiveness

CSS properties and values that trigger reflows are particularly expensive. They can slow user interface responsiveness—page rendering, animation smoothness, and scroll performance—especially on low-powered devices such as phones and smart TVs.

What is a reflow?

A **reflow** is any operation that changes the layout of part or all of a page. Examples include changing the dimensions of an element or updating its left position. They're because they force the browser to recalculate the height, width, and position of other elements in the document.

Repaints are similar to reflows in that they force the browser to re-render part of the document. Changing the color of a button when in a `:hover` state is one example of a repaint. They're a bit less troublesome than reflows because they do not affect the dimensions or position of nodes; however, repaints should still be kept to a minimum.

Reflows and repaints are most often triggered by DOM operations; for example, adding to or removing elements. But they can also be caused by changes to properties that affect the dimensions, visibility, or position of an element. This is true whether the change is caused by JavaScript or a CSS-based animation.

 Page Loads

Page loads will always trigger reflow and repaints as the browser parses the initial HTML, CSS, and JavaScript.

It's difficult to completely banish repaints and reflows from a project. We can, however, identify them and reduce their impact using timeline tools.

Timeline Tools

Timeline tools are a bit befuddling at first. They measure the performance of your front end, capturing how much time it takes for various tasks to complete. By recording activity while interacting with our pages, we can spot what lines of our CSS may be causing performance bottlenecks.

To use the timeline, click the timeline tab in the developer tools interface. In Chrome, Opera, and Firefox, it's appropriately named **Timeline**. Safari makes it plural, so it's **Timelines**. Internet Explorer 11 uses the more descriptive **UI Responsiveness**.[2]

In any browser, press the **Record** button to start the recording process. Interact with the problematic portions of the page and, when you're done, click the appropriate button to stop recording.

---

[2] In Firefox, you may have to enable the timeline feature in the Web Inspector. You can find this setting under **Toolbox Options**.

Depending on which browser you use, you may see data immediately or after you stop recording. Safari and Firefox display data in real time, while Chrome, Opera, and Internet Explorer render a performance chart after you stop recording.

Document loads, function calls, DOM events, style recalculations, and paint actions are all logged in every browser, giving us an overview of performance bottlenecks. What we're looking for, at least as far as CSS performance is concerned, are two related aspects:

- large numbers of style recalculation and paint operations
- operations that take a long time, as indicated by larger blocks in the timeline

To see what this looks like in practice, we'll compare two basic documents, Examples A and B. In both cases, we're moving a series of `div` elements from an x-position of zero to an x-position of 1,000. Both examples use CSS transitions. In Example A, however, we're going to animate the `left` property. In Example B, we're going to use a translation transform and animate the `transform` property.

Our markup for both is the same (the result can be seen in Figure 3.16):

```
<!DOCTYPE html>
  <html lang="en-US">
  <head>
      <meta charset="utf-8">
      <title>Performance example</title>
      <style type="text/css">
          /* CSS will go here. */
      </style>
  </head>
  <body>
      <button type="button" id="move">Move</button>
      <div></div>
      <div></div>
      <div></div>
      <div></div>
      <div></div>
      <div></div>
      <div></div>
      <div></div>
      <div></div>
      <div></div>
```

```
        <script type="text/javascript" src="toggle-move-class.js">
➡</script>
    </body>
</html>
```

Figure 3.16. Our HTML demo page of div elements in Safari

Our JavaScript for both documents is also the same. Clicking the **Move** button toggles the moved class on each div element:

```
var move = document.getElementsById('move');
move.addEventListener('click', function(e) {
    var objs = document.body.querySelectorAll('div');
    Array.prototype.map.call(objs, function(o){
        o.classList.toggle('moved');
    });
});
```

Our CSS is where matters diverge. The CSS used in Example A follows:

```
div {
    background: #36f;
    margin-bottom: 1em;
    width: 30px;
    height: 30px;
    position: relative;
    left: 0;
    transition: left 2s ease-in;
}

.moved {
    left: 1000px;
}
```

When triggered, this animation will generate a lot of style calculation and repaint indicators in our timeline. The images that follow show timeline output for this transition in Safari (Figure 3.17), Chrome (Figure 3.18), Internet Explorer (Figure 3.19), and Firefox (Figure 3.20).

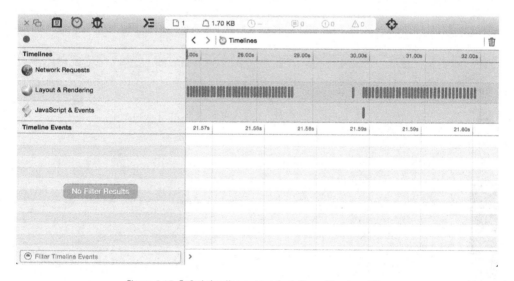

Figure 3.17. Safari timeline output for left-position transition

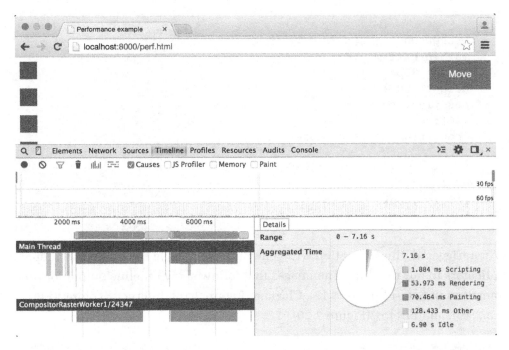

Figure 3.18. The same again in Chrome

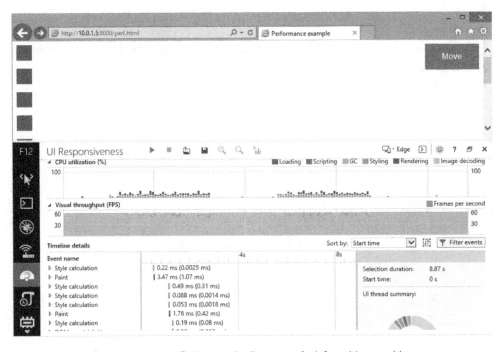

Figure 3.19. Internet Explorer 11 timeline output for left-position transition

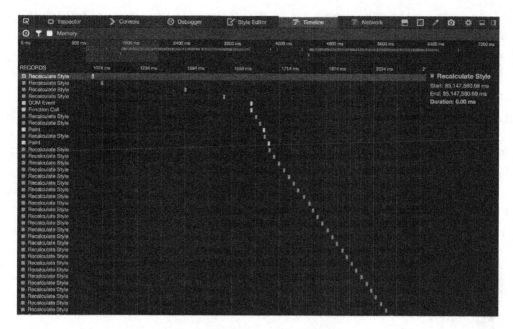

Figure 3.20. And how it looks in Firefox

The reason for the style calculations and repaints has to do with the property we're transitioning: `left`. The `left` property triggers a reflow whenever it is changed, even if that change is caused by an animation or transition.

Now, let's take a look at the CSS for Example B:

```css
div {
    background: #f3f;
    margin-bottom: 1em;
    width: 30px;
    height: 30px;
    position: relative;
    left: 0;
    transition: transform 2s ease-in;
    transform: translateX(0);

}
```

```
.moved {
    transform: translateX(1000px);
}
```

Here we're using a transform and transitioning bteween `translateX(0)` and `translateX(1000px)`.

In most browsers, transforms don't trigger reflows, and our timelines will contain far fewer repaint operations. This is evident in Safari (Figure 3.21), Chrome (Figure 3.22), and Internet Explorer (Figure 3.23). Firefox is the exception here; compare Figure 3.20 to Figure 3.24. The timelines for a `left` transition and a translation transformation are very similar.

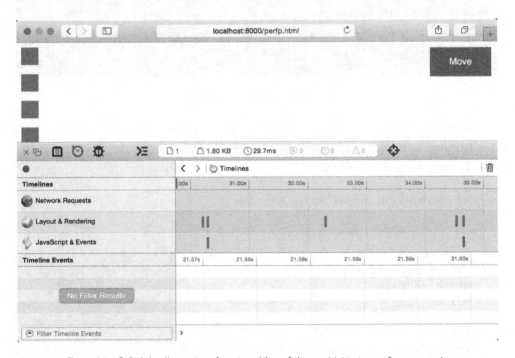

Figure 3.21. Safari timeline output for a transition of the `-webkit-transform` property

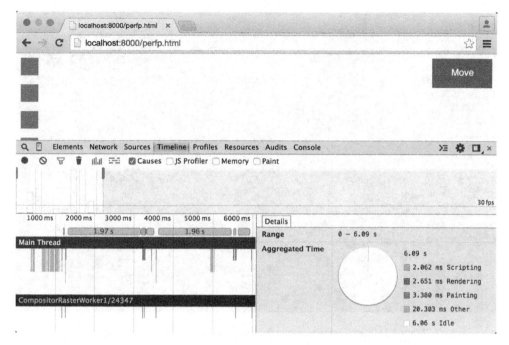

Figure 3.22. The same for Chrome, this time utilizing the `transform` property

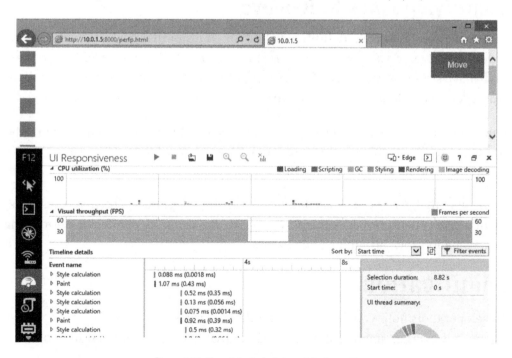

Figure 3.23. How it looks in Internet Explorer 11

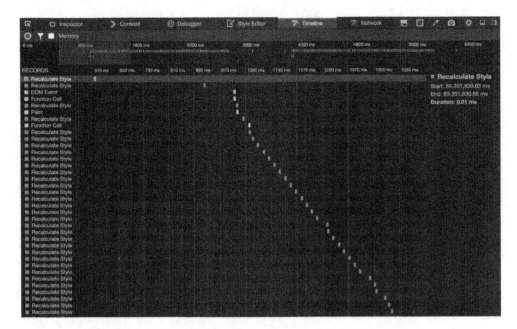

Figure 3.24. Firefox timeline output for a transition of the transform property

Identifying Lines to Remove

Unfortunately, there is no definitive list of which properties cause reflows and re-paints. Paul Lewis' CSS Triggers comes closest,[3] but it's Chrome-specific. Browsers do behave similarly for many of these properties, however, so this resource will at least give you an idea of what properties may be causing trouble.

Once you know which properties *could* be problematic, the next step is to test the hypothesis. Disable that property—either with a comment or by adding a temporary x- prefix—and rerun the timeline test.

Remember that performance is relative, not absolute or perfect. The goal is improvement: make it perform better that it did before. If a property or effect is performing unacceptably slow, eliminate it altogether.

Minification

Developer tools help you find and fix rendering issues, but what about efficiency: are our file sizes as small as they can be? For that, we need **minification** tools.

---

[3] http://csstriggers.com/

Minification in the context of CSS simply means "removing excess characters." Consider, for example, this block of code:

```
h1 {
    font: 16px / 1.5 'Helvetica Neue', arial, sans-serif;
    width: 80%;
    margin: 10px auto 0px;
}
```

That's 98 bytes long, including line breaks and spaces. Let's look at a minified example:

```
h1{font:16px/1.5 'Helvetica Neue',arial,sans-serif;width:80%;
➥margin:10px auto 0}
```

Now our CSS is only 80 bytes long—an 18% reduction. Fewer bytes, of course, means faster download times and data transfer savings for you and your users.

In this section, we'll look at CSS Optimizer, or CSSO, a minification tool that runs on Node.js.[4] To install CSSO, you'll first have to install Node.js and NPM.[5] NPM is installed as part of the Node.js installation process, so you'll only need to install one package.

Using CSSO does require you to be comfortable using the command-line interface. Linux and OS X users can use the Terminal application (**Applications** > **Terminal.app** for OS X). If you're using Windows, utilize the command prompt. Go to the **Start** or **Windows** menu and type cmd in the search box.

Installing CSSO

Once you have set up Node.js and NPM , you can install CSSO. At a command line prompt, type:

```
npm install -g csso
```

The -g flag installs CSSO globally so that we can use it from the command line. OS X and Linux users may need to use sudo (sudo npm install -g csso). You'll know

---

[4] http://nodejs.org
[5] https://www.npmjs.com/

it's installed when NPM prints its installation path to the command line window, and the command line prompt reappears, as depicted in Figure 3.25.

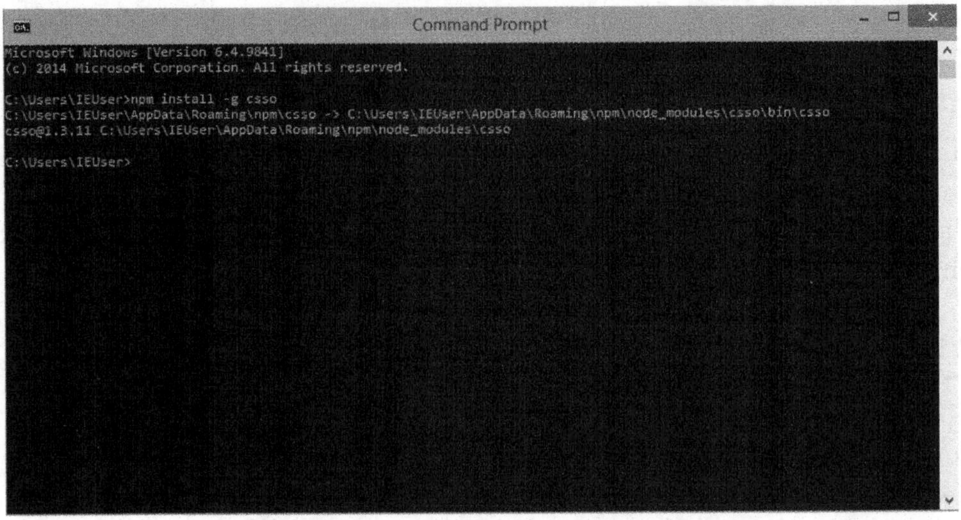

Figure 3.25. Installing CSSO using Windows' command prompt

Now we're ready to minify our CSS.

Minification with CSSO

To minify CSS files, run the `csso` command, passing the name of a file as an argument:

```
csso style.css
```

This will perform basic compression. CSSO strips unneeded whitespace, removes superflous semicolons, and deletes comments from your CSS input file.

Once complete, CSSO will print the optimized CSS to standard output, meaning the current terminal or command prompt window. In most cases, however, we'll want to save that output to a file. To do that, pass a second argument to `csso`—the name of the minified file. For example, if we wanted to save the minified version of **style.css** as **style.min.css**, we'd use the following:

```
csso style.css style.min.css
```

By default, CSSO will rearrange parts of your CSS. It will, for example, merge declaration blocks with duplicated selectors and remove some overriden properties. Consider the following CSS:

```
body {
    margin: 20px 30px;
    padding: 100px;
    margin-left: 0px;
}

h1 {
    font: 200 36px / 1.5 sans-serif;
}

h1 {
    color: #ff6600;
}
```

In this snippet, `margin-left` overrides the earlier `margin` declaration. We've also repeated `h1` as a selector for consecutive declaration blocks. After optimization and minification, we end up with this:

```
body{padding:100px;margin:20px 30px 20px 0}h1{font:200 36px/1.5
➡ sans-serif;color:#f60}
```

CSSO removed extraneous spaces, line breaks, and semicolons, and shortened `#ff6600` to `#f60`. CSSO also merged the `margin` and `margin-left` properties into one declaration (`margin: 20px 30px 20px 0`) and combined our separate h1 selector blocks into one.

Now, if you're skeptical of how CSSO will rewrite your CSS, you can disable its restructuring features. Just use the `--restructure-off` or `-off` flags. For example, running `csso style.css style.min.css -off` gives us the following:

```
body{margin:20px 30px;padding:100px;margin-left:0}h1{font:200 36px/
➡1.5 sans-serif}h1{color:#f60}
```

Now our CSS is minified, but not optimized. Disabling restructuring will keep your CSS files from being as small as they could be. Avoid disabling restructuring unless you run into problems.

Preprocessors, introduced in Chapter 9, offer minification as part of their tool set; however, using CSSO can shave additional bytes from your file sizes.

Code-quality Tools

Finally, let's discuss tools that help you analyze the quality of your CSS. Though several CSS code-quality tools exist, in this section we'll focus on three:

- CSS Lint
- analyze-css
- UnCSS

The first two tools, CSS Lint and analyze-css, check your CSS for problems such as inefficient selectors, invalid rules, or unnecessary specificity. These have the greatest impact on CSS maintainability, although inefficient selectors can also affect front-end performance.

The third tool, UnCSS, checks your CSS for unused selectors and style rules. It parses a stylesheet and a list of HTML pages, and returns a CSS file that's stripped of unused rules.

All of these tools are available as Node.js packages, and can also be installed using NPM.

If you're working on a small site, such as a few pages that are updated infrequently or a personal blog, many of the problems that these tools flag can safely be ignored. You'll spend time refactoring for little gain in maintainability and speed. For larger projects, however, they're invaluable. They'll help you head off maintability problems before they start.

CSS Lint

CSS Lint is the grandmother of these code-quality tools. Created by Nicole Sullivan and Nicholas Zakas, it's available both as an NPM package and online at CSS-Lint.net.[6] We'll discuss the NPM package here.

Installation

Install CSS Lint as you would any other NPM package:

```
npm install -g csslint
```

Basic Usage

To check for errors, or lint your CSS, run the CSS Lint command passing the path to your CSS filename as an argument:

```
csslint stylesheet.css
```

Running this command causes CSS Lint to return a list of issues with your CSS, as evidenced in Figure 3.26.

---

[6] http://csslint.net/

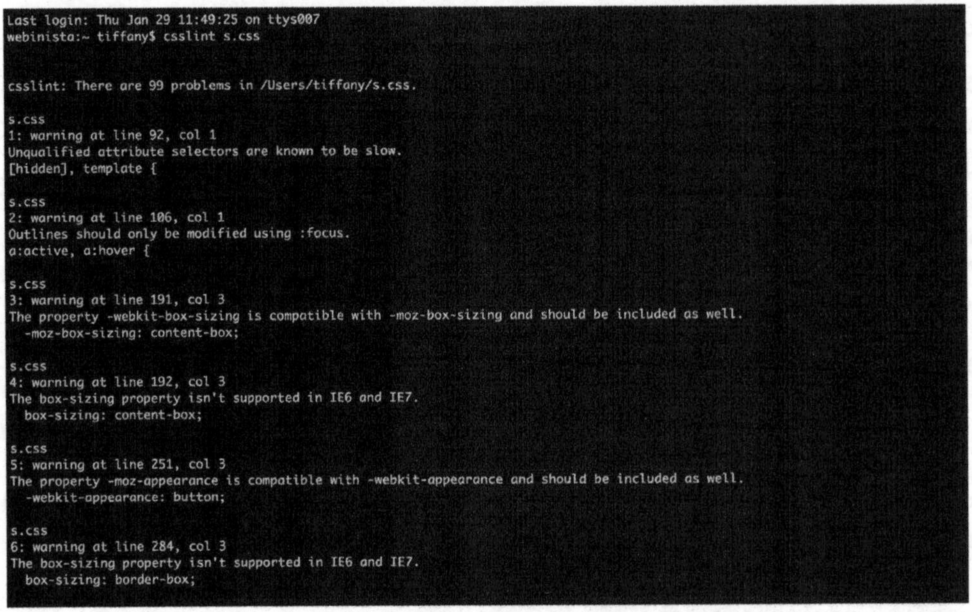

```
Last login: Thu Jan 29 11:49:25 on ttys007
webinista:~ tiffany$ csslint s.css


csslint: There are 99 problems in /Users/tiffany/s.css.

s.css
1: warning at line 92, col 1
Unqualified attribute selectors are known to be slow.
[hidden], template {

s.css
2: warning at line 106, col 1
Outlines should only be modified using :focus.
a:active, a:hover {

s.css
3: warning at line 191, col 3
The property -webkit-box-sizing is compatible with -moz-box-sizing and should be included as well.
  -moz-box-sizing: content-box;

s.css
4: warning at line 192, col 3
The box-sizing property isn't supported in IE6 and IE7.
  box-sizing: content-box;

s.css
5: warning at line 251, col 3
The property -moz-appearance is compatible with -webkit-appearance and should be included as well.
  -webkit-appearance: button;

s.css
6: warning at line 284, col 3
The box-sizing property isn't supported in IE6 and IE7.
  box-sizing: border-box;
```

Figure 3.26. Terminal output from CSS Lint

CSS Lint inspects your stylesheets for four kinds of CSS problems:

Compatibility: problems that affect a particular browser version

Performance: problems that can cause slow page loads and rendering

Maintainability and duplication problems: issues that will make your colleagues pull their hair out and perhaps yours as well

Accessibility: CSS that has a negative impact on users of assistive software

It reports each error separately as a separate block of text, with each block containing the following:

- filename (here, that's s.css)

- error location; for example, warning at line 92, col 1

- guideline of which you've run afoul (for example, "unqualified attribute selectors are known to be slow" or "outlines should only be modified using :focus")

- selector or declaration at fault

CSS Lint prints output to the terminal window. If you'd rather save it as a file, use the redirection operator. This applies to most systems, whether Linux, OS X, or Windows:

```
csslint stylesheet.css > csslintoutput.txt
```

CSS Lint is also configurable; you can disable checks for any of its rules by using the `--ignore` flag. Say that you've finally dropped support for Internet Explorer 6 and 7. You can tell CSS Lint to ignore the box-sizing rule by passing `--ignore=box-sizing` as an argument:

```
csslint /path/to/stylesheet.css --ignore=box-sizing
```

CSS Lint is more pragmatic than bleeding edge. It will raise vendor-prefix warnings for properties such as transitions that you may not need to include, depending on the browser distribution of your site's audience. If your site's visitors use modern browsers, you may be able to disable the following rules:

- `gradients`
- `box-sizing`
- `compatible-vendor-prefixes`
- `fallback-colors` (enable if you still have a significant share of IE8 users)

To view a list of rule identifiers and what they mean, use `csslint --list-rules`. Type `csslint --help` for the full menu of CSS Lint options. For more in-depth documentation, consult the CSS Lint Wiki.[7]

analyze-css

Like CSS Lint, analyze-css inspects your CSS for complexity and performance. It does not, however, check for accessibility or compatibility. Instead, it produces a series of metrics and offending selectors that you should examine further.

---

[7] https://github.com/CSSLint/CSSLint/wiki

Installation

You're probably sensing a pattern here. Install analyze-css using NPM with the following command:

```
npm install -g analyze-css
```

Basic Usage

analyze-css can handle both local files and URLs. To analyze a local file, use the --file flag:

```
analyze-css --file stylesheet.css
```

To analyze a remote asset instead, use the --url flag:

```
analyze-css --url http://example.com/css/stylesheet.css
```

analyze-css outputs JSON-formatted data to standard output (again, this means the terminal or command prompt window) by default. But we'll redirect it to a file:

```
analyze-css --file stylesheet.css > nameoffile.json
```

analyze-css reports a variety of details about your CSS in a metrics field. These include oldPropertyPrefixes (the number of properties that no longer require a vendor prefix), and length (file size in bytes). But the real meat of the report lies in the offenders field. Below is a snippet of output from analyze-css:

```
{
  "generator": "analyze-css v0.9.1",
  "metrics": {...
  },
  "offenders": {
    "universalSelectors": [
      "[type=submit] @ 108:3",
      "[type=submit]:hover @ 116:3",
      "[type=submit]:focus @ 116:3",
      "[disabled] @ 133:1",
      "[id=landing] @ 173:3",
      "[id=landing] header @ 174:3"
    ],
```

```
    "oldPropertyPrefixes": [
      "[id=landing] .logo { -moz-transition: transform 150ms ease-in
➥ 10ms, opacity 150ms ease-in } // was required by firefox 15 and
➥ earlier @ 182:5",
      "[id=landing] .logo { -o-transition: transform 150ms ease-in
➥ 10ms, opacity 150ms ease-in } // was required by opera 12 and
➥ earlier @ 184:5",
    ],
    "qualifiedSelectors": [
      "span.error @ 147:1"
    ],
    "multiClassesSelectors": [
      ".dance.logo @ 186:5"
    ], ...
  }
}
```

offenders lists potential problems with your CSS. For example, the qualifiedSe-
lectors property lists every class selector that's overly qualified by an element.
Here it's span.error on line 147, character 1 of our CSS file. The multiClassesSe-
lectors property lists instances of selectors that combine two or more class names;
in this case .dance.logo on line 186. In both cases, we're sending overly specific
CSS that uses more bytes than we need.

A full stylesheet analysis might include the incidences of !important (the import-
ants property), a list of color declarations, Internet Explorer hacks (oldIEFixes),
and duplicated properties or selectors.

UnCSS

UnCSS parses your HTML and CSS files, removing unused CSS. If your projects
include a CSS framework such as Bootstrap or use a reset stylesheet, consider adding
UnCSS to your workflow. It will shave unnecessary CSS—and bytes—from your
code.

Installation

As with other NPM packages, you can install UnCSS using the following command:

```
npm install -g uncss
```

Using UnCSS from the Command Line

UnCSS requires the filepath or URL of an HTML page that contains a linked CSS file; for example:

```
uncss http://sitepoint.com/
```

UnCSS will parse the HTML and its linked stylesheets, and print the optimized CSS to standard output. To redirect to a file, use the redirect operator (>):

```
uncss http://sitepoint.com/ > optimized.css
```

You can also pass multiple filepaths or URLs to the command line. CSS will analyze each file and dump optimized CSS that contains rules affecting one or more pages:

```
uncss index.html article-1.html article-2.html > optimized.css
```

For a full list of commands—and an example of how to use UnCSS with a Node.js script—consult the UnCSS docs.[8]

Consider a Task Runner

This probably sounds like a lot of extra time and steps to add to your workflow, but you should consider a task runner such Grunt[9] or build system such as Gulp.[10] It's where automation can help quite a bit.

Grunt is the more established of the two tools, so there are more plugins and a larger community. I happen to be partial to Gulp's syntax. Use whichever tool works best for you and your colleagues.

What's great about Grunt and Gulp is that you can assemble a toolchain that will automatically run concatenation, minification, and optimization tasks for CSS, JavaScript, and image files. Because the configuration and build script files are JSON

---

[8] https://github.com/giakki/uncss
[9] http://gruntjs.com
[10] http://gulp.js

and JavaScript, you can easily reuse them across projects or share them with a team. CSS Lint, UnCSS, and CSSO are all available as both Grunt and Gulp plugins, making them easier to integrate.

Getting started with Grunt or Gulp can be intimidating. Luckily, a few developers have demystified them both. Grunt newbies should read Chris Coyier's *24 Ways* article, "Grunt for People Who Think Things Like Grunt are Weird and Hard."[11] SitePoint's Craig Buckler wrote a nice tutorial for getting started with Gulp.js.[12]

It's very easy to become overwhelmed by the options. Take a pragmatic approach to building your toolkit. Add tools that you think will enhance your workflow and improve the quality of your output.

Conclusion

In this chapter, we've looked at some tools to help you diagnose, debug, and optimize your CSS. In the next chapter, we'll look at advanced layout techniques, including Flexbox.

---

[11] http://24ways.org/2013/grunt-is-not-weird-and-hard/
[12] http://www.sitepoint.com/introduction-gulp-js/

Complex Layouts

In this chapter, we'll dig into a few CSS layout topics. In the first half, we'll tackle two fundamentals of CSS layout: the box model and stacking context. Understanding these concepts will help you create complex layouts and diagnose layout bugs.

In the second half of the chapter, we'll look at two newer layout-related CSS specifications: the CSS multicolumn layout module and the flexible box module (better known as flexbox). Both modules allow developers to create layouts that are robust and adaptable across a range of device sizes.

Managing the CSS Box Model

Perhaps the most important point to understand about CSS is this: **Everything is a box**. More specifically, every element in a document generates a box. This box may be a block-level box, or it may be an inline-level box. The box type determines how the element affects page layout.

Whether or not an element creates a box and which type of box it creates will depend on the markup language. CSS developed as a way to style HTML documents so, as a result, much of the CSS visual rendering model is rooted in HTML4's distinction between block-level and inline elements. By default, elements such as p and section create block-level boxes but a, span, and em create inline boxes. SVG, on the other hand, does not use the box model, so most layout-related CSS properties fail to work with SVG. (This is covered in Chapter 8.)

Block-level boxes create new blocks of content as can be seen in Figure 4.1. Block-level boxes are rendered vertically according to their source order and (except for tables) expand to fill the available width of their containing element. This is known as **normal flow**. Block-level boxes have a display value of block, list-item, table, or any of the table-* values (for example, table-cell).

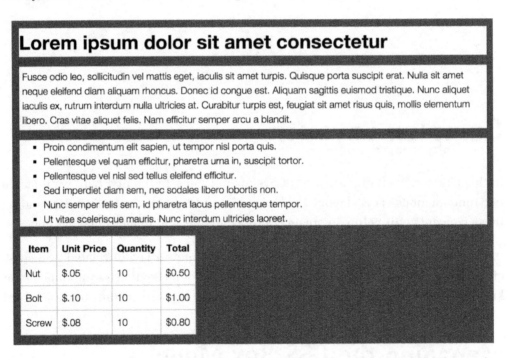

Figure 4.1. Block-level boxes featuring h1, p, ul, and table elements within a containing element (gray area)

Inline-level boxes, by contrast, do not form new blocks of content. Instead, these boxes make up the lines inside a block box. They're displayed horizontally and fill the width of the containing box, wrapping across lines if necessary, as shown in Figure 4.2. Inline-level boxes have a display value of inline, inline-block, inline-table, or ruby.

Fusce odio leo, sollicitudin vel mattis eget, iaculis sit amet turpis. Quisque porta suscipit erat. Nulla sit amet neque eleifend diam aliquam rhoncus. Donec id congue est. Aliquam sagittis euismod tristique. Nunc aliquet iaculis ex, rutrum interdum nulla ultricies at. Curabitur turpis est, feugiat sit amet risus quis, mollis elementum libero. Cras vitae aliquet felis. Nam efficitur semper arcu a blandit. Proin condimentum elit sapien, ut tempor nisl porta quis. Pellentesque vel quam efficitur, pharetra urna in, suscipit tortor.

Pellentesque vel nisl sed tellus eleifend efficitur. Sed imperdiet diam sem, nec sodales libero lobortis non. Nunc semper felis sem, id pharetra lacus pellentesque tempor. Ut vitae scelerisque mauris. Nunc interdum ultricies laoreet. Nam a dui luctus, egestas enim sit amet, blandit quam. Phasellus lorem libero, sollicitudin id hendrerit a, faucibus eget nisi.

Figure 4.2. An example of an inline box with `margin: 1em` and `padding: 5px` applied

But how are the dimensions of the box calculated? Here is where it becomes more complicated. As seen in Figure 4.3, box dimensions are the sum of the box's content area, plus its padding width, and border width as defined in CSS2.[1] The margin width creates a margin box for the element, and affects other elements in the document; however, the margin width has no effect on the dimensions of the box itself.

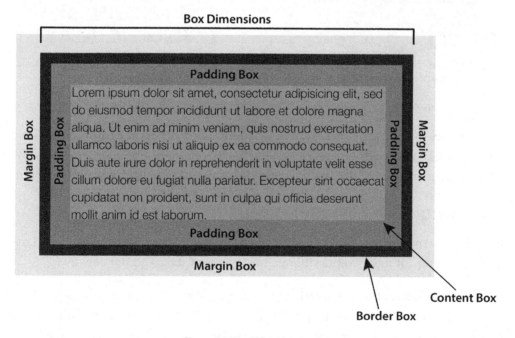

Figure 4.3. The CSS 2.1 box model

For instance, a p element with `width: 300px`, `padding: 20px`, and `border: 10px` has a calculated width of 360 pixels. That's the sum of its width, left and right padding, and left and right `border-width` properties. To create an element that is

---

[1] http://dev.w3.org/csswg/css2/box.html

300 pixels wide with 20 pixels of padding and a 10 pixel border, the width needs to be 240px. Most leading browsers calculated the width in just this way. Internet Explorer 5.5, however, did not.

Instead, IE5.5 used the width property as the final arbiter of box dimensions, with padding and border drawn inside the box as seen in Figure 4.4. Both values were, in effect, subtracted from width, decreasing the size of the content area. Though it's the exact opposite of the behavior defined in the specification, many web developers thought it was the more sensible approach.[2]

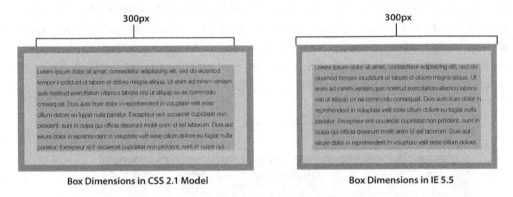

Box Dimensions in CSS 2.1 Model   Box Dimensions in IE 5.5

Figure 4.4. The CSS 2.1 box model versus the old Internet 5.5 "quirks mode" box model

Partly as a way to resolve these competing models, the CSS working group introduced the box–sizing property. It lets us choose the box model implementation that we prefer, and greatly simplifies calculations when working with responsive designs.

Choosing a Box Model with `box-sizing`

The box-sizing property is defined in the CSS Basic User Interface Module Level 3 specification.[3] It has two possible values: content-box and border-box.

Initially, the value of box-sizing is content-box. With this value, setting the width and height properties of an element affect the size of its content area. This matches the behavior defined by the CSS 2.1 specification, and it's the default behavior in modern browsers (as presented in Figure 4.4).

---

[2] A great tool for visualizing these differences is Caroline Artz' Box Sizing Demo. [http://codepen.io/carolineartz/full/ogVXZj/]

[3] http://www.w3.org/TR/css3-ui/#box-sizing

Setting the value of box-sizing to border-box creates a little bit of magic. Now, the values of width and height will be applied to the outer border edge instead of the content area. Borders and padding are drawn inside the element box, matching the old Internet Explorer 5.5 behavior. Let's look at an example that mixes percentage widths and px units for padding and borders:

```
<div class="wrapper">
    <article>
    <h2>This is a headline</h2>
    <p>Lorem ipsum dolor sit amet, consectetur adipisicing ... </p>
    </article>
    <aside>
    <h2>This is a secondary headline</h2>
    <p>Lorem ipsum dolor sit amet, consectetur adipisicing ... </p>
    </aside>
</div>
```

Both our article and aside elements have the following CSS applied, which gives us the layout shown in Figure 4.5 where the first element has a width of 60% while the second has a width of 40%:

```
article, aside {
    background: #FFEB3B;
    border: 10px solid #9C27B0;
    float: left;
    padding: 10px;
}
article {
    width: 60%;
}
```

```
aside {
    width: 40%;
}
```

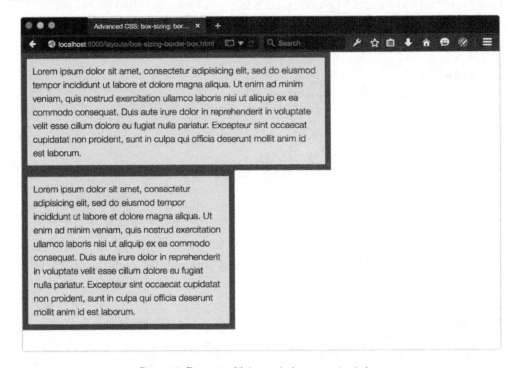

Figure 4.5. Elements with box-sizing: content-box

By default, both `aside` and `article` have a `box-sizing` value of `content-box`. The `border-width` and `padding` values add 40 pixels to the width of each element, which throws off the 60%/40% split considerably. Now let's add `box-sizing: border-box` to the `article` and `aside` elements:

```
article, aside {
    box-sizing: border-box;
}
```

You can see the change in Figure 4.6: the elements have the same width, but the `box-sizing: border-box` means that the width includes the border and padding. Because the `width` property applies to the border edge instead of the content area, our elements now fit side by side.

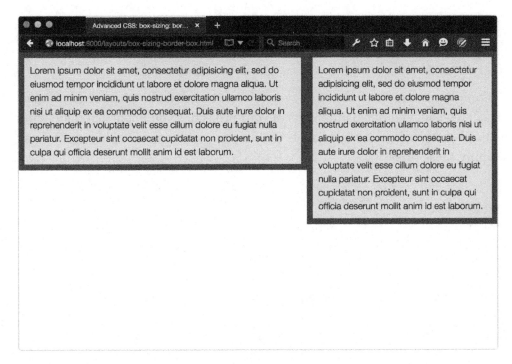

Figure 4.6. Elements with `box-sizing: border-box`.

I'd suggest that you use `box-sizing: border-box` in your projects. It makes life easier, as there's no need to calculate the `width` value to account for the values of `padding` and `border`, and boxes behave more predictably.

The best way to apply `box-sizing: border-box` is with reset rules. The following example is from Chris Coyier's CSS-Tricks post, "Inheriting `box-sizing` Probably Slightly Better Best-Practice"[4]:

```
html {
    box-sizing: border-box;
}
```

---

[4] https://css-tricks.com/inheriting-box-sizing-probably-slightly-better-best-practice/

```
*, *:before, *:after {
    box-sizing: inherit;
}
```

This applies `border-box` sizing to every element by default, without affecting the box-sizing behavior of existing parts of your project. If you *know* that there will be no third-party or legacy components that rely on `content-box` behavior, you can simplify these rules:

```
*,
*:before,
*:after {
    box-sizing: border-box;
}
```

Table 4.1 shows curent bowser support for `box-size: border-box`

Table 4.1. Browser support for `box-size: border-box`

Internet Explorer	Firefox	Safari	Chrome	Opera	Android
8+	2+ (versions < 29 require `-moz-` prefix)	3.1+ (versions < 5.1 require `-webkit-` prefix)	4+ (versions < 9 require `-webkit-` prefix)	10.1+	2.1+ (versions < 4 require `-webkit-` prefix)

Managing the box model is just one ingredient in understanding how to create complex layouts. Let's dig into layering elements in the next section.

Managing Layers with `position` and `z-index`

Every element in a document participates in a stacking context. The **stacking context** is a model—a set of rules, really—for how elements are painted to the screen. If you've ever used the `z-index` property, you've worked with stacking contexts.

The root `html` element creates a **root stacking context**. Some CSS properties and values can also trigger a **local stacking context** for the elements to which they're applied. Whether part of a root or local context, children within a stacking context are painted to the screen from back-to-front as follows:

1. Child stacking contexts with a negative stack level (for example, positioned and `z-index: -1`)

2. Non-positioned elements

3. Child stacking contexts with a stack level of 0 (for example, positioned and `z-index: auto`)

4. Child stacking contexts with positive stack levels (for example, positioned and `z-index: 1`)[5]

If two elements have the same stack level, they'll be layered according to their order in the source HTML.[6]

Let's look at an example. Here's our HTML:

```
<div id="a">
    <p><b>div#a</b></p>
</div>
<div id="b">
    <p><b>div#b</b></p>
</div>
<div id="c">
    <p><b>div#c</b></p>
</div>
<div id="d">
    <p><b>div#d</b></p>
</div>
 <div id="e">
    <p><b>div#e</b></p>
</div>
```

And here's our CSS:

---

[5] An element is **positioned** if its `position` value is something other than `static`.

[6] This is discussed in far greater detail in Appendix E of the CSS2 specification. [http://dev.w3.org/csswg/css2/zindex.html]

```
#a {
    background: rgba(233, 30, 99, 0.5);
}

#b, #c, #d, #e {
    position: absolute;
}

#b {
    background: rgba(103, 58, 183, 0.8);
    bottom: 120px;
    width: 410px;
    z-index: 2;
}

#c {
    background: rgba(255, 235, 59, 0.8);
    top: 190px;
    z-index: 1;
}

#d {
    background: #03a9f4;
    height: 500px;
    top: 10px;
    z-index: -1;
}

#e {
    background: rgba(255, 87, 34, 0.7);
    top: 110px;
    z-index: 1;
}
```

This will produce the stacking order shown in Figure 4.7. The bottom-most layer is #d because its z-index value is -1. Since #a isn't positioned, it sits above #d, but below the positioned elements (#b, #c, and #e). The next layer is #c, followed by #e. Since both elements have the same z-index value, #e is stacked higher because it's last in the source order. The top-most layer is #b, due to its z-index of 2.

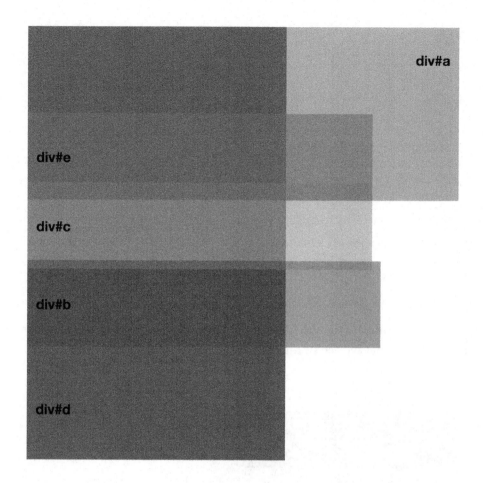

Figure 4.7. A stacking context with positioned and unpositioned elements of varying z-index values

All the elements in the previous example are part of the root stacking context. But let's see how stacking is affected by a property that forces a local context: opacity when its value is less than 1. Consider the following HTML:

```
<div id="f">
  <p><b>div#f</b></p>
</div>
<div id="g">
  <p><b>div#g</b></p>
</div>
```

It's paired with this CSS:

```
#f, #g {
    position: absolute;
}
#f {
    background: rgba(255,193,7,.9);
}
#f p {
    background: rgb(34,34,34);
    color: whitesmoke;
    position: relative;
    z-index: 1;
}
#g {
    background: rgba(3,169,244,.7);
    top: 50px;
    left: 100px;
}
```

According to the rules of the stacking context, #f p occupies the top-most layer in the stack. That's what we see in Figure 4.8.

Figure 4.8. The rendered version of our sample HTML and CSS

But if we change our CSS and add opacity: .99 to the #f rule set, something interesting happens:

```
#f {
    background: rgba(255,193,7,.9);
    opacity: .99;
}
```

The `opacity` property creates a new stacking context any time its value is less than 1. As a result, the `z-index` for its child element becomes relative to its parent rather than the root stacking context. You can see how this works in Figure 4.9. Notice that #g now occupies the top-most layer.[7]

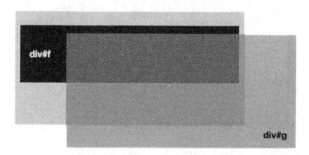

Figure 4.9. How `opacity` affects stacking order

Let's add an absolutely positioned `div` element to #f and give it a `z-index` value of 2. Now `div` is stacked on top of #f p (see Figure 4.10), but it's still layered behind #g because #f has a local stacking context. Children of a local stacking context can only be reordered relative to that context. Elements that sit in other contexts can't be layered within a local one.

---

[7] A handful of other property-value combinations also trigger a new stacking context. The stacking context [https://developer.mozilla.org/en-US/docs/Web/Guide/CSS/Understanding_z_index/The_stacking_context] from Mozilla Developer Network details them all.

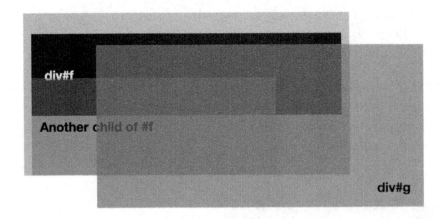

Figure 4.10. Multiple elements in a stacking context

 Handling Undesired Behaviors with `opacity`

Because `opacity` triggers a new stacking context, you may run into undesired behavior when transitioning the `opacity` of layers that overlap. To work around this, use `rgba()` or `hsla()` values for `color` or `background-color` and transition those instead.

Let's look at an example of using the stacking context to manage layers and positioned elements. In this case, we'll create a menu that slides in from the top of the screen. But rather than slide in *over* the logo and **Menu** button, we'll make it slide in beneath it. First our HTML:

```
                                    04-layouts/stacking-context.html (excerpt)

<header>
    <img src="dont-awesomenews.svg">
    <button type="button" id="menu">
        <img src="dont-menu.svg">
    </button>
    <nav>
        <ul id="menu-list">
            <li><a href="/sports">Sports</a></li>
            <li><a href="/politics">Politics</a></li>
            <li><a href="/arts">Arts &amp; Entertainment</a></li>
```

```
            <li><a href="/business">Business</a></li>
            <li><a href="/travel">Travel</a></li>
        </ul>
    </nav>
</header>
```

Clicking the button element causes the element to slide into view. Now for our (edited) CSS:

```
header {
    background: #222629;
    color: whitesmoke;
    position: fixed;
    top: 0;
    width: 100%;
}
nav {
    background: #222629;
    position: absolute;
    width: 100%;
    left: 0;
    top: -33vw;
    transition: top 500ms;
}
.open {
    top: 9vw;
}
```

This CSS above creates a menu that slides down from the top when triggered. But as it slides in, it passes over the AwesomeNews logo as you can see in Figure 4.11.

Figure 4.11. The menu slides over the *AwesomeNews* logo

Our menu (the nav element) slides over the logo and **Menu** button because it has a higher stack level. Remember that when multiple elements have the same z-index value, the last one in the source will be the top-most layer.

Let's change this. What happens when we add z-index: -1 to the nav rule set? Well, you get the mess you see in Figure 4.12.

Figure 4.12. Adding `z-index: -1` forces `nav` to the bottom of the stack

The navigation slides in behind the logo and **Menu** button, but it also slides in behind the content. It's hard to read and impossible to click.

Because its parent element (`header`) has a `z-index` of `auto`, the `nav` element is still part of the root stacking context. Adding `z-index: -1` shoves it to the bottom of the root element's stack, which means it sits behind other elements in the root stacking context.

So how do we fix this? By creating a new stacking context for `nav`. We already know that the `opacity` property will create a new stacking context when its value is less than 1. But positioned elements can also create a new stacking context if the `z-index` value is something other than `auto` or 0. Our `header` element already has `position: fixed`. Now we just need to add `z-index: 1` to its rule set:[8]

---

[8] WebKit- and Blink-based browsers create a new stacking context whenever an element has `position: fixed`, even if its `z-index` value is `auto`. Firefox and Internet Explorer do not.

css/chapter4/menu.css *(excerpt)*

```css
header {
    background: #222629;
    color: whitesmoke;
    position: fixed;
    top: 0;
    width: 100%;
    z-index: 1;
}
```

Now our nav element is contained within the stacking context of its parent. Since header has a stack level of 1 and nav is its child, the menu sits above the rest of our content. But because nav has a negative stack level, it sits at the bottom of the header element's stacking context, as illustrated in Figure 4.13.

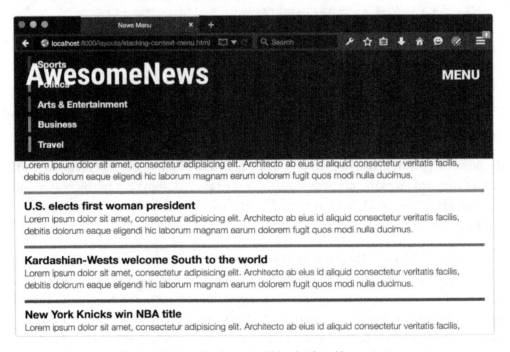

Figure 4.13. Managing elements within a local stacking context

For the rest of this chapter, we'll switch gears and talk about two modules for creating complex layouts: multiple column and flexible layout. Both modules make previously difficult layouts straightforward, and previously impossible layouts possible.

With them, we can create adaptive columns and grid-based layouts without the need for extra wrapping `div` elements or expensive DOM manipulations.

Using CSS Multicolumn Layout

Multiple-column (multicolumn) layout allows text and elements to flow from one column to another, and automatically adjust to the width of the viewport or container. With it, we can create text layouts that mimic those found in newspapers, magazines, and ebooks. We can also use it to create space-efficient user interfaces.

Although the specification is mature, the state of browser support is so-so. Basic support for multiple-column layout is quite good. All major browsers support the ability to create columns (`columns` property), set an optimal column width (`column-width`), set the size of the gutter (`column-gap`), and add rules between columns (`column-rule`).

Chrome ≤ 45 / Opera ≤ 30 and Firefox ≤ 41 do require vendor prefixes: `-webkit-` and `-moz-` respectively. To date, Chrome and Opera lack support for `column-fill` (or `-webkit-column-fill`) while Firefox lacks support for `column-span` (or `-moz-column-span`). Neither Internet Explorer 10+ nor Safari 9+ require vendor prefixes.

Support for `break-before`, `break-after`, and `break-inside`, on the other hand, is less robust. These properties specify how the children of a multicolumn element should be distributed across columns or pages. Internet Explorer supports these properties, while Firefox does not. Safari, Chrome, and Opera currently support the non-standard `-webkit-column-break-before`, `-webkit-column-break-after`, and `-webkit-column-break-inside` properties instead. Table 4.2 details the level of browser support for multicolumn layout.

Table 4.2. Browser support for multiple-column layout (source: CanIUse.com[9]).

Internet Explorer	Firefox	Safari	Chrome	Opera	Android
10+	2+ (partial; requires `-moz-` prefix)	9+ (versions < 9 have partial support, require `-webkit-` prefix; uses non-standard properties)	1+ (partial; requires `-webkit-` prefix)	11.5+ (partial; requires `-webkit-` prefix in versions 15+)	2.1+ (partial; requires `-webkit-` prefix)

Despite the current state of support, it's safe to use these properties in projects. Multicolumn layout is a progressive enhancement. If the browser does not support it, text will default to the normal flow.

Defining Column Number and Width Using `columns`

To create multiple columns, set the `columns` property:

```
<div style="columns: 2">
    <p>Lorem ipsum dolor sit amet, consectetur adipisicing ... </p>
    <p>Duis aute irure dolor in reprehenderit in voluptate ... </p>
</div>
```

The `columns` property is a shorthand property for `column-width` and `column-number`. With `columns`, the first value that can be interpreted as a length becomes the value of `column-width`. The first value that can be interpreted as an integer becomes the value of `column-number`. The order in which you specify each value is of no consequence. As has been shown, there's no need to specify both. Unspecified values default to their initial values of `auto`. All of the following examples are valid values for `columns`:

- `columns: 10em 3` (Same as `column-width: 10em; column-number: 3`)
- `columns: 3` (Same as `column-width: auto; column-number: 3`)

---

[9] http://caniuse.com/#feat=multicolumn

▨ `columns: 3 20em`

▨ `columns: 10em (Same as column-width: 10em; column-number: auto)`

▨ `columns: 4 auto`

Avoid Being Caught Short Using Firefox

Firefox only supports the `-moz-columns/columns` shorthand. Setting `column-number` or `-moz-column-number` will fail to work.

Setting `column-width` determines the *optimal size* for each column. Its value should be in length units; for example, `column-width: 200px` or `column-width: 10em`. Percentages will not work, and its initial value is `auto`.

"Optimal," of course, means that `column-width` sets the *ideal* width, not necessarily its actual width. Columns may be wider or narrower depending on the available space and/or viewport size. In Figure 4.14, for example, the container is 760 pixels wide and the `column-width` value is 15em. That gives us three columns.

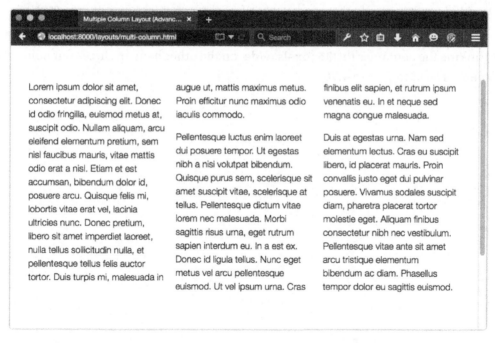

Figure 4.14. A multicolumn layout with `column-width: 15em` at a container width of 760px

But if we expand the container to 1080 pixels wide as in Figure 4.15, there's now room for four columns.

Figure 4.15. A container width of 1080px provides room for four columms when the `column-width` property value is 15em

Shrinking the container to 335 pixels wide, on the other hand, reduces our columns to one, as seen in Figure 4.16.

Figure 4.16. When the container is 355px wide, we only have room for one column at 15em

Setting the `column-number` property, on the other hand, defines the optimal number of columns to create. Its value must be an integer greater than 0. If `column-width` is something other than `auto`, the browser will create columns of that width up to the number of columns specified by `column-number`. If `column-width: auto`, the browser will create the number of columns specified by `column-number`. That's a bit tricky to understand, so let's illustrate with some screenshots.

In the figures that follow, our container has a `column-number` value of 3, and a `column-width` value of `auto`. Whether our container is 760 pixels wide (as in Figure 4.17) or 355 pixels wide (as in Figure 4.18), we still have three columns.

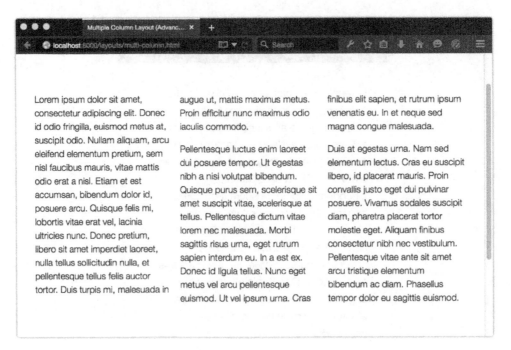

Figure 4.17. When `column-width` is `auto` and `column-number: 3` in a 760px container

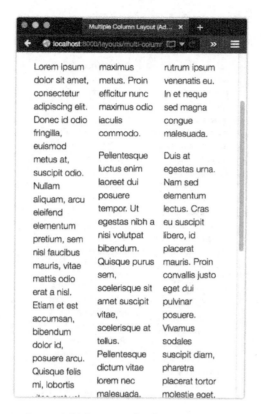

Figure 4.18. When `column-width` is `auto` and `column-number: 3` in a 355px container

Now, compare these to Figure 4.19, where our container has a `column-number` value of 3, and a `column-width` value of 8em. Inside a 760 pixels wide container, our number of columns remains the same. But when our container is 355 pixels wide, we can only fit two columns.

Figure 4.19. `column-width: 8em` and `column-number: 3` in a 355px container

This goes out of the window entirely, though, if we set the `height` of a column container. Setting a fixed height on a container forces the browser to create additional columns to accommodate the container's content. In this case, the `column-number` property will be ignored.

Spacing Columns with `column-gap` and `column-rule`

How many columns will fit in a container also depends on the value of `column-gap`. Known as the gutter in print design, the **column gap** sets the distance between each column. The initial value of `column-gap` is `normal`. In most browsers, that's about `1em`.

Increasing or decreasing its width has no effect on the width of each column, just the space in between. If an element is `45em` wide with `column-width: 15em` and `column-gap: normal` applied, the content will be divided into two columns rather than three, as can be seen in Figure 4.20.

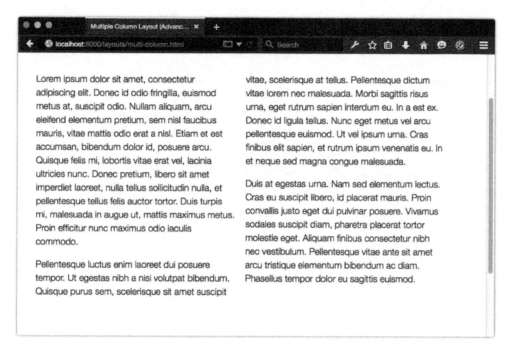

Figure 4.20. Columns that are 15em wide inside a 45em container with the default `column-gap` value

Changing `column-gap` to 0, however, gives us our full three-column layout as shown in Figure 4.21. Without a `column-gap`, there's now sufficient room for three columns.

As with `column-width`, the value of `column-gap` should be either 0 or a positive length value. Negative lengths such as `-2em` are invalid.

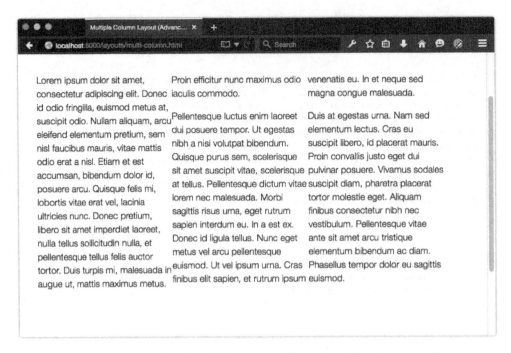

Figure 4.21. 15em wide columns inside a 45em wide container with `column-gap: 0`

With `column-rule`, we can add lines to visually separate columns. It functions similarly to `border`, and accepts the same values. For example:

```
.multi-col {
    -webkit-column-rule: thin dashed #607d8b;
    -moz-column-rule: thin dashed #607d8b;
    column-rule: thin dashed #607d8b;
}
```

Like `border`, `column-rule` is really a shorthand for the `column-rule-width`, `column-rule-style`, and `column-rule-color` properties. Each `column-rule-*` property accepts the same values as its `border` counterpart, and is demonstrated in Figure 4.22.

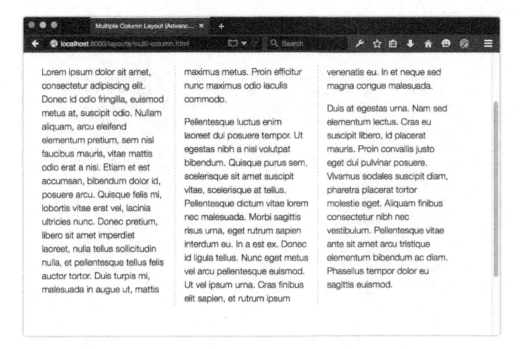

Figure 4.22. Adding a `column-rule`

Column width is not affected by changes to `column-rule`. Instead, column rules sit at the midpoint of the column gap. If the width of the rule exceeds that of the gap, the column rule will render beneath the columns' contents as shown in Figure 4.23.

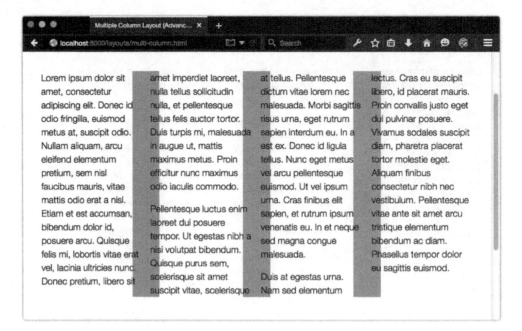

Figure 4.23. What happens when the width of a column rule exceeds the column gap

Images Within Columns

If the width of an image exceeds that of its column, the overflowing portion of that image will be hidden, as shown in Figure 4.24. This is the behavior outlined in the multicolumn specification, and it's what Internet Explorer, Chrome, Safari, and Opera do.

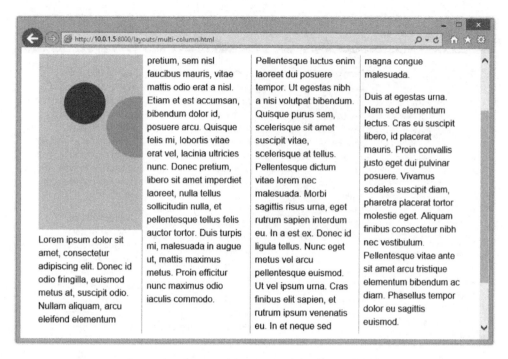

Figure 4.24. Images are clipped to the width of their column

Unfortunately, Firefox version 42 (and prior) is yet to follow suit. As witnessed in Figure 4.25, images overflow the column width and are positioned at the bottom of the stacking context in Firefox.

Figure 4.25. Images within a column sit at the bottom of the stacking context in Firefox   41

You can work around this by adding a `width: 100%` declaration to the image or object. Doing so constrains the width of the image to that of the column box as shown in Figure 4.26.

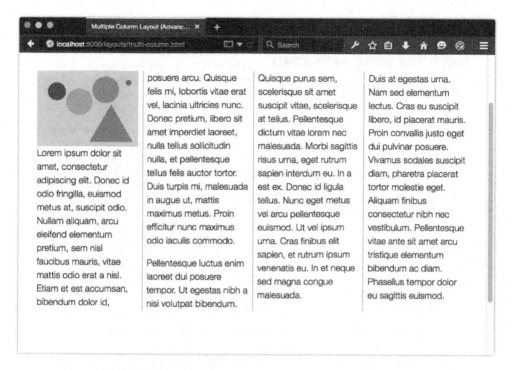

Figure 4.26. Using `img{width: 100%}` inside a multicolumn container

Making Elements Span Columns

We can also make a particular element span columns with the `column-span` property. This property accepts two values: `none` and `all`. Using `none` means that the element will be part of the normal column flow; `all` will make the element span every column.

It's currently not possible to make an element span *a particular number of columns*. We're limited to specifying whether it should span all columns or none at all. Consider the layout shown in Figure 4.27.

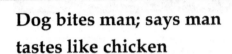

Figure 4.27. How an h1 element fits into the multicolumn layout flow

Here the h1 element (the article headline "Dog bites man ...") is part of the multi-column layout flow. It sits within a column box, wrapping as appropriate. Now let's add column-span: all:[10]

```
article > h1 {
    -webkit-column-span: all;
    column-span: all;
}
```

This gives us the layout shown in Figure 4.28, with a headline that spans both columns.

---

[10] Firefox ≤ 41 is without support for column-span, even with a prefix.

Figure 4.28. Using `column-span` to make an element span multiple columns

Managing Column Breaks

In a multiple-column layout, a long block of text may start in one column and end in another, as shown in Figure 4.29.

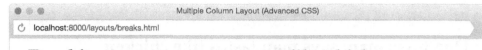

Dog bites man; says man tastes like chicken

Lorem ipsum dolor sit amet, consectetur adipiscing elit. Nam non feugiat ligula. Integer felis erat, consectetur eget libero vitae, feugiat faucibus turpis. In hac habitasse platea dictumst.

Fusce quis arcu vel mi fringilla imperdiet sit amet sit amet felis. Sed et sollicitudin nisl. Donec gravida arcu sodales sodales tristique. Donec posuere nisi nec sem ullamcorper venenatis. Ut et tincidunt sapien, ultricies luctus diam.

Cras tincidunt tincidunt ex, pulvinar viverra ex rutrum ut. Fusce felis tortor, sodales nec ligula in, lacinia viverra turpis. Donec ut eros quam.

Aenean non purus ante. Donec egestas feugiat semper. Nulla pharetra mauris ipsum, vel

facilisis nisi commodo a. Nunc et lacus imperdiet, sodales augue sit amet, consectetur sapien. Proin nec feugiat ligula. Nunc aliquet elit dolor, et tempor quam accumsan sed.

Fusce sollicitudin metus non volutpat bibendum. Donec velit sem, rhoncus nec nunc non, vulputate porta lectus. Praesent a sem eu est aliquam pharetra. Etiam pharetra lacus id tempus semper. Nulla quis metus dolor.

Donec a tortor accumsan, scelerisque odio quis, congue sem. Pellentesque luctus, quam ac mollis maximus, eros ex consectetur erat, eget molestie ex velit a quam. Duis ultricies, elit ac efficitur sodales, felis purus egestas erat, sit amet posuere elit nulla vel dolor. In in est sit amet turpis mattis malesuada.

Figure 4.29. Elements may break across columns in a multicolumn layout

To prevent this, use `break-inside: avoid` or `break-inside: avoid-column`. The `break-inside` property applies to the children of a multicolumn container. For example, to prevent all children of `.multi-col` from breaking across column boxes, use the following:[11]

```
.multi-col > * {
    break-inside: avoid-column;
}
```

Now the purple paragraph no longer breaks across columns, as can be seen in Figure 4.30. The `break-inside` property also affects paged media,[12] which explains why there are both `avoid` and `avoid-column` values. The difference is that `avoid-column` prevents a box from breaking across columns while `avoid` prevents a box from breaking across columns *and pages*.

---

[11] WebKit- and Blink-based browsers currently use the non-standard `-webkit-column-break-inside` property. It works the same way, but `avoid` is its only valid value.

[12] http://www.w3.org/TR/css3-page/

Multiple Column Layout (Advanced CSS)

localhost:8000/layouts/breaks.html

Dog bites man; says man tastes like chicken

Lorem ipsum dolor sit amet, consectetur adipiscing elit. Nam non feugiat ligula. Integer felis erat, consectetur eget libero vitae, feugiat faucibus turpis. In hac habitasse platea dictumst.

Fusce quis arcu vel mi fringilla imperdiet sit amet sit amet felis. Sed et sollicitudin nisl. Donec gravida arcu sodales sodales tristique. Donec posuere nisi nec sem ullamcorper venenatis. Ut et tincidunt sapien, ultricies luctus diam.

Cras tincidunt tincidunt ex, pulvinar viverra ex rutrum ut. Fusce felis tortor, sodales nec ligula in, lacinia viverra turpis. Donec ut eros quam.

Aenean non purus ante. Donec egestas feugiat semper. Nulla pharetra mauris ipsum, vel facilisis nisi commodo a. Nunc et lacus imperdiet, sodales augue sit amet, consectetur sapien. Proin nec feugiat ligula. Nunc aliquet elit dolor, et tempor quam accumsan sed.

Fusce sollicitudin metus non volutpat bibendum. Donec velit sem, rhoncus nec nunc non, vulputate porta lectus. Praesent a sem eu est aliquam pharetra. Etiam pharetra lacus id tempus semper. Nulla quis metus dolor.

Donec a tortor accumsan, scelerisque odio quis, congue sem. Pellentesque luctus, quam ac mollis maximus, eros ex consectetur erat, eget molestie ex velit a quam. Duis ultricies, elit ac efficitur sodales, felis purus egestas erat, sit amet posuere elit nulla vel dolor. In in est sit amet turpis mattis malesuada.

Figure 4.30. Preventing column breaks inside elements with `break-inside`

CSS Fragmentation Module Level 3

The CSS Fragmentation Module Level 3[13] specification is closely related to the multiple-column and paged media specifications. It further defines how block boxes should break across columns, pages, and regions.

It's also possible to force a break before or after an element using `break-before` and `break-after`. Let's force a column break before the third paragraph:

```
.multi-col p:nth-of-type(3) {
    background-color: #e91e63;
    break-before: column;
}
```

Here we've used the `column` value to force a column break before the selected element (see Figure 4.31). The `break-after` property works similarly, forcing a column break *after* the selected element. The `always` value also forces column breaks, but `always` will also force a column break in paged media.

---

[13] http://dev.w3.org/csswg/css-break-3/

Figure 4.31. Forcing a column break before an element

Webkit- and Blink-based browsers use `-webkit-column-break-before` and `-webkit-column-break-after`. Both properties are holdovers from an earlier version of the specification. For those properties, the `column` value is unsupported, so use `always` instead. Firefox is yet to support any of these values, or support a vendor-prefixed equivalent.

Optimizing the User Interface

Arranging paragraphs of text isn't the only use case for multiple-column layouts. We can also use it with lists to make use of horizontal space. Consider the layout shown in Figure 4.32.

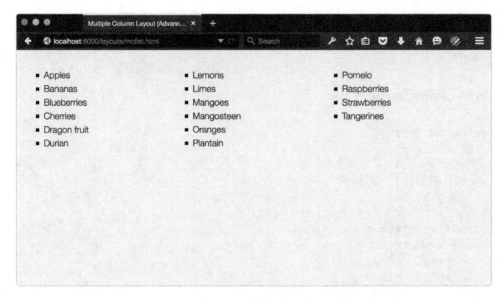

Figure 4.32. A list split into three columns

The old-school way of creating this layout is to split our list into three separate ones and float them to the left or right of a containing element. Here's what the markup might look like:

```
<div class="clearfix">
    <ul class="column-float-left">
        <li>Apples</li>
        <li>Oranges</li>
        <li>Bananas</li>
        <li>Dragon fruit</li>
    </ul>
    <ul class="column-float-left">
        <li>Cherries</li>
        <li>Strawberries</li>
        <li>Blueberries</li>
        <li>Raspberries</li>
    </ul>
    <ul class="column-float-left">
        <li>Durian</li>
        <li>Mangosteen</li>
```

```
        <li>Mangoes</li>
    </ul>
</div>
```

And the accompanying CSS:

```
.columned-list {
    float:left;
    width: 33%;
    min-width: 150px;
    margin: 0;
}
.clearfix::after {
    clear:both;
    content: ' ';
    display: block;
}
```

While this approach works, it requires more markup than a single-list element. We're using three `li` elements instead of one. And we have to manage floated elements and clearing those floats. With a multiple-column layout, we can use a single element without worrying about clearing floats:

```
<ul style="columns: 3">
    <li>Apples</li>
    <li>Oranges</li>
    <li>Bananas</li>
    <li>Dragon fruit</li>
    <li>Cherries</li>
    <li>Strawberries</li>
    <li>Blueberries</li>
    <li>Raspberries</li>
    <li>Durian</li>
    <li>Mangosteen</li>
    <li>Mangoes</li>
</ul>
```

 Blink- and WebKit-based Browsers

Blink- and WebKit-based browsers remove bullets and numbers from some or all list items in a multicolumn layout. As a workaround, add a left margin (or right margin in a right-to-left language) of at least 20px to `li` elements within a multi-column container.

Another use-case for multicolumn layouts is wrangling lists of checkbox inputs. Here, too, we can maximize the use of horizontal space to create more compact forms, as shown in Figure 4.33.

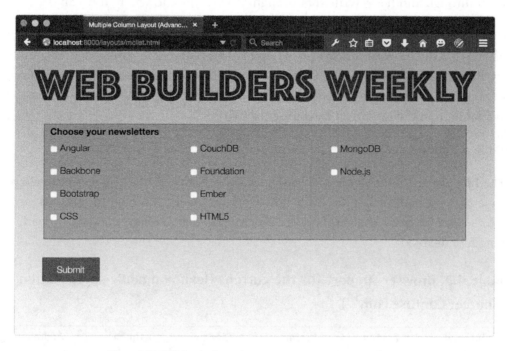

Figure 4.33. Utilizing horizontal space to create more compact forms

Use multicolumn layout when you have blocks of content to be automatically distributed and evenly spaced across several columns. It *is not* a great choice for overall page layouts. It *is* a great choice for components.

Creating Flexible Layouts with Flexbox

A better choice for page layouts is flexbox, or the Flexible Box Layout Module.[14] **Flexbox** provides an easy way to align elements and create flexible components and grids.

---

[14] http://dev.w3.org/csswg/css-flexbox-1/

Flexbox is approaching maturity as a specification. The latest versions of most browsers now support its properties and values without a vendor prefix.

Before we dig into flexbox, here's a quick review of its history: the original 2009 specification went through a huge rewrite in 2012 where several properties and values were renamed and some behaviors were adjusted. And then the specification went through another rewrite that brought it very close to where it began.

Different browser vendors implemented the specification at different points, which means that the browser landscape is fragmented. Safari ≤ 6, Android ≤ 4.3, and UC Browser support the original 2009 version of the flexbox specification.[15] Internet Explorer 10 implements the 2012 version, details of which implementation are available from the Microsoft Developer Network.[16]

Table 4.3 shows current browser support for flexbox.

The full history of the flexbox rewrite process is buried in the annals of the www-style@w3.org mailing list archives; however, the specification editor Tab Atkins wrote two blog posts that explain the differences. See Atkins' "Flexbox is dead, long live flexbox!"[17].

Table 4.3. Browser support for the current flexbox module specification (Source: CanIUse.com[18])

Internet Explorer	Firefox	Safari	Chrome	Opera	Android
11	28+	6.1+ (versions 9 require -webkit- prefix)	21+ (versions 28 require -webkit- prefix)	12.1+ (versions 15 and 16 require -webkit- prefix)	4.4+

---

[15] http://www.w3.org/TR/2009/WD-css3-flexbox-20090723/#packing

[16] https://msdn.microsoft.com/en-us/library/hh673531(v=vs.85).aspx

[17] http://www.xanthir.com/blog/b4Dm0

[18] http://caniuse.com/#feat=flexbox

The upside, however, is that the latest versions of all major browsers support the latest version of the flexbox specification. That's the version we'll focus on here.[19]

A basic flexible box layout is very simple to create: add `display: flex` or `display: inline-flex` to the containing element. Safari 8 and UC Browser 9.9 do require a vendor prefix. In those browsers, you'll need to use `display: -webkit-flex` or `display: -webkit-inline-flex`.

When you add `display: flex` or `display: inline-flex` to a containing element, its immediate children become **flex items**, shown in Figure 4.34. If no other properties are set, each flex item will:

- have the same height as its tallest element, and
- stack horizontally with no space between the edges of each box

Figure 4.34. A list with `display: flex` applied to the `ul` containing element (note how each child `li` stacks horizontally)

---

[19] If you'd like an introduction to cross-browser flexbox that includes older versions of the specification, read Chris Mills' piece, "Advanced cross-browser flexbox" [https://dev.opera.com/articles/advanced-cross-browser-flexbox/].

That may not seem like such a big deal, but it simplifies the CSS necessary for a range of user interface patterns. One use case is creating the Holy Grail of layout.[20] Here's our markup:

```
<div class="flex">
    <div>...</div>
    <div>...</div>
    <div>...</div>
</div>
```

Now all we need to do is add `.flex {display: flex;}` to our CSS to end up with the layout shown in Figure 4.35. The length of the content in the middle column affects the height of the exterior columns.

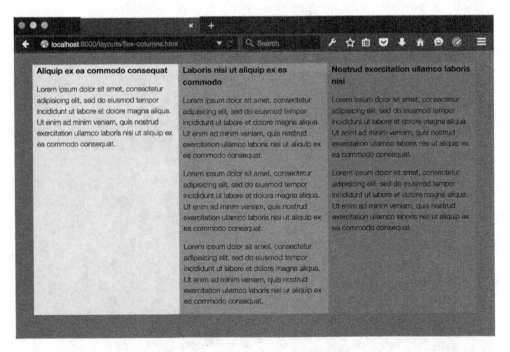

Figure 4.35. Flexbox makes columns easy

Using flexbox for page layout does have its risks, though, as that wasn't what it was originally designed to do. Because content affects layout, users with slower connections may experience a jump in the page layout as the document loads. This is explained in greater detail in Jake Archibald's "Don't use flexbox for overall page

---

[20] https://en.wikipedia.org/wiki/Holy_Grail_(web_design

layout."[21] A better option for layout would be CSS Grid, which we'll take a look at in Chapter 10.

Creating Simple Grids with `flex-wrap`

Flexbox also makes it easy to create components in a grid with the `flex-wrap` property. Initially, the value of `flex-wrap` is `nowrap`. Flex items will simply fill the width of the container, growing or shrinking as necessary to fit on one line. If we set it to `flex-wrap: wrap`, however, flex items will drop to the next line if their width exceeds that of the container.

Let's build a four-across grid based on the markup:

```
<div class="grid">
    <div class="alpha">A</div>
    <div class="beta">B</div>
    <div class="gamma">C</div>
    <div class="delta">D</div>
    <div class="epsilon">E</div>
    <div class="zeta">F</div>
    <div class="eta">G</div>
</div>
```

We've added `display: flex` to our `.grid` rule set to trigger a flexible layout context. We've also added `flex-wrap: wrap` so that our flex items will wrap:

```
.grid{
    display: flex;
    flex-wrap: wrap;
}

.grid > * {
    flex: 0 0 25%;
}
```

Our `.grid > *` rule set uses the `flex` property to give all items a `flex-basis` (a width) of 25%. This gives us two rows of evenly sized boxes, shown in Figure 4.36.

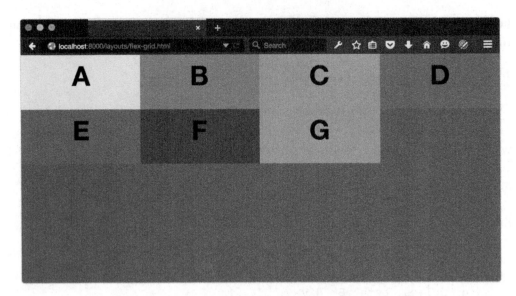

Figure 4.36. Creating components in a grid with flexbox

This grid looks a bit awkward, though: our second row has a gap. Let's fix that. We just need to change our `flex-grow` value:

```
.grid > * {
    flex: 1 0 25%;
}
```

Now the elements in our second row will expand evenly to fill the container, as presented in Figure 4.37.

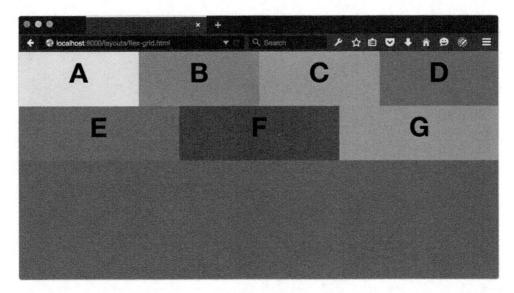

Figure 4.37. Gridded items in a flex container can also expand to fill available space

To evenly distribute items across the width of a flex container, use `justify-content: space-between` or `justify-content: space-around`. The former evenly distributes the space between flex items, aligning the first and last items with the edges of the container (Figure 4.38). The latter centers flex items and evenly distributes space around them (Figure 4.39).

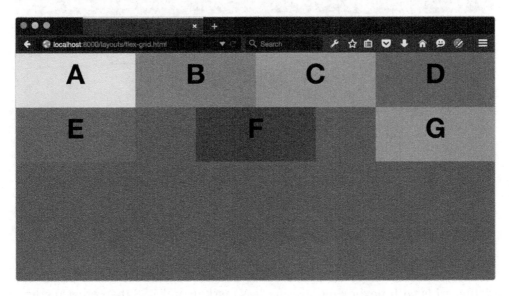

Figure 4.38. Distributing flex items with `justify-content: space-between`

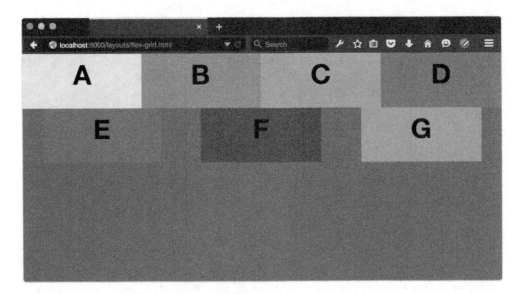

Figure 4.39. Distributing flex items with `justify-content: space-around`

It's also possible to center flex items in a row with `justify-content: center`, as seen in Figure 4.40. In that case, the items in our second row will be centered in the middle of the row.

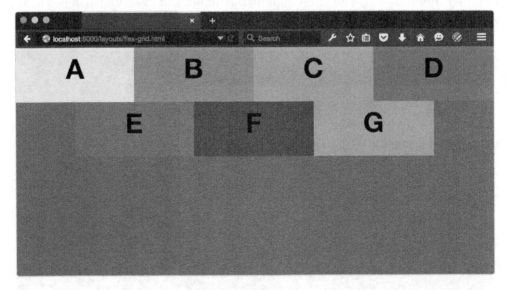

Figure 4.40. Distributing flex items with `justify-content: center`

Creating grids with flexbox requires far less markup and CSS than other methods.

Creating Flexible Components with `flex`

Another use case for flexbox is creating flexible, vertically aligned form components. Consider the interface pattern shown in Figure 4.41.

Figure 4.41. A form field with an adjacent button

Here we have a form input control and an adjacent button. Both are vertically aligned, and our button is 110 pixels wide.

What if we want our `input` element to expand to fill the available space in its container? Without flexbox, we'd require some JavaScript and hand-waving to update the width of `input` in response to changes in the width of its parent. With flexbox, however, we can just use `flex`.

The `flex` property is actually shorthand for three other properties:

`flex-grow:`   indicates that an element should grow if necessary and must be a positive integer; initial value is `0`

`flex-shrink:`   indicates that an element should shrink if necessary and must be a positive integer; initial value is `1`

`flex-basis:`   indicates the initial or minimum width (when the flex axis is horizontal) or height of an element (when it's vertical); may be a length or percentage, or `auto`, and its initial value is `auto`

Though it's possible to set each of these individually, the specification strongly recommends using the `flex` shorthand. Here's an example:

```
div {
    display: flex;
    justify-content: center;
}

input[type="text"],
```

```
button {
    border:0;
    display: inline;
    font: inherit;
}

input[type="text"] {
    flex: 1 0 auto;
}

button {
    background: #003;
    color: whitesmoke;
    display: block;
    text-align: center;
    flex: 0 0 110px;
}
```

Remember the Prefix for WebKit-based Browsers

Just a reminder that some recent versions of WebKit browsers require a `-webkit-` prefix for flexbox properties. For those browsers, `justify-content` needs to be `-webkit-justify-content` and `flex` should be `-webkit-flex`.

Here we've used `flex: 1 0 auto` for our `input` element. Since its `flex-grow` value is 1, it will grow to fill the available space of its parent. For the `button` element, however, we've used `flex: 0 0 110px`. The 0 values for `flex-grow` and `flex-shrink` prevent the width of the button from increasing or decreasing, while the `flex-basis` value of 110px sets its width.

As you can see in Figure 4.42, our button remains the same size, but the width of `input` expands to fill the remaining space.

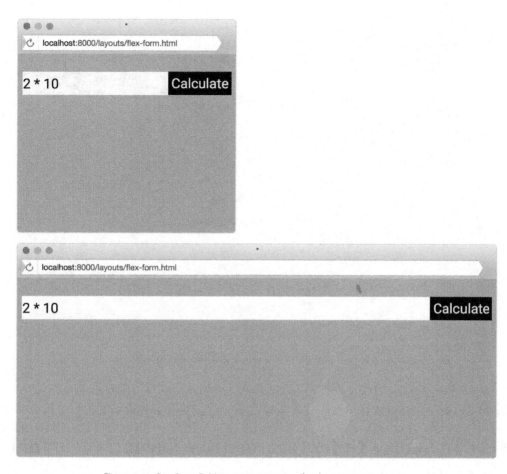

Figure 4.42. Our form field component at 330 (top) and 840-pixels wide

Here's the tricky bit about `flex-grow` and `flex-shrink` values: they're proportional. Yes, `flex: 1 0 auto` means our `input` element will be wider than our button. But changing the value of our button's `flex` property to `flex: 1 0 auto` doesn't necessarily mean that both elements will have the same size, as shown in Figure 4.43.

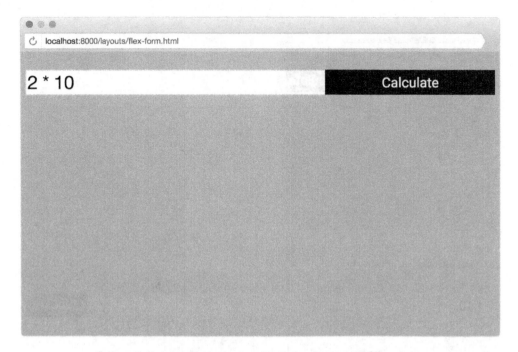

Figure 4.43. Both items have the same `flex` value, but are still different sizes

Instead, flex items will be resized to fill the container, taking their used `min-width` and `max-width` values into account (which may be their initial values).

Letting Source Order Diverge from Layout: the `order` Property

The source order of a document is important. Whether a search box comes before or after the sitemap links in your footer has implications for assistive technology and flexibility of layout. Take a look at the footer component shown in Figure 4.44.

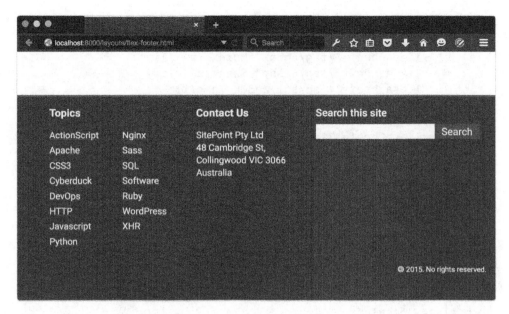

Figure 4.44. Distributing flex items with `justify-content: center`

Here our **Topics** subsection comes first, followed by the **Contact Us**, **Search this site**, and a "copyleft" notice. But this is what our markup looks like:

```
                                    04-layouts/flex-footer.html (excerpt)
<footer class="flex align-top wrap">
    <!-- Search form -->
    <form class="flex wrap">
        <div><label>Search this site</label></div>
        <p class="flex same-height">
            <input type="search">
            <button type="submit">Search</button>
        </p>
    </form>
    <!-- Topics -->
    <section id="topics">
        <h2>Topics </h2>
        <ul class="taglist">
            <li><a href="/tag/actionscript">ActionScript</a></li>
            <li><a href="/tag/apache">Apache</a></li>
            <li><a href="/tag/css3/">CSS3</a></li>
            <li><a href="/tag/cyberduck/">Cyberduck</a></li>
            <li><a href="/tag/devops/">DevOps</a></li>
            <li><a href="/tag/http/">HTTP</a></li>
```

```
            <li><a href="/tag/javascript/">JavaScript</a></li>
            <li><a href="/tag/python/">Python</a></li>
            <li><a href="/tag/nginx">Nginx</a></li>
            <li><a href="/tag/sass/">Sass</a></li>
            <li><a href="/tag/sql/">SQL</a></li>
            <li><a href="/tag/software/">Software</a></li>
            <li><a href="/tag/ruby/">Ruby</a></li>
            <li><a href="/tag/wordpress/">WordPress</a></li>
            <li><a href="/tag/xhr/">XHR</a></li>
        </ul>
    </section>
    <!-- Contact -->
    <section id="contact">
        <h2>Contact Us</h2>
        <p>SitePoint Pty Ltd<br>48 Cambridge St,<br>Collingwood VIC
layouts-tabflexbox 3066<br>Australia</p>
    </section>
    <!-- Copyleft -->
    <p class="copyleft">
        <b>&copy;</b> 2015. No rights reserved.
    </p>
</footer>
```

Our source order doesn't match our rendering order. In the source, our search box is first, followed by the list of tags, address, and copyleft notice. What kind of trickery is this? Here are the relevant portions of our CSS:

04-layouts/flex-footer.html *(excerpt)*

```
form {
  flex-wrap: wrap;
  flex: 0 0 30%;
  order: 1
}

[id=topics] {
  flex: 1 1 auto;
  order: -1
}

[id=copyleft] {
  flex: 0 0 100%;
  order: 1;
}
```

```
[id=contact] {
  flex: 0 0 25%;
}
```

Each rule set has an `order` property—that is, except for `[id=contact]`. We'll come back to that point in a moment. The `order` property determines the sequence of flex items on screen. Its value must be an integer and negative values are perfectly valid. Its initial value is 0.

With `order`, the actual number matters less than its value relative to the `order` property of its siblings. As you can see in the previous example, a flex item with `order: 1` will succeed a flex item with an `order` value of 0. This is true whether `order: 0` is declared or computed. That's why `[id=contact]` is the second item in our display order. A flex item with `order: -1`, on the other hand, will precede a flex item with an `order` value of 0. Two items with the same `order` value will be displayed according to their order in the source.

Vertical Centering with Flexbox

Finally, let's take a look at how to vertically center content with flexbox. Vertically centering elements is one of the more difficult tasks to achieve with CSS, particularly if the height of your content is unknown. But with flexbox, we require just one line of CSS: `align-items: center`:

```
.flex-container {
    display: flex;
    align-items: center;
}
```

This will position flex items so that there is an equal amount of space above and below the row, as in Figure 4.45.

Figure 4.45. Distributing flex items with `justify-content: center`

But that's not all. If our flex items wrap, those rows will also be centered within its parent.

In Figure 4.46, our rows of flex items are centered, but there's still a great deal of space between each row.

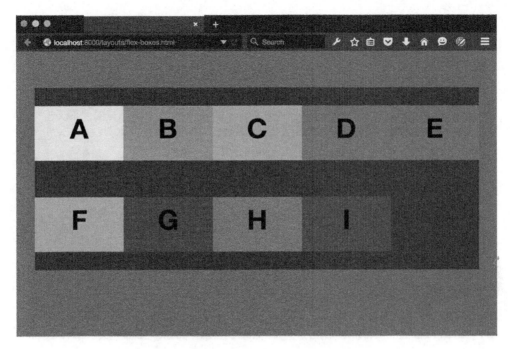

Figure 4.46. Vertically centering rows of flex items

We can manage this space with the `align-content` property. Using `align-content: center` eliminates the space between rows, as in Figure 4.47.

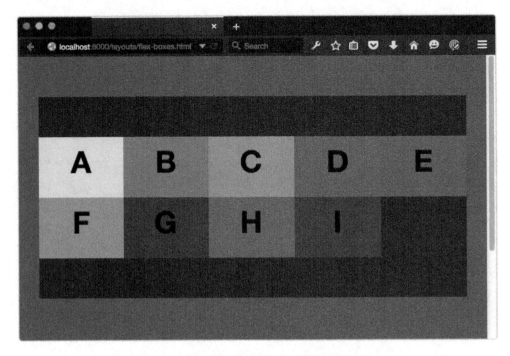

Figure 4.47. Eliminating space between rows of flex items using `align-content: center`

We can use `align-content: center` with `align-items: center`, or by itself. The CSS that follows will also create the layout shown in Figure 4.47:

```
.flex-container {
    display: flex;
    align-content: center;
}
```

The `align-content` property only has an effect, however, when there are mutiple rows of flex items. Otherwise, `align-items` is sufficient.

 Vertical Centering with Box Alignment

It's worth noting that the Box Alignment module[22], currently in working draft, should bring vertical centering to all layout methods, including block.

---

[22] http://www.w3.org/TR/css-align-3/

There's a bit more to flexbox than what we've covered here. CSS-Tricks' "A Guide to flexbox"[23] digs into all the properties and values. You can also check out Philip Walton's "Solved by flexbox,"[24] which showcases several UI patterns that are made easier with flexbox.

Conclusion

Now that this chapter is complete, you should understand some of the tricks and challenges of creating complex layouts. Specifically, you should now understand:

- why and how to use the `box-sizing` property
- how stacking contexts work and how to create them
- when and how to use multiple-column layout
- what kinds of layout challenges you can solve with flexbox

Stacking context comes up again in Chapter 6, in which we discuss transforms. But first, let's look at CSS transitions.

---

[23] https://css-tricks.com/snippets/css/a-guide-to-flexbox/
[24] http://philipwalton.github.io/solved-by-flexbox/

Chapter 5

Transitions and Animation

Now that we've covered some advanced CSS layouts, let's look at how to add some whimsy, delight, and polish to our documents with CSS transitions and animations. Transitions and animations can often clarify the effect of an action. A menu that slides into view, for example, is less abrupt and jarring than one that appears suddenly after a button is clicked. Transitions and animations can also draw attention to a page change or problem. You might, for instance, transition the border color of a form field to highlight that its value is invalid.[1]

This is probably a good time to explain how animations and transitions differ. With a **transition**, you define start and end states, and the browser fills in the states in between. With **animations**, on the other hand, you can define those in-between states and control how the animation progresses.

---

[1] "Animation for Attention and Comprehension" [http://www.nngroup.com/articles/animation-usability/] from the Nielsen Norman Group is a nice backgrounder on how animations and transitions can enhance usability.

CSS Transitions

CSS transitions[2] are a CSS-based way to update the value of a CSS property over a specified duration. Given a start value and an end value, the browser will interpolate in-between values over the course of the transition. They're great for simple effects where you don't mind giving up control over how the animation progresses.

In my own work, I often use transitions for :hover states. I also use them when revealing or concealing content, such as showing an off-screen menu. You *could* create animations for such effects, but animations are generally more verbose, as you'll see later in the chapter.

Browser support for CSS transitions is quite good (see Table 5.1), with the latest versions of all major desktop and mobile browsers supporting them. In most—UC Browser being the exception—no vendor prefix is necessary. Of course, if your audience is still heavy with people who use older versions of Firefox or Safari, you'll want to include the appropriate prefixes (-moz- and -webkit- respectively).

Table 5.1. Browser support for CSS transitions (Source CanIUse.com[3])

Chrome	Firefox	Internet Explorer	Opera	Safari	Android	UC Browser
4+ (versions < 26 require -webkit- prefix)	4+ (versions < 16 require -moz- prefix)	10+	10.5+ (versions < 12.1 require -o- prefix)	3.1+ (versions 6.1 require -webkit- prefix)	2.1 (versions < 4.4 require -webkit- prefix)	9+ (require -webkit- prefix)

Transitions also degrade gracefully. In browsers without support for them, users will just see a transition-free change between the two values. This may be jarring—for example, when showing or hiding content—but it won't break your site's functionality. An alternative is to use a JavaScript library. jQuery, for example, has several simple animation methods.[4] First test to see whether the browser supports transitions (or animations), and fall back to JavaScript methods if it does not.

---

[2] http://dev.w3.org/csswg/css-transitions/
[3] http://caniuse.com/#search=transitions
[4] http://api.jquery.com/category/effects/

Not all properties can be animated or transitioned. Only properties that accept *interpolatable* values can. Interpolation is a method of calculating values that fall within a range. Interpolatable values are typically numeric unit values such as lengths, percentages, or colors, so they can't be used with properties such as `visibility` or `display`. Nor can we animate to or from `auto` values.[5]

Creating Your First Transition

In this example, we'll make our link color transition from blue to pink when users move their mouse over it, and back to blue when users moves their mouse off it.

Here's our bare-bones HTML:

05-animations/transitions/simple.html (excerpt)

```
<!DOCTYPE html>
    <html lang="en-US">
    <head>
        <link rel="stylesheet" href="style.css">
    </head>
    <body>
        <p>Mouse over <a href="http://sitepoint.com/">this link</a>
➥ to see the transition effect.</p>
    </body>
</html>
```

This gives us the page shown in Figure 5.1.

---

[5] The CSS Transitions specification includes a list of animatable CSS properties and values [http://dev.w3.org/csswg/css-transitions-1/#animatable-css].

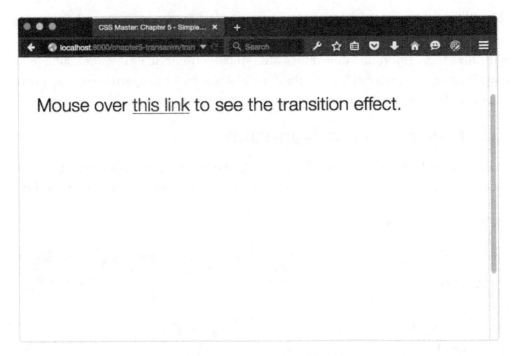

Figure 5.1. A basic HTML page with a link

Now let's add the following CSS to our **style.css**

```
a {
    transition: 1s;
}
a:link {
    color: #309;
}
a:hover {
    color: #f0c;
}
```

This is the bare minimum CSS required for a transition to work: a start value (`color: #309`), an end value (`color: #f0c`), and a transition duration (`transition: 1s;`). When you mouse over the link, you'll see a gradual transition from blue to hot pink, as illustrated in Figure 5.2.

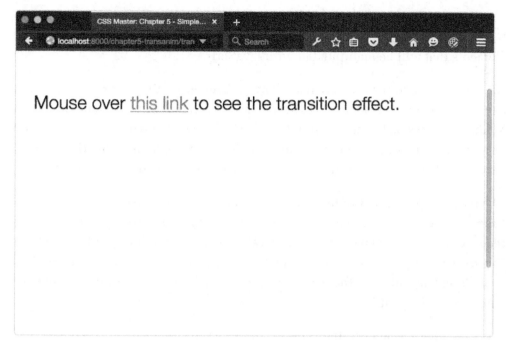

Figure 5.2. Once the transition has completed

Transitions need to be triggered by some kind of event. Often, this is a user interaction. We might transition between colors when entering and leaving a :hover state, as we've done here. But we can also trigger a transition by adding or removing a class name using JavaScript. In the example following, we've modified element's classList attribute to do just that:

```
05-animations/transitions/simple-withjs.html (excerpt)

<script type="text/javascript">
    var btn = document.querySelector('button');
    btn.addEventListener('click', function() {
        document.body.classList.toggle('change');
    });
</script>
```

In the code, we've first defined a variable named btn. If you're unfamiliar with programming, a variable is simply a bucket of sorts that holds a value. We can then use the variable anywhere we need that value. The value of btn is our button element, as returned by document.querySelector('button'). The document.querySelector() method is defined by the Selectors API specification.[6] It accepts any CSS selector as its argument, and returns the first item that matches. It's a way to select elements that will be manipulated with JavaScript.

Next, we've added what's known as an **event listener** for the click event using addEventListener. The addEventListener method is part of the Document Object Model. It allows us to define a function that will be called when a particular event occurs. This function is known as an **event handler** or **callback function**. In this case we're listening—or waiting—for a click event on the button element.

The magic happens within the click event handler. We're using the classList.toggle() method to add or remove the change class from the body element (document.body). When the classList value changes, it will trigger the animation. The classList property is a newer part of the Document Object Model API. It provides a handful of methods that simplify the process of manipulating the class names of an element.[7]

If you'd rather use jQuery, the syntax looks like this:

```
$('button').on('click', function() {
    $('body').toggleClass('change');
});
```

jQuery uses a $() function to select elements. This function accepts a CSS selector string as an argument, and returns a list of elements that match. When we call a method on this list of elements, it's applied to each item in the list. Here, it's the on method. It works similarly to addEventListener, and also accepts two arguments. The first is the event to listen for and the second is the function to invoke.

Within our event handler function, we've used the library's toggleClass method to add the change class to the body element. As with the plain JavaScript example, this is what triggers our transition.

---

[6] http://www.w3.org/TR/selectors-api2/

[7] The classList property is also known as DOMTokenList. It's defined in the Document Object Model specification. [http://www.w3.org/TR/dom/] Internet Explorer 9 lacks support for classList, however. If you still need to support IE9, use the className property, or a polyfill.

Lacking confidence with JavaScript?

If any of that went over your head, don't worry. Web Platform Docs explains these concepts in its guide to programming basics,[8] or pick up Darren Jones' *JavaScript: Novice to Ninja*.[9] Using jQuery? Try the jQuery Learning Center.[10]

Now let's look at our CSS. It's only a few lines long:

```css
body {
    background: #fcf;
    transition: 5s;
}

.change {
    background: #0cf;
}
```

Here we've defined a starting background color for our body element, and a transition. We've also defined a .change class, which has a different value for background. When our event handler runs, it will add the change class to our body element. This will trigger a transition from the original background color to the one defined in the .change declaration block, as shown in Figure 5.3.

If you want a transition to work in both directions—for example, when the class is both added and removed—you should add it to whichever declaration block is your start state. We've done that here by including the transition property in the body declaration block. If we moved the transition to the change class, our transition would only work when change was added to our body element, but not when it was removed.

---

[8] https://docs.webplatform.org/wiki/concepts/programming/programming_basics
[9] https://www.sitepoint.com/premium/books/javascript-novice-to-ninja
[10] http://learn.jquery.com/

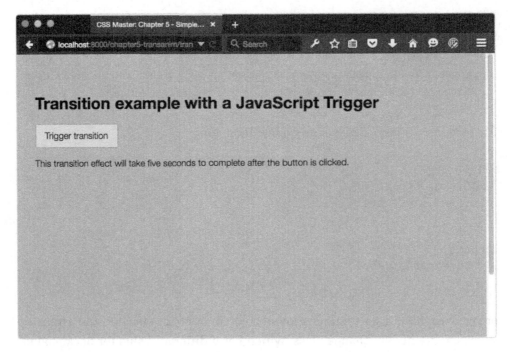

Figure 5.3. Creating a transition triggered by JavaScript

In the examples mentioned, we've used the `transition` shorthand property. It's a condensed way of specifying four "longhand" properties, which are listed in Table 5.2.

Table 5.2. CSS transition properties

Property	Description	Initial value
`transition-duration`	How long the transition should last	`0s` (no transition)
`transition-property`	Which property to transition	`all` (all animatable properties)
`transition-timing-function`	How to calculate the values between the start and end values	`ease`
`transition-delay`	How long the browser should wait between changing the property and starting the transition	`0s` (no delay)

Each longhand property has an *initial* value. It's a default value that the browser will use unless the property is explicitly set. For example, the initial value of transition-property is all (all properties), and the initial value of transition-timing-function is ease. When we set a transition duration—whether using the transition or transition-duration property—those values for transition-property and transition-timing-function are implied. This is why we can get away with setting the transition property and nothing else.

Using the transition Property

As we've already seen in the previous examples, time units are one acceptable value for the transition property. The CSS Values and Units Module Level 3 specification[11] defines two kinds of time units for use with transitions and animations: s for seconds, and ms for milliseconds. We can also collapse values for transition-timing-function, transition-delay, and transition-property into this shorthand transition property:

```
body {
    background: red;
    transition: background 500ms linear 1s;
}
```

Here we've told the browser to transition the background property. The duration will last 500 milliseconds (which we could also write as .5s). It will use the linear timing function (discussed later in this chapter), and the start of the transition will be delayed by 1 second. It's a compact version of the following CSS:

```
body {
    background: red;
    transition—property: background;
    transition—duration: 500ms;
    transition—timing—function: linear;
    transition—delay: 1s;
}
```

Order matters somewhat when using the transition shorthand property. The first value that can be interpreted as a time will become the transition duration no matter where it sits in the value string. The second time value will determine the transition delay. In other words, we could reorder the values in our transition property like so:

---

[11] http://www.w3.org/TR/css3-values/

```
body {
    background: red;
    transition: 500ms 1s background linear;
}
```

Using the `transition` property is the most concise way to define a transition; however, there may be cases in which you want to define a global transition effect (for example, `transition: 500ms ease`) in one part of your CSS, and limit it to specific CSS properties (for example, `transition-property: color`) in another. This is where the longhand properties are useful.

Transition Durations and Delays

The `transition-duration` property sets the duration of the transition, or how long it will take to complete. The `transition-delay` property determines how much time should lapse before the transition begins. Both properties accept time units as a value. These can be seconds or milliseconds; `1s`, `2.5s`, and `200ms` are all valid values.

Both `transition-duration` and `transition-delay` have an initial value of `0s`, or zero seconds. For `transition-duration`, this means there will be no gradual transition between the start and end states. For `transition-delay`, this means the transition will occur immediately.

With `transition-duration`, you must use values greater than zero, such as `.5s` or `2500ms`. Negative values will be treated like a value of `0s`, and the transition will fail to execute, as illustrated in Figure 5.4.

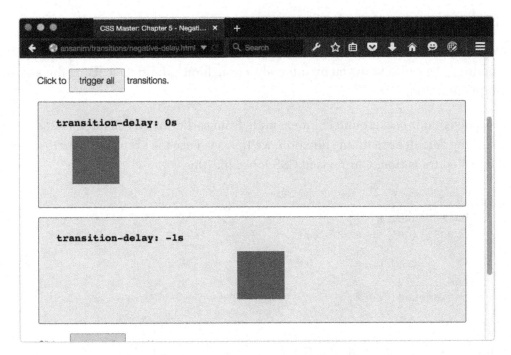

Figure 5.4. The effect of a negative transition delay

Negative values are valid for `transition-delay`, though. Positive `transition-delay` values shift the start of the animation by the specified amount of time. Negative values, however, offset the beginning of the transition, as seen in Figure 5.4. Using `transition-duration: 2s; transition-delay: -1s` will cause the transition to jump one second into the play cycle before continuing. Using a negative `transition-delay` value can create a snappier transition experience by shortening its perceived duration.

Timing Functions

We can also shape transition effects using the `transition-timing-function` property. Timing functions are formulae of sorts that determine how the in-between values of a transition are calculated. Which timing function you use will depend on what kind of transition effect you'd like to achieve: a stepped transition or a smooth gradual one.

Stepped Transitions

With stepped transitions, the play cycle is divided into intervals of equal value and duration. We can set how many intervals a transition should have using the `steps` timing function.

Let's revisit our background color example from earlier in this chapter. Instead of using the default `ease` timing function, we'll instead use the `steps` function to create a five-step transition. Our revised CSS looks like this:

```
body {
    background: #f0f;
    transition: 5s steps(5);
}

.change {
    background: #0cf;
}
```

Rather than a smooth, gradual shift between colors, this transition will cycle through five distinct color states.

There are also two keywords we can use to create stepped animations: `step-start` and `step-end`. These are equivalent to `steps(1, start)` and `steps(1, end)`. With these keywords (or their `step` function equivalents), the transition will have exactly one interval between the start value and end value.

Smooth Transitions

Smooth transitions use the `cubic-bezier` function to interpolate values. Understanding *how* this function works involves a bit of math, along with some handwaving and magic. Read Pomax' "A Primer on Bézier Curves"[12] if you're interested in the intimate details. What follows is a simplified explanation.

The cubic Bézier function is based on the cubic Bézier curve. In general, a Bézier curve consists of a start point and an end point, and one or more control points that affect the shape of the curve. A *cubic* Bézier curve always has two of these control points, which can be seen in Figure 5.5. Curves are drawn from the start point to the end point, towards the control points.

---

[12] http://pomax.github.io/bezierinfo/#explanation

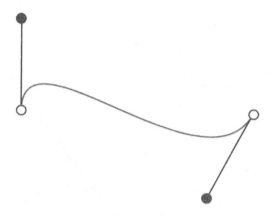

Figure 5.5. A cubic Bézier curve, where the filled circles are the control points

The arguments passed to the `cubic-bezier` function represent the coordinates of those control points: *x1, y1, x2, y2*. But there's a constraint on these points: X values—the first and third parameters—must fall between 0 and 1. Y values (the second and fourth parameters) can exceed this range in either direction. In other words, `cubic-bezier(0, 1.02, 1, 0)` and `cubic-bezier(0, 1.08, .98, -0.58)` are valid values, but `cubic-bezier(2, 1.02, -1, 0)` is not.[13]

Graphs are the best way to illustrate how `cubic-bezier` works. The X-axis is a function of the transition's duration, and can be seen in Figure 5.6. The Y-axis is a function of value of the property that's being transitioned. The outputs for these functions determine the values of the property at a particular point in the transition. Changes in the graph match the changes in speed over the course of a transition.

---

[13] Lea Verou's cubic-bezier.com [http://cubic-bezier.com/] is a great tool for experimenting with the `cubic-bezier` function.

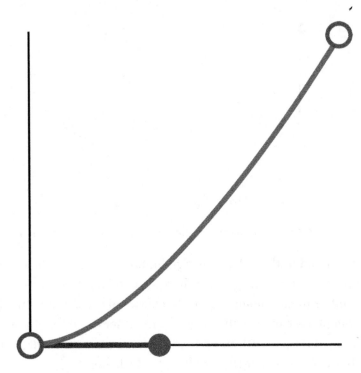

Figure 5.6. A graph of `cubic-bezier(0.42, 0, 1, 1)`

In most cases, it's easier to use a timing function keyword. We mentioned `step-start` and `step-end` in the previous section, but there are five more keywords, each of which is an alias for `cubic-bezier` values. They're listed in Table 5.3.

Table 5.3. Timing function keywords and their function equivalents

Keyword	Equivalent function	Effect
ease	cubic-bezier(0.25, 0.1, 0.25, 1)	Begins slowly, accelerates quickly, then slows towards the end of the transition
ease-in	cubic-bezier(0.42, 0, 1, 1)	Begins quickly, then accelerates slowly but steadily until the end of the transition
ease-out	cubic-bezier(0, 0, 0.58, 1)	Accelerates quickly but slows towards the end of the transition
ease-in-out	cubic-bezier(0.42, 0, 0.58, 1)	Begins slowly, accelerates quickly, then decelerates towards the end of the transition
linear	cubic-bezier(0, 0, 1, 1)	Speed remains consistent over the course of the animation

Transitioning Multiple Properties

It's possible to transition multiple properties of a single element using a transition list. Let's look at an example:

```css
div {
    background: #E91E63;
    height: 200px;
    width: 200px;
    margin: 10px 0;
    position: relative;
    left: 0;
    top: 3em;
    transition: left 4s cubic-bezier(0.175, 0.885, 0.32, 1.275),
    background 2s 500ms;
}

.transthem {
    left: 30%;
    background: #00BCD4;
}
```

Here, we've defined transitions for the `left` and `background` properties. The difference is that each item is separated by a comma. The `left` transition will last four seconds and use a `cubic-bezier` timing function. The `background` transition will only last two seconds, but it will begin after a half-second (`500ms`) delay.

Occasionally, you may need to detect when a transition ends in order to take another action. For example, if you transition the `opacity: 1` to `opacity: 0`, it's a good idea to add a `hidden` attribute to the element for improved assistive technology support. This is where the `transitionend` event comes in handy.[14]

When a transition completes, the browser fires a `transitionend` event on the affected element—one for each property.[15] We can listen for these events using `addEventListener`:

---

[14] In older versions of Chrome (< 26) and Safari (< 6), this event is prefixed `webkitTransitionEnd`. In older versions of Opera, it is `oTransitionEnd` (10.5) or `otransitionend` (12). Other browsers and versions use no prefix.

[15] There is no corresponding `transitionstart` event; nor does HTML define an `ontransitionend` event attribute.

```
var element, transitionEndHandler;
transitionEndHandler = function(evt) {
    // Do something.
}
element = document.getElementById('el');
element.addEventListener('transitionend', transitionEndHandler);
```

Are you using jQuery? The function definition stays the same, but the last two lines can be combined:

```
$('#el').on('transitionend', transitionEndHandler);
```

Let's put this knowledge to use. In this example, we'll hide unselected form options when the user picks one. Our (simplified) HTML follows:

05-animations/transitions/transition-end.html (excerpt)

```
<h1>Please select your favorite color of the ones shown below.</h1>
<form>
  <ul>
      <li>
          <input type="radio" name="favecolor" id="red"><label
➥ for="red">Red</label>
      </li>
      <li>
          <input type="radio" name="favecolor" id="yellow"><label
➥ for="yellow">Yellow</label>
      </li>
      <li>
          <input type="radio" name="favecolor" id="blue"><label
➥ for="blue">Blue</label>
      </li>
  </ul>

  <div id="thanks" hidden>Thank you for selecting your
➥ favorite color.</div>
  <button type="reset">Reset</button>
</form>
```

And here's our (also simplified) CSS:

```
li {
    transition: 500ms;
}

.fade {
    opacity: 0;
}

/* For browsers that don't support the hidden attribute */
[hidden] {
    display: none;
}
```

Add some styles for color and font size, and we end up with the example in Figure 5.7.

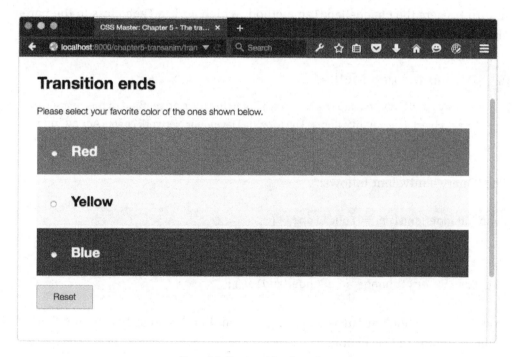

Figure 5.7. Our transition demo form

Now let's tie it together with JavaScript. First, let's define an action that adds the fade class—in this case, a change event handler:

```
                          05-animations/transitions/transition-end.html (excerpt)

var form, changeHandler;
changeHandler = function() {
    // Select unchecked radio buttons. Returns a NodeList.
    var notfave = document.querySelectorAll('input:not(:checked)');

    // Treat the NodeList like an array
    Array.prototype.map.call(notfave, function(nf) {
        // Find the parent node, and add a 'fade' class
        nf.parentNode.classList.add('fade');
    });
};
form.addEventListener('change', changeHandler);
```

When the user selects a color, our form element will receive a change event. That in turn triggers the changeHandler method, which adds a fade class to the parent element of each radio button. This is what triggers our transition.

 Using the map Method

Array.prototype.map.call is a way of using the map method of the JavaScript array object for array-like items. The Mozilla Developer Network covers Array.prototype.map[16] in depth.

The jQuery equivalent follows:

```
var changeHandler = function() {
    // Select unchecked radio buttons. Returns a NodeList.
    $('input').not(':checked').parent().addClass('fade');
};
$('form').on('change', changeHandler);
```

Now let's take a look at our transitionend handler. It's slightly different from the other examples in this chapter:

---

[16] https://developer.mozilla.org/en-US/docs/Web/JavaScript/Reference/Global_Objects/Array/map

```
var transitionendHandler = function(eventObject) {
    eventObject.target.setAttribute('hidden', '');
    document.getElementById('thanks').removeAttribute('hidden');
};
document.addEventListener('transitionend', transitionendHandler);
```

Our `transitionendHandler` accepts a single event object argument. Here we've named it `eventObject`, but you could name it `evt`, `foo`—just about anything. This event object is passed automatically, according to behavior defined by the Document Object Model, Level 2 specification. In order to reference this event object within our handler, we need to define it as a parameter for our function.

Every event object includes a `target` property. This is a reference to the element that received the event. In this case it's a list item, and we're adding a `hidden` attribute to each (`eventObject.target.setAttribute('hidden', '')`). The last line of our event handler removes the `hide` class from our "Thank you" message, as seen in Figure 5.8.

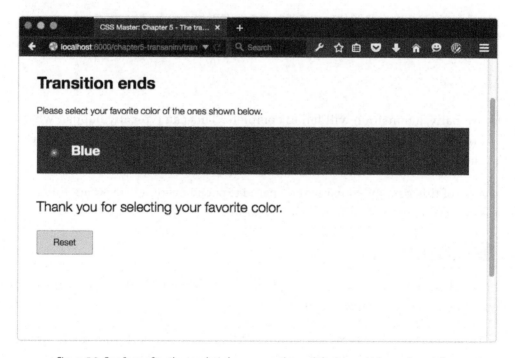

Figure 5.8. Our form after the user has chosen an option and the `transitionend` event fires

The jQuery equivalent follows:

```
var transitionendHandler = function(eventObject) {
    $(eventObject.target).attr('hidden', '');
    $('#thanks').removeAttr('hidden');
};

$(document).on('transitionend', transitionendHandler);
```

Here we're using jQuery's methods to add a hidden attribute to each list item, and to remove it from #thanks.

Multiple Transitions and `transitionend` Events

Compound transitions—that is, a transition of multiple properties—trigger multiple transitionend events. A transition such as `transition: left 4s cubic-linear, background 2s 500ms;` will trigger two `transitionend` events: one for the `left` property and another for `background`. To determine which transition triggered the event, you can check the `propertyName` property of the event object:

```
var transitionendHandler = function(eventObject) {
    if( eventObject.propertyName === 'opacity' ){
        // Do something based on this value.
    }
};
```

Occasionally, a transition will fail to complete. This can typically happen when the property is overridden while it's in progress—perhaps a user action removes the class name. In those situations, the `transitionend` event won't fire.

Because of this risk, avoid using the `transitionend` event to trigger anything "mission critical," such as a form submission.

CSS Animation

Think of CSS animation as the more sophisticated sister to CSS transitions. Animations differ from transforms in a few key ways:

- Animations do not degrade gracefully. If there's no support from the browser, the user is out of luck. The alternative is to use JavaScript.

- Animations can repeat, and repeat infinitely. Transitions are always finite.

▧ Animations use keyframes, which offer the ability to create more complex effects.

▧ Animations can be paused in the middle of the play cycle.

The latest versions of all major browsers support CSS animation, proxy browsers excepted. Versions of Safari prior to 9, versions of Chrome prior to 43, and UC Browser versions up to and including 9 require a `-webkit-` prefix. See Table 5.4 for more information.

Table 5.4. Browser support for CSS animation (Source: CanIUse.com[17])

Chrome	Firefox	Internet Explorer	Opera	Safari	Android	UC Browser
4+ (versions 43 require `-webkit-` prefix)	5+ (versions 15 require `-moz-` prefix)	10+	12.1+ (versions 15 require `-webkit-` prefix)	4+ (versions 9.0 require `-webkit-` prefix)	2.1 (versions 4.3 require `-webkit-` prefix, 4.3 has partial support)	9+ (requires `-webkit-` prefix)

Firefox versions 15 and earlier require a `-moz-` prefix; later versions do not. Internet Explorer 10+ also supports animations without a prefix. Earlier versions of IE do not support animations at all.

We can check for CSS animations support in a few ways. The first is by testing for the presence of `CSSKeyframeRule` as a method of the `window` object:

```
var hasAnimations = 'CSSKeyframeRule' in window;
```

If the browser supports the `@supports` rule and `CSS.supports()` API (discussed in Chapter 6), we can use that instead:

---

[17] http://caniuse.com/#feat=css-animation

```
var hasAnimations = CSS.supports('animation-duration','2s');18
```

The other option is to use the Modernizr JavaScript library[19] and its `Modern-izr.cssanimations` property.

Creating Your First Animation

We first have to define an animation using an `@keyframes` rule. The `@keyframes` rule has two purposes:

- sets the name of our animation
- groups our keyframe rules

Let's create an animation named `pulse`:

```
@keyframes pulse {

}
```

Our keyframes will be defined within this block. In animation, a **keyframe** is a point at which the action changes. With CSS animations specifically, keyframe rules are used to set property values at particular points in the animation cycle. Values that fall between the values in a keyframe rule are interpolated.

At the minimum we require two keyframes: a `from` keyframe, which is the starting state for our animation and a `to` frame, which is its end state. Within each individual keyframe block, we can define which properties to animate:

css/chapter5/animsimple.css *(excerpt)*

```
@keyframes pulse {
    from {
        transform: scale(0.5);
        opacity: .8;
    }

    to {
```

---

[18] In older versions of WebKit/Blink-based browsers, this needs to be `CSS.supports('-webkit-animation-duration','2s');`

[19] http://modernizr.com/

```
            transform: scale(1);
            opacity: 1;
        }
    }
```

This code will scale our object from half its size to its full size, and change the opacity from 80% to 100%.[20]

The keyframes rule only *defines* an animation, though. Nothing is actually made to move. For that, we need to apply it. Let's also define a pulse class that we can use to apply this animation to any element:

```
.pulse {
    animation: pulse 500ms;
}
```

Here we've used the animation shorthand property to set the animation name and duration. In order for an animation to play, we need the name of an @keyframes rule (in this case, pulse) and a duration. Other properties are optional.

The order of properties for animation is similar to that of transition. The first value that can be parsed becomes the value of animation-duration. The second value becomes the value for animation-delay. Words that aren't CSS-wide keywords or animation property keyword values are assumed to be @keyframe rule set names.

As with transition, animation also accepts an animation list. The **animation list** is a comma-separated list of values. We could, for example, split our pulse animation into two rules: pulse and fade:

```
@keyframes pulse {
    from {
        transform: scale(0.5);
    }
    to {
        transform: scale(1);
    }
}
```

---

[20] Use @-webkit-keyfames to support older versions of Chrome (< 43) and Safari (< 9). Use @-moz-keyframes if you need to support older versions of Firefox (< 16).

```
@keyframes fade {
    from {
        opacity: .5;
    }
    to {
        opacity: 1;
    }
}
```

Then we could combine them as part of a single animation:

```
.pulse-and-fade {
    animation: pulse 500ms, fade 500ms;
}
```

Animation Properties

Though the `animation` property is shorter, sometimes longhand properties are clearer. Longhand animation properties are listed in Table 5.5.

Table 5.5. Animation properties

Property[a]	Description	Initial value
`animation-delay`	How long to wait before executing the animation	`0s` (executes immediately)
`animation-duration`	How long the cycle of an animation should last	`0s` (no animation occurs)
`animation-name`	The name of a `@keyframes` rule	`none`
`animation-timing-function`	How to calculate the values between the start and end states	`ease`
`animation-iteration-count`	How many times to repeat the animation	`1`
`animation-direction`	Whether or not the animation should ever play in reverse	`normal` (no reverse)
`animation-play-state`	Whether the animation is running or paused	`running`
`animation-fill-mode`	Specifies what property values are applied when the animation isn't running	`none`

[a] To date, these properties must be prefixed for WebKit/Blink-based browsers (that is, `-webkit-animation-name` and `-webkit-animation-duration`).

The `animation-delay` and `animation-duration` properties function like `transition-delay` and `transition-duration`. Both accept time units as a value, either in seconds (s) or milliseconds (ms) units. Negative time values are valid for `animation-delay`, but not `animation-duration`.

Let's rewrite our `.pulse` rule set using longhand properties. Doing so gives us the following:

```
.pulse {
    animation-name: pulse;
    animation-duration: 500ms;
}
```

The `animation-name` property is fairly straightforward. Its value can be either `none`, or the name of the `@keyframes` rule. Animation names have few restrictions. CSS keywords such as `initial`, `inherit`, `default`, and `none` are forbidden. Most punctuation characters won't work, while letters, underscores, digits, and emoji (and other Unicode) characters usually will. For clarity and maintainability, it's a good idea to give your animations descriptive names, and avoid using CSS properties as names.

To Loop or Not to Loop: The `animation-iteration-count` Property

If you're following along with your own code, you'll notice that this animation only happens once. We want our animation to repeat. For that, we'll need the `animation-iteration-count` property.

The `animation-iteration-count` property accepts most numeric values. Whole numbers and decimal numbers are valid values. With decimal numbers, however, the animation will stop part-way through the last animation cycle, ending in the `to` state. Negative `animation-iteration-count` values are treated the same as 1.

To make an animation run indefinitely, use the `infinite` keyword. The animation will play an infinite number of times. Of course, `infinite` really means until the document is unloaded, the browser window closes, the animation styles are removed, or the device shuts down. Let's make our animation infinite:

```
.pulse {
    animation-name: pulse;
    animation-duration: 500ms;
    animation-iteration-count: infinite;
}
```

Or, using the `animation` shorthand property:

```
.pulse {
    animation: pulse 500ms infinite;
}
```

Playing Animations: the animation-direction Property

There's still a problem with our animation, however. It doesn't so much *pulse* as repeat our scaling-up animation. What we want is for this element to scale up and down. Enter the animation-direction property.

The animation-direction property accepts one of four values:

normal:	the initial value, playing the animation as specified
reverse:	flips the from and to states and plays the animation in reverse
alternate:	plays even-numbered animation cycles in reverse
alternate-reverse:	plays odd-numbered animation cycles in reverse

To continue with our current example, reverse would scale down our object by a factor of 0.5. Using alternate would scale our object up for the odd-numbered cycles, down for the even-numbered. Conversely, using alternate-reverse would scale our object down for the odd-numbered cycles and up for the even ones. Since this is the effect we want, we'll set our animation-direction property to alternate-reverse:

```
.pulse {
    animation-name: pulse;
    animation-duration: 500ms;
    animation-iteration-count: infinite;
    animation-direction: alternate-reverse;
}
```

Or, using the shorthand property:

```
.pulse {
    animation: pulse 500ms infinite alternate-reverse;
}
```

Using Percentage Keyframes

Our previous example was a simple pulse animation. We can create more complex animation sequences using percentage keyframes. Rather than using from and to, **percentage keyframes** indicate specific points of change over the course of the animation. Below is an example using an animation named wiggle:

css/chapter5/animspctkeyframes.css *(excerpt)*

```
@keyframes wiggle {
    25% {
        transform: scale(.5) skewX(-5deg) rotate(-5deg);
    }
    50% {
        transform: skewY(5deg) rotate(5deg);
    }
    75% {
        transform: skewX(-5deg) rotate(-5deg) scale(1.5);
    }
    100% {
        transform: scale(1.5);
    }
}
```

We've used increments of 25% here, but these keyframes could be 5%, 10%, or 33.2%. As the animation plays, the browser will interpolate the values between each state. As with our previous example, we can assign it to a selector:

```
/* Our animation will play once */
.wiggle {
    animation-name: wiggle;
    animation-duration: 500ms;
}
```

Or using the animation shorthand property:

```
.wiggle {
    animation: wiggle 500ms;
}
```

There's just one problem here. When our animation ends, it goes back to the original, pre-animated state. To prevent this, we use the `animation-fill-mode` property.

The `animation-fill-mode` Property

Animations have no effect on properties before they begin or after they stop playing. But as you've seen with the `wiggle` example, once an animation ends, it reverts to its pre-animation state. With `animation-fill-mode`, we can fill in those states before the animation starts and ends.

The `animation-fill-mode` property accepts one of four values:

none: the animation has no effect when it is not executing

forwards: when the animation ends, the property values of the end state will still apply

backwards: property values for the first keyframe will be applied during the animation delay period

both: effects for both `forwards` and `backwards` apply

Since we want our animated element to remain in its final, scaled-up state, we're going to use `animation-fill-mode: forwards` (`animation-fill-mode: both` would also work).

The effect of `animation-fill-mode: backwards` is most apparent when the `animation-delay` property is set to a `500ms` or higher. When `animation-fill-mode` is set to `backwards`, the property values of the first keyframe are applied, but the animation is not executed until the delay elapses.

Pausing Animations

As has been mentioned, animations can be paused. Transitions can be reversed mid-way, or stopped altogether by toggling a class name. Animations, on the other hand, can be paused part-way through the play cycle using `animation-play-state`. It has two defined values: `running` and `paused`, and its initial value is `running`.

Let's look at a simple example of using `animation-play-state` to play or pause an animation.[21] First, our CSS:

```
.wobble {
    animation: wobble 3s ease-in infinite forwards alternate;
    animation-play-state: paused;
}

.running {
    animation-play-state: running;
}
```

Here we have two declaration blocks: `wobble`, which defines a wobbling animation, and `running`, which sets a play state. As part of our `animation` declaration, we've set an `animation-play-state` value of `paused`. To run our animation, we'll add the `running` class to our element. Let's assume that our markup includes a **Run animation** button with an `id` of `trigger`:

```
var trigger = document.querySelector('#trigger');
var moveIt = document.querySelector('.wobble');

trigger.addEventListener('click', function() {
    moveIt.classList.toggle('running');
});
```

Using jQuery, this would be:

```
$('#trigger').on('click', function(){
    $('.wobble').toggleClass('running');
});
```

Adding `.running` to our element overrides the `animation-play-state` value set in `.wobble`, and causes the animation to play.

---

[21] Some browsers support adding the `animation-play-state` value to the `animation` declaration, but not Safari and Internet Explorer.

Detecting When Animations Start, End, or Repeat

Like transitions, animations fire an event when they end: animationend. Unlike transitions, animations also fire animationstart and animationiteration events when they begin or repeat. As with transitions, you might use these events to trigger another action on the page. Perhaps you'd use animationstart to contextually reveal a **Stop Animation** button, or animationend to reveal a **Replay** button.

We can listen for these events with JavaScript. Below, we're listening for the animationend event:

```
var animate = document.getElementById('#animate');

animate.addEventListener('animationend', function(eventObject) {
    // Do something
});
```

The code is slightly different if you're using jQuery:

```
$('#animate').on('animationend', function(eventObject) {
    // Do something
});
```

 Vendor Prefixing

In Chrome < 43 and Safari < 9, these events still require a vendor prefix. They're also camel-cased: webkitAnimationStart, webkitAnimationEnd, and webkitAnimationIteration.

Here, too, the event handler function receives an event object as its sole argument. In order to determine which animation ended, we can query the animationName property of the event object.

A Note About Accessibility

Transitions and animations can enhance the user experience by making interactions smooth rather than jumpy, otherwise bringing delight to the interface; however, they still have accessibility risks. Large spinning animations, for example, can cause dizziness or nausea for people with vestibular disorders, such as vertigo[22]. Flashing animations can trigger seizures in some people with photosensitive epilepsy[23]. Use them sparingly, and strongly consider giving users the ability to turn them off.

A Note About Performance

Some properties create better-performing transitions and animations than others. If an animation updates a property that triggers a reflow or repaint, its performance may be poor on low-powered devices such as phones and tablets.

Properties that trigger a reflow are ones that affect layout. These include the following animatable properties:

- `border-width` (and `border-*-width` properties)
- `border` (and `border-*` properties)
- `bottom`
- `font-size`
- `font-weight`
- `height`
- `left`
- `line-height`
- `margin` (and `margin-*` properties)
- `min-height`
- `min-width`
- `max-height`
- `max-width`
- `padding` (and `padding-*` properties)
- `right`
- `top`
- `vertical-align`
- `width`

---

[22] "Infinite Canvas 6: Vestibular Disorders and Accessible Animation" [https://www.youtube.com/watch?v=QhnIZh0xwk0]is a great introduction to the subject of vestibular disorders and animation.

[23] WCAG 2.0 provides guidelines [http://www.w3.org/WAI/WCAG20/quickref/Overview.php#seizure] for avoiding flashes and animations that are known to trigger seizures.

When these properties are animated, the browser must recalculate the size and position of the affected—and often neighboring—elements. Use Chapter 6 where you can. Transitioning or animating a translation transform [that is, `transform: translate(100px,200px)`] can replace `top`, `left`, `right`, and `bottom` properties. In some cases, `height` and `width` animations can be replaced with a `scale` transformation.

Sometimes, triggering a reflow (or layout update) is unavoidable. In those cases, minimize the number of elements affected and use tricks (such as negative delays) to shorten the perceived animation duration.

Properties that trigger a repaint are typically those that cause a color change. These include:

- `background`
- `background-image`
- `background-position`
- `background-repeat`
- `background-size`
- `border-radius`
- `border-style`
- `box-shadow`
- `color`
- `outline`
- `outline-color`
- `outline-style`
- `outline-width`

Changes to these properties are less expensive to calculate than those that affect layout, but they do still have a cost. Changes to `box-shadow` and `border-radius` are especially expensive to calculate, especially for low-powered devices. Use caution when animating these properties.

Conclusion

In this chapter, we've looked at how to add motion to web pages using CSS transitions and animations, and why you might like to do so. We've also touched on performance and accessibility concerns, and explained the finer points of the `cubic-bezier` function.

As you use transitions and animations, consider *how* you are using them. They're best used to focus the user's attention or clarify an action. But they can also be used to add whimsy and delight.

Chapter

6

CSS Transforms

Transforms allow us to create effects and interactions that are otherwise impossible. When combined with transitions and animations, we can create elements and interfaces that rotate, dance, and zoom. Three-dimensional transforms, in particular, make it possible to mimic physical objects.

Take, the humble postcard received from a friend, for example. Its front face contains a photo of the destination from which your friend sent the card (Figure 6.1). When you flip it over, you see expanded information about the photo and your friend's journey (by the way, he wishes you were there).

Figure 6.1. Greetings from Hollywood[1]

A postcard isn't a web interface, obviously, but it is a metaphor for the kind of interfaces that we can create. Perhaps you want to build a weather widget that functions similarly to a postcard. The front of our widget contains a current weather summary, which can be seen in Figure 6.2. Flipping it over—triggered by a tap or swipe—might show an expanded weather forecast, or reveal a settings panel as seen in Figure 6.3.

---

[1] Photo by the author.

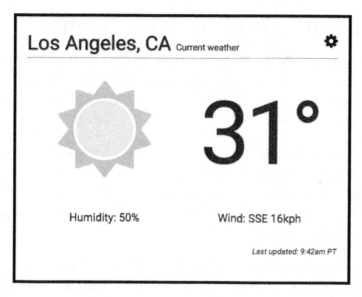

Figure 6.2. An example weather widget

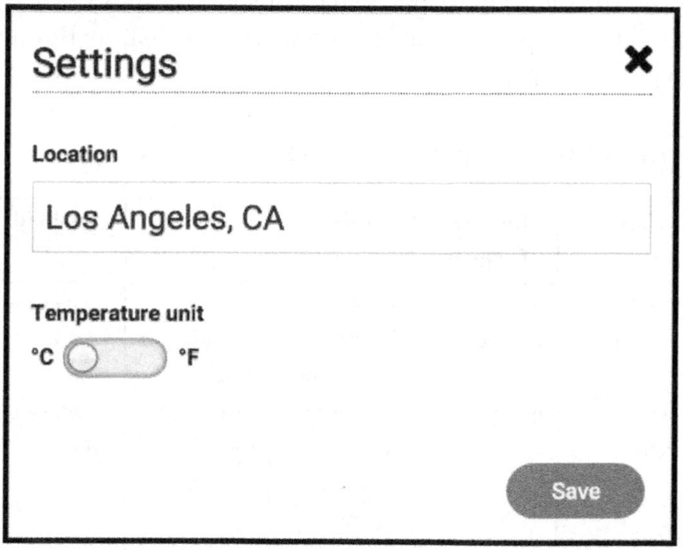

Figure 6.3. Our widget's settings panel

Card-style interfaces are a great example of what we can build with transforms. In this chapter, we'll do a deep dive into the details of how they work, but first: the current state of transforms.

The Current State of Transforms

Transforms are defined by the CSS Transforms specification.[2] At one point, two-dimensional and three-dimensional transforms were defined by two separate specifications. As you move through the chapter, you'll notice a bit of redundancy in function names.

Because the specifications for 2D and 3D transforms were drafted separately, the landscape of browser support is a little complicated. The latest versions of most browsers support both. Safari ≤ 8, Blackberry, and UC Browser still require the -webkit- vendor prefix. Most other browsers support transforms without a vendor prefix. That's the good news.

The bad news is that not all browsers completely support all features. Internet Explorer 10 and 11 offer support for 3D transforms, but their lack of support for the transform-style property means that 3D transforms can't be nested. This is not true of Microsoft Edge, the recently released browser for Windows 10, which supports all transforms-related properties. Table 6.1 and Table 6.2 show the state of browser support for 2D and 3D transforms.

Table 6.1. Current browser support for 2D transforms

Chrome	Firefox	Internet Explorer	Opera	Safari	Android	UC Browser
4+ (versions 35 require -webkit- prefix)	3.5+ (versions 15 require -moz- prefix)	9+ (versions < 10 require -ms- prefix)	11.5+ (versions 11.5 require -o- prefix, while versions 15–22 require -webkit- prefix)	3.1+ (versions 8 require -webkit- prefix)	2.1 (versions 4.4.4 require -webkit- prefix)	9+ (require -webkit- prefix)

---

[2] http://dev.w3.org/csswg/css-transforms/

Table 6.2. Current browser support for 3D transforms

Chrome	Firefox	Internet Explorer	Opera	Safari	Android	UC Browser
12 (versions 12-35 require -webkit- prefix)	10+ (versions 10-15 require -moz- prefix)	10+ (no support for `transform-style: preserve-3d`)	15+ (versions 15-22 require -moz- prefix)	3.2+ (versions 8 require -webkit- prefix)	2.1 (versions 4.4.4 require -webkit- prefix)	9+ (requires -webkit- prefix)

Of course, some web users aren't using up-to-date browsers. If you need to support ancient browsers (Firefox ≤ 10, Chrome ≤ 11, Safari 3, Opera ≤ 14, and Android ≤ 2.3), ensure that your content still looks good and works well without transforms.

How Transforms Affect Layout

Before we go too much further, there are a few details you should know about how the `transform` property affects layout. When you apply the `transform` property to an element and its value is other than `none`, three things happen.

- The element becomes a containing block for child elements.
- It establishes a new stacking context for the element and its children.
- It imposes a local coordinate system within the element's bounding box.

Let's look at these concepts individually.

`transform` Creates a Containing Block

When an element is positioned—that is, when the value of the `position` property is something other `static`—it is drawn relative to a containing block. A containing block is the closest positioned ancestor or, failing that, the root element (such as `html` or `svg`) of a document.

In Figure 6.4, the child rectangle has a `position` value of `absolute`. Its `right` and `bottom` properties are both set to 0. Its parent element has a `position` value of `relative`. Because the parent in this case is positioned, it becomes a containing block for the child. If the parent rectangle was not positioned, this child element would instead be drawn at the bottom right of the browser window.

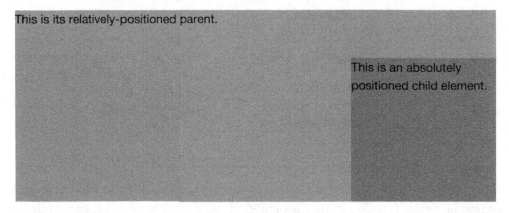

Figure 6.4. A child element with `position: absolute` inside a container with `position: relative`

Transforms work similarly. Setting the value of `transform` to something other than `none` turns the transformed element into a containing block. Positioned children of a transformed element are positioned relative to that element, as seen in Figure 6.5.

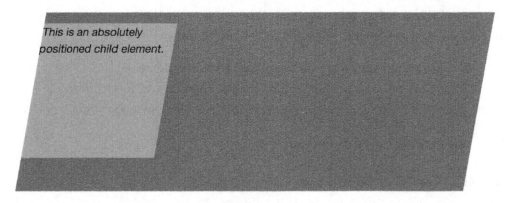

Figure 6.5. A child element with `position: absolute` nested within an element with `transform: skewX(-15deg)`

Note that in Figure 6.5, the parent element is not positioned. The `transform` property is what's creating this containing block.

`transform` Creates a New Stacking Context

Transforms also create a new stacking context for the element to which it's applied. As you may recall from Chapter 4, elements within a stacking context are painted from back to front as follows:

1. Child-stacking contexts with a negative stack level (for example, positioned `z-index: -1`)

2. Nonpositioned elements

3. Child-stacking contexts with a stack level of 0 (for example, positioned and `z-index: 0;` or `z-index: auto;`)

4. Child-stacking contexts with positive stack levels (for example, `z-index: 1`) sit at the top of the stack

Setting the value of `transform` to something other than `none` puts the element's stack level at 0, and will cause a transformed element to be stacked in front of nonpositioned elements. The `z-index` values of each child element will be relative to the parent. Let's update our example from Chapter 4 to see how this works:

```
<div style="position:relative;">
    <div id="a">
        <p><b>div#a</b></p>
    </div>

    <div id="b" style="transform: scale(2) translate(25%, 15%);">
        <p><b>div#b</b></p>
    </div>

    <div id="c" style="position:relative; z-index: 1">
        <p><b>div#c</b></p>
    </div>
    <div id="d" style="position:absolute; z-index: -1">
        <p><b>div#d</b></p>
    </div>
</div>
```

In this case (see Figure 6.6), `div#d` sits at the bottom of the stack, and `div#a` sits above it. But `div#b` comes next because the `transform` property forces its `z-index` value to be 0 instead of `auto`. With `z-index: 1`, `div#c` sits at the top of the stack.

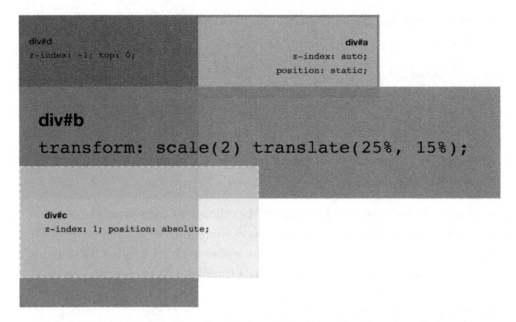

Figure 6.6. A stacking context with positioned and unpositioned elements with varying z-index values

Three-dimensional transforms add additional complexity. An element shifted along the Z-axis may render on a different plane than its container. Elements may also intersect with other elements across layers. Still, the basic rules of the stacking order apply.

Transformed elements may also overlap other elements on the page, and prevent them from receiving mouse, touch, or pointer events. One option for fixing this is to change the `position` and `z-index` values of the transformed or overlapped element.

In browsers that support it, you can also use the `pointer-events` CSS property with a value of `none`. Apply it to the transformed element that's overlapping content. The `pointer-events` property lets us control whether an element receives pointer events (for example, `click` or `mousedown`) events. The latest versions of all major browsers support the `pointer-events` property for use with HTML. Use `z-index` as a fall back for older browsers.[3] It originated with the Scalable Vector Graphics specification,[4] but recent versions of CSS have defined its behavior for more general markup use.

---

[3] The `pointer-events` CSS property is distinct from the PointerEvents DOM event object.

[4] http://www.w3.org/TR/SVG11/interact.html#PointerEventsProperty

Transforms are applied after elements have been sized and positioned. Unlike floated elements, transformed elements have no effect on content flow.[5] Floating an element removes it from the normal flow, and causes other elements to wrap around it. For transformed elements, this is not the case.

Transforms don't affect CSS layout, although transformed child elements may overflow the parent element's bounding box. Because transforms are applied after the layout has been calculated, they do not affect the `HTMLElement.offsetLeft` or `HTMLElement.offsetTop` DOM properties. Using these properties to detect the rendered position of an element will give you inaccurate results.

Transforms do, however, affect client rectangle values and visual rendering of elements. To determine the rendered left and top positions of an element, use the `HTMLElement.getClientRects()` or `HTMLElement.getBoundingClientRect()` DOM methods (for example, `document.getElementById('#targetEl').getClientRects()`).

Because they don't force the browser to calculate page layout, transforms typically perform better than properties such as `left` and `height` when animated.

transform Creates a Local Coordinate System

You may recall from geometry class that the Cartesian coordinate system is a way of specifying points in a plane. You may also recall that a plane is a flat two-dimensional surface that extends infinitely along the horizontal and vertical axes. These axes are also known as the X-axis and Y-axis.

Point values along the X-axis increase as you move from left to right, and decrease from right to left. Y-axis point values increase as you move up, and decrease as you move down. The X and Y axes are perpendicular to each other. Where they cross is known as the *origin*, and the coordinates of its location are always (0,0) Figure 6.7 illustrates this.

---

[5] Document flow is described by the Visual formatting model [http://www.w3.org/TR/CSS21/visuren.html] section of the CSS2.1 specification. Updates to this model are partly described by CSS Display Module Level 3. [http://dev.w3.org/csswg/css-display/]

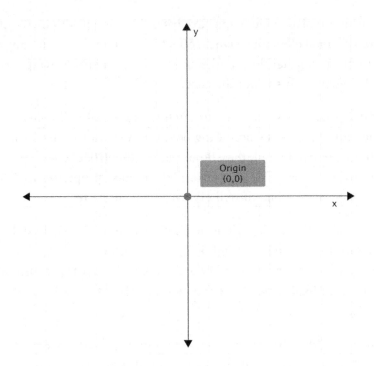

Figure 6.7. A two-dimensional coordinate system

In a three-dimensional coordinate system, there's also a Z-axis. This axis is perpendicular to both the X and Y axes, as well as the screen (see Figure 6.8). The point at which the Z-axis crosses the X and Y axes is also known as the origin. Its coordinates are (0,0,0).

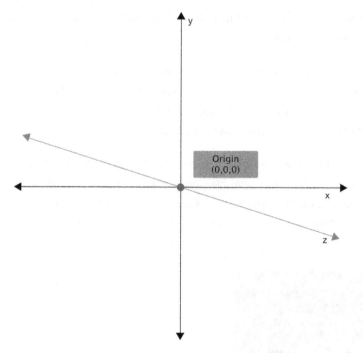

Figure 6.8. A three-dimensional coordinate system

A rendered HTML document is, essentially, a coordinate system. The top-left corner is the origin, with coordinates of (0,0) or (0,0,0). Values increase along the X-axis as you move right. Values increase along the Y-axis as you move down the screen or page. Z-axis values increase as elements move towards the viewer and decrease as they move away from the viewer.

Setting the value of `transform` to a value besides none adds a **local coordinate system** to the selected elements. The origin—point (0,0) or (0,0,0)—in this local coordinate system sits at the center of the element's bounding box. We can change the position of the origin, however, by using the `transform-origin` property. Points within the element's bounding box are then transformed relative to this local origin.

The `transform-origin` Property

The `transform-origin` property accepts up to three values: one for each of the X, Y, and Z positions. For example, `transform-origin: 300px 300px` for a 2D transformation, or `transform-origin: 0 0 200px` for a 3D transformation.

If one value is specified, the second value is assumed to be center, and the third value is assumed to be 0px.

Both the X and Y coordinates may be percentages, lengths, or positioning keywords. Positioning keywords are left, center, right, top, and bottom. The Z position, however, must be a length. In other words, transform-origin: left bottom 200px works, but transform-origin: left bottom 20% does not.

The position of the transform origin is relative to the element being transformed. It moves the (0,0) point of the local coordinate system to a new location within the element's bounding box. This, of course, modifies the transformation, sometimes radically. Figure 6.9 shows a transform-origin point of 50% 50% and one at 0px 0px.

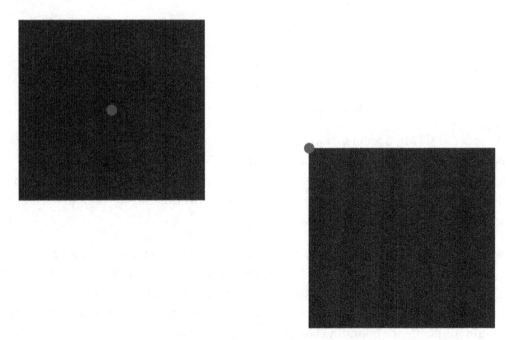

Figure 6.9. Rectangles with transform-origin values of 50% 50% (left) and 0 0 (right)

Now that you know a little more about how transforms affect layout, let's dig into the transform functions. This is how we make the magic. Transforms let us rotate, flip, skew, and scale elements. When combined with animations and transitions, we can create sophisticated motion graphic effects.

Transforms can be grouped into two categories: 2D and 3D. Each group contains functions for rotating, skewing, scaling, and translating. 2D functions are concerned with transformations of points along the X and Y axes. 3D functions add the third dimension of depth and affect points along the Z-axis.

2D Transform Functions

Two-dimensional transform functions enjoy the widest browser support. They're supported without vendor prefixes in Internet Explorer 10+, Firefox 15+, Chrome 35+, and Opera 23+.

Safari ≤ 8, UC Browser, and Android 4 (or earlier) require a `-webkit-` prefix for all transforms. So do older versions of Chrome (4 to 35) and Opera (15 to 23). Firefox versions 10 through 14 and older require a `-moz-` prefix. Support in Internet Explorer 9 is available with an `-ms-` prefix, while IE8 does not support transforms.

As we've mentioned, 2D transforms affect points in the X and Y dimensions. There are four primary functions: `rotate`, `scale`, `skew`, and `translate`. There are also functions that let us transform an element in one dimension: `scaleX` and `scaleY`; `skewX` and `skewY`; and `translateX` and `translateY`.

rotate()

A rotation transform spins an element around its origin by the angle specified around the point specified. Using `rotate()` tilts an element clockwise (positive angle values) or counter-clockwise (negative angle values). Its effect is much like a windmill or pinwheel, as seen in Figure 6.10.

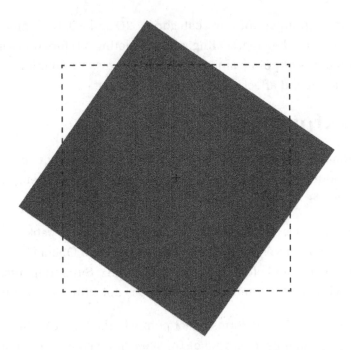

Figure 6.10. The purple box has been rotated 55 degrees from its start position, shown by the dotted line

The `rotate()` function accepts values in angle units. Angle units are defined by the CSS Values and Units Module Level 3.[6] These may be `deg` (degrees), `rad` (radians), `grad` (gradians), or `turn` units. One complete rotation is equal to `360deg`, `6.28rad`, `400grad`, or `1turn`.

Rotation values that exceed one rotation (say, `540deg` or `1.5turn`) are rendered according to their remaindered value, unless animated or transitioned. In other words, `540deg` is rendered the same as `180deg` (540 degrees minus 360 degrees) and `1.5turn` is rendered the same as `.5turn` (1.5 - 1). However, a transition or animation from `0deg` to `540deg` or `1turn` to `1.5turn` will rotate the element one-and-a-half times.

2D Scaling Functions: `scale`, `scaleX`, and `scaleY`

With the scaling functions, we can increase or decrease the rendered size of an element in the X-dimension (`scaleX`), Y-dimension (`scaleY`), or both (`scale`). Scaling is illustrated in Figure 6.11, where the border illustrates the original boundaries of the box, and the + marks its center point.

---

[6] http://dev.w3.org/csswg/css-values-3/#angles

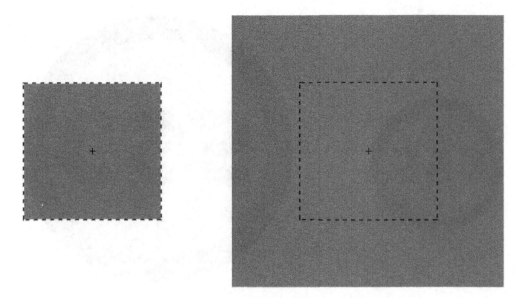

Figure 6.11. A box (left) is scaled by a factor of 2 (right)

Each scale function accepts a multiplier or factor as its argument. This multiplier can be just about any positive or negative number. Percentage values, however, aren't supported. Positive multipliers greater than 1 will increase the size of an element. For example, `scale(1.5)` will increase the size of the element in the X and Y directions 1.5 times. Positive multipliers between 0 and 1 will reduce the size of an element.

Values less than 0 still cause an element to scale up or down in size; however, using a negative scaling value causes a reflection (flip) transform. In Figure 6.12, the right figure has been scaled in both dimensions by a factor of -2 (`scale(-2)`), flipping it horizontally and vertically.

Figure 6.12. An element at its original size (left) and with `transform: scale(-2)` applied

 Multipliers of Zero

Using `scale(0)` will cause the element to disappear, because multiplying a number by zero results in a product of zero.

Using `scale(1)` creates an **identity transformation**, which means it's drawn to the screen as if no scaling transformation was applied. Using `scale(-1)` will not change the drawn size of an element, but the negative value will cause the element to be reflected.

It's possible to scale the X and Y dimensions separately using the `scale` function. Just pass it two arguments: `scale(1.5, 2)`. The first argument scales the X-dimension; the second scales the Y-dimension. We could, for example, reflect an object along the X-axis alone using `scale(-1, 1)`. Passing a single argument scales both dimensions by the same factor.

2D Translation Functions: `translateX`, `translateY`, and `translate`

Translating an element offsets its painted position from its layout position by the specified distance. As with other transforms, translating an element doesn't change its `offsetLeft` or `offsetTop` positions. It does, however, affect where it's visually positioned on screen.

Each 2D translation function—`translateX`, `translateY`, and `translate`—accepts lengths or percentages for arguments. Length units include pixels (`px`), `em`, `rem`, and viewport units (`vw` and `vh`).

The `translateX` function changes the relative horizontal rendering position of an element. If an element is positioned zero pixels from the left, `transform: transitionX(50px)` would shift its rendering 50 pixels to the right of its original position. Similarly, `translateY` changes the vertical rendering position of an element. A transform of `transform: transitionY(50px)` offsets the element vertically by 50 pixels.

With `translate()`, we can shift an element vertically and horizontally using a single function. It accepts up to two arguments: the X translation value, and the Y translation value. Figure 6.13 shows the effect of an element with a `transform` value of `translate(120%, -50px)`, where the left green square is the original position, and the right green square is translated 120% horizontally and -50px vertically from its containing element (the dashed border).

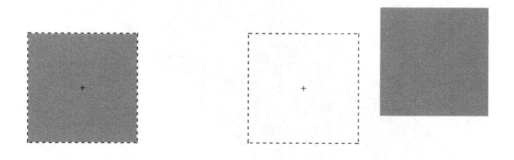

Figure 6.13. The effect of having an element with a `transform` value of `translate(120%, -50px)`

Passing a single argument to `translate` is the equivalent of using `translateX`; the Y translation value will be set to 0. Using `translate()` is the more concise option.

Applying `translate(100px, 200px)` is the equivalent of `translateX(100px)` `translateY(200px)`.

Positive translation values move an element rightward (for `translateX`) or downward (for `translateY`). Negative values move an element to the left (`translateX`) or up (`translateY`).

Translations are particularly great for moving items left, right, up, or down. Updating the value of the `left`, `right`, `top`, and `bottom` properties forces the browser to recalculate layout information for the entire document. But transforms are calculated *after* the layout has been calculated. They affect where the elements *appear* on screen, but not their actual dimensions. Yes, it's weird to think about document layout and rendering as separate concepts, but in terms of browsers, they are.[7]

skew, skewX, and skewY

Skew transformations shift the angles and distances between points while keeping them in the same plane. Skew transformations are also known as shear transformations, and they distort the shapes of elements as seen in Figure 6.14, where the dashed line represents the original bounding box.

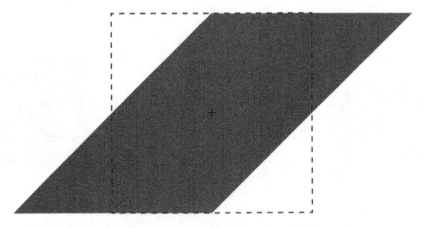

Figure 6.14. A rectangle is skewed 45 degrees along its X-dimension

[7] Google's Optimizing Performance [https://developers.google.com/web/fundamentals/performance/] discusses some of the differences between layout or rendering, and painting or drawing.

The skew functions—skew, skewX, and skewY—accept most angle units as arguments. Degrees, gradians, and radians are valid angle units for the skew functions, while turn units, perhaps obviously, are not.

The skewX function shears an element in the X or horizontal direction (see Figure 6.15). It accepts a single parameter, which again must be an angle unit. Positive values shift the element to the left, and negative values shift it towards the right.

Figure 6.15. The left image is not transformed, while the right image reveals the effect of transform: skewX(30deg)

Similarly, skewY shears an element in the Y or vertical direction, where Figure 6.16 shows the effect of transform: skewY(30deg). Points to the right of the origin are shifted downward with positive values. Negative values shift these points upward.

Figure 6.16. Again, the left image remains untransformed, and the right image is skewed vertically by 30 degrees

This brings us to the skew function. The skew function requires one argument, but accepts up to two. The first argument skews an element in the X direction, and the second skews it in the Y direction. If only one argument is provided, the second value is assumed to be zero, making it the equivalent of skewing in the X direction alone. In other words, skew(45deg) renders the same as skewX(45deg).

Current Transform Matrix

So far, we've discussed transform functions separately, but they can also be combined. Want to scale and rotate an object? No problem, use a **transform list**, for example:

```
.rotatescale {
    transform: rotate(45deg) scale(2);
}
```

This produces the results you see in Figure 6.17.

Figure 6.17. The original element (left) and after a combined rotation and scaling transformation is applied (right)

Now, the order of transform functions matters quite a bit. This is a point that's better shown than talked about, so let's look at an example to illustrate. This CSS skews and rotates an element:

```
.transformEl {
    transform: skew(10deg, 15deg) rotate(45deg);
}
```

It gives us the result you see in Figure 6.18.

Figure 6.18. An element after a transformation of skew(10deg, 15deg) rotate(45deg)

But what if you want to rotate an element first and then skew it? The CSS looks like this:

```
.transformEl {
    transform:  rotate(45deg) skew(10deg, 15deg);
}
```

But the effect, shown in Figure 6.19, is quite different.

Figure 6.19. An element after it has been rotated and then skewed

Each of these transforms has a different *current transform matrix* created by the order of its transform functions. To fully understand why this is, we'll need to learn a little bit of *matrix multiplication*. This will also help us understand the `matrix` and `matrix3d` functions.

Matrix Multiplication and the Matrix Functions

A matrix is an array of numbers or expressions arranged in a rectangle of rows and columns. All transforms can be expressed using a 4×4 matrix as seen in Figure 6.20.

$$\begin{bmatrix} m_{11} & m_{21} & m_{31} & m_{41} \\ m_{12} & m_{22} & m_{32} & m_{42} \\ m_{13} & m_{23} & m_{33} & m_{43} \\ m_{14} & m_{24} & m_{34} & m_{44} \end{bmatrix}$$

Figure 6.20. The 4×4 matrix for 3D transforms

This matrix corresponds to the `matrix3d` function, which accepts 16 arguments, one for each value of the 4×4 matrix. Two-dimensional transforms can also be expressed using a 3×3 matrix, seen in Figure 6.21.

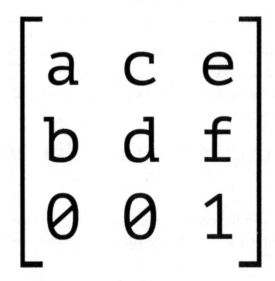

$$\begin{bmatrix} a & c & e \\ b & d & f \\ 0 & 0 & 1 \end{bmatrix}$$

Figure 6.21. A 3×3 matrix used for 2D transforms

This 3×3 matrix corresponds to the `matrix` transform function. The `matrix()` function accepts six parameters, one each for values a through f.

Each transform function can be described using a matrix and the `matrix` or `matrix3d` functions. Figure 6.22 shows the 4×4 matrix for the `scale3d` function, where sx, sy, and sz are the scaling factors of the X, Y, and Z dimensions respectively.

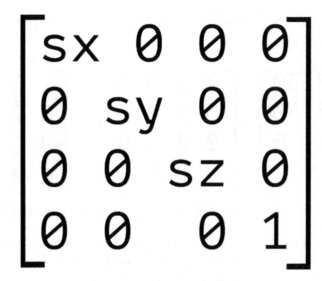

Figure 6.22. The 4×4 scaling transform matrix

When we combine transforms—such as `transform: scale(2) translate(30px, 50px)`—the browser multiplies the matrices for each function to create a new matrix. This new matrix is what's applied to the element.

But here's the thing about matrix multiplication: it isn't commutative. With simple values, the product of 3×2 is the same as 2×3. With matrices, however, the product of $A \times B$ is not necessarily the same as the product of $B \times A$. Let's look at Figure 6.23 as an example. We'll calculate the matrix product of `transform: scale(2) translate(30px, 50px)`.

$$
\begin{bmatrix} 2 & 0 & 0 & 0 \\ 0 & 2 & 0 & 0 \\ 0 & 0 & 1 & 0 \\ 0 & 0 & 0 & 1 \end{bmatrix} \times \begin{bmatrix} 1 & 0 & 0 & 30 \\ 0 & 1 & 0 & 50 \\ 0 & 0 & 1 & 0 \\ 0 & 0 & 0 & 1 \end{bmatrix} = \begin{bmatrix} 2 & 0 & 0 & 60 \\ 0 & 2 & 0 & 100 \\ 0 & 0 & 1 & 0 \\ 0 & 0 & 0 & 1 \end{bmatrix}
$$

Figure 6.23. The product of the matrices for `scale(2)` and `translate(30px, 50px)`

Our element has been scaled by a factor of two, and then translated 60 pixels horizontally and 100 pixels vertically. We can also express this product using the `matrix` function: `transform: matrix(2, 0, 0, 2, 60, 100)`. Now let's switch the order of these transforms; that is, transform: translate(30px, 50px) scale(2). The results are shown in Figure 6.24.

$$
\begin{bmatrix} 1 & 0 & 0 & 30 \\ 0 & 1 & 0 & 50 \\ 0 & 0 & 1 & 0 \\ 0 & 0 & 0 & 1 \end{bmatrix} \times \begin{bmatrix} 2 & 0 & 0 & 0 \\ 0 & 2 & 0 & 0 \\ 0 & 0 & 1 & 0 \\ 0 & 0 & 0 & 1 \end{bmatrix} = \begin{bmatrix} 2 & 0 & 0 & 30 \\ 0 & 2 & 0 & 50 \\ 0 & 0 & 1 & 0 \\ 0 & 0 & 0 & 1 \end{bmatrix}
$$

Figure 6.24. The product of the matrices for translate(30px, 50px) and scale(2)

Notice that our object is still scaled by a factor of two, but here it's translated by 30 pixels horizontally and 50 pixels vertically instead. Expressed using the matrix function, this is transform: matrix(2, 0, 0, 2, 30, 50).

It's also worth noting that inherited transforms function similarly to transform lists. Each child transform is multiplied by any transform applied to its parent. For example:

```
<div style="transform: skewX(25deg)">
    <p style="transform: rotate(-15deg)"></p>
</div>
```

is rendered the same as:

```
<div>
    <p style="transform: skewX(25deg) rotate(-15deg)"></p>
</div>
```

The current transform matrix of the p element will be the same in both cases. Though we've focused on 2D transforms so far, the above also applies to 3D transforms. The third dimension adds the illusion of depth. It also brings some additional complexity in the form of new functions and properties.

3D Transform Functions

There are nine functions for creating 3D transforms. Each of these functions modifies the Z-coordinates of an element and/or its children. Remember, Z-coordinates are points along the plane that sit perpendicular to the viewer. With the exception of rotateZ(), these functions create and change the illusion of depth on screen.

rotateX() and rotateY()

The rotateX() and rotateY() functions rotate an element around the X and Y axes respectively. Using rotateX() creates a somersault effect, causing an object to flip top-over- tail around a horizontal axis. With rotateY(), the effect is more like that of a spinning top, rotating around a vertical axis.

Like rotate(), both rotateX() and rotateY() accept an angle measurement as an argument. This angle can be expressed in degrees (deg), radians (rad), gradians (grad), or turn units. As mentioned earlier in the chapter, rotateZ() works the same way as rotate(). It's a relic from when 2D and 3D transforms were defined in separate specifications.

Positive angle values for rotateX() cause an element to tilt backwards, as shown in Figure 6.25.

Figure 6.25. An element with transform: rotate(45deg) applied

Negative angle values for rotateX() do the opposite, causing the element to tilt forward as is shown in Figure 6.26.

Figure 6.26. An element with a negative rotation (`transform: rotate(-45deg)`) applied

Negative angles for `rotateY()` cause the element to tilt counter-clockwise. In Figure 6.27, the element has has a rotation of -55 degrees around the Y-axis.

Figure 6.27. An element with `transform: rotateY(-55deg)` applied

Positive values tilt it clockwise, as shown in Figure 6.28.

Figure 6.28. An element with `transform: rotateY(55deg)` applied

The containing element in Figure 6.26, Figure 6.27, and Figure 6.28 has a `perspective` value of 200px. We'll discuss the `perspective` property later in this chapter.

For now, it's enough to know that this property adds a sense of depth and exaggerates the effect of the three-dimensional rotation. Compare Figure 6.29 to Figure 6.28. Both have been rotated along the Y-axis by 55°, but in Figure 6.29, the parent container has a `perspective` value of `none`. Our object looks more squished than rotated. Use `perspective` on a container element when creating a 3D transform.

Figure 6.29. An element with `transform: rotateY(55deg)`, nested within a container with `perspective:none`

 Beware Infinitesimal Thickness

There's another facet to be aware of when working with 3D rotations. Rotating an element by ±90° or ±270° can sometimes cause it to disappear from the screen. Each element on a page has an infinitesimal thickness. By rotating it a quarter or three-quarters of a turn, we're looking at its infinitesimally thin side. It's kind of like looking at the edge of a sheet of paper that's perpendicular to your face. Adjusting the `perspective` and `perspective-origin` values of a parent element can prevent this behavior in some cases, but not all of them.

Rotating around Multiple Axes with `rotate3d()`

Sometimes, we want to rotate an object around more than one axis. Perhaps you want to rotate an element counter-clockwise and tilt it by 45° as in Figure 6.30. This is what `rotate3d()` does.

Figure 6.30. Rotating around both the X and Y axes by 45°

The rotate3d() function accepts four arguments. The first three make up an X, Y, Z direction vector, and each of these arguments should be a number. The fourth argument for rotate3d() should be an angle. The transformed object will be rotated by the angle around the direction vector defined by the first three arguments.

What those first three numbers actually are matters less than the ratio between them. For example, transform: rotate3d(100,5,0,15deg); and transform: rotate3d(20,1,0,15deg); have equivalent 3D matrices and produce the same effect.

That said, because of how the rotate3d matrix is calculated,[8] something like transform: rotate3d(1, 500, 0, 15deg); won't produce a significantly different effect than transform: rotate3d(1, 1, 0, 15deg);.

Just about any non-zero value for any of the first three parameters will create a tilt along that axis. Zero values will prevent a tilt. As you may have guessed, rotateX(45deg) is the equivalent of rotate3d(1, 0, 0, 45deg) and rotateY(25deg) could also be written as rotate3d(0, 1, 0, 25deg).

If the first three arguments are 0 (such as transform: rotate3d(0, 0, 0, 45deg)), the element won't be transformed. Using negative numbers for the X, Y, or Z vector

---

[8] http://dev.w3.org/csswg/css-transforms-1/#Rotate3dDefined

arguments is valid; it will just negate the value of the angle. In other words, `rotate3d(-1, 0, 0, 45deg)` is equivalent to `rotate3d(1, 0, 0, -45deg)`.

Using `rotate3d()` rotates an element by the given angle along multiple axes at once. If you want to rotate an element by different angles around multiple axes, you should use `rotateX()`, `rotateY()`, and `rotate()` or `rotateZ()` separately.

perspective() Function

The `perspective()` function controls the foreshortening of an object when one end is tilted towards the viewer. **Foreshortening** is a specific way of drawing perspective; that is, simulating three dimensions when you only have two dimensions. With foreshortening, the end of objects that are tilted towards the viewer appear larger, and the end furthest from the viewer appears smaller. It mimics the distortion that occurs when you view an object up close versus viewing it at a distance.

The more technical definition, pulled from the transforms specification,[9] says that `perspective()` "creates a perspective projection matrix." The definition continues:

> This matrix scales points in X and Y based on their Z value, scaling points with positive Z values away from the origin, and those with negative Z values towards the origin. Points on the Z=0 plane are unchanged.

In practice, this means that `perspective()` will have a visible effect only when some of an object's points have a non-zero Z-coordinate. Use it with another 3D function in a transform list (for example, `transform: perspective(400px) rotateX(45deg)`), or apply it to the child of a transformed parent.

The `perspective()` function accepts a single argument. This argument must be a length greater than zero. Negative values are invalid, and the transform will not be applied. Lower values create a more exaggerated foreshortening effect, as you can see in Figure 6.31. In this image, the value of our `transform` is `perspective(10px) rotate3d(1,1,1,-45deg)`.

---

[9] http://dev.w3.org/csswg/css-transforms/#funcdef-perspective

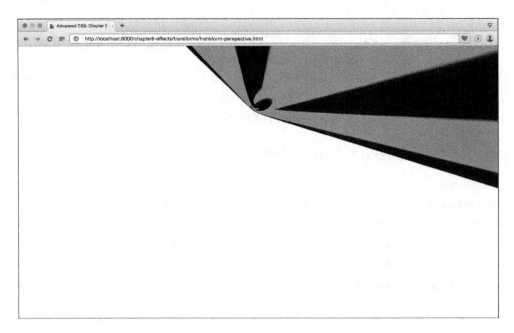

Figure 6.31. An element with a transform value of perspective(10px) rotate3d(1,1,1,-45deg)

Higher values create a moderate amount of foreshortening. Figure 6.32 illustrates the impact of a higher perspective value. Its transform property value is perspective(500px) rotate3d(1,1,1,-45deg).

Figure 6.32. An element with a `transform` value of `perspective(500px)` `rotate3d(1,1,1,-45deg)`

Order really matters when working with the `perspective()` function. A good rule of thumb is to list it first, as we've done in the examples here. You *can* list it elsewhere in the transform list (for example, `rotate3d(1,0,1,-45deg)` `perspective(100px)`), but the resulting current transform matrix doesn't create much of an effect.

There's also a point of diminishing returns with the `perspective()` function (and with the `perspective` property, for that matter). Increasing the argument's value beyond a certain threshold will create little difference in how the element and its children are painted to the screen.

The `perspective()` Function vs. the `perspective` Property

A word of caution: the transforms specification defines both a `perspective()` function and a `perspective` property. Though both are used to calculate the perspective matrix, they differ in how they're used. The `perspective` property affects—and must be applied to—the containing element. It sets an imaginary distance between the viewer and the stage. The `perspective()` function, on the other hand, can be applied to elements as part of a `transform` list.

Translating Depth with `translateZ()` and `translate3d()`

Earlier in this chapter, we discussed how to translate an element horizontally or vertically using `translateX()` and `translateY()`. We can also, however, translate along the Z-axis. There are two functions that allow us to do this: `translateZ()` and `translate3d()`. When combined with transitions, these functions make it possible to create interesting zoom effects.[10]

The `translateZ()` function accepts a single length parameter as its argument. Length units are the only valid units for this function; percentages won't work. The `translateZ()` function shifts the object towards or away from the user by the specified number of pixels. Negative values shift the element or group away from the user, in effect shrinking it, as can be seen in Figure 6.33.

---

[10] The 2011 Beer Camp [http://2011.beercamp.com/] site has one of the more memorable examples of this technique.

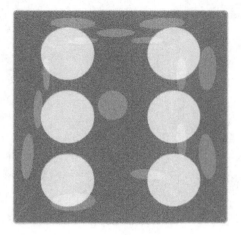

Figure 6.33. The effect of `transform: translateZ(-150px)`

Positive values shift the element towards the user where it appears larger. Sometimes the effect is to fill the entire viewport, appearing to engulf the user as in Figure 6.34.

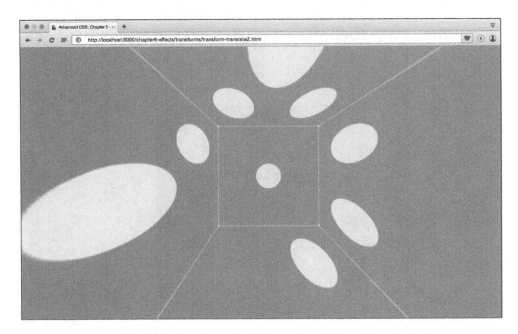

Figure 6.34. The effect of transform: translateZ(150px)

If the value of translateZ() is large enough, the element will be disappear from view. It's actually moved behind the viewer in this imagined 3D space. Similarly, if the value of translateZ() is small enough, say translateZ(-40000px), the element will disappear from view because it is now "too far" from the user and too small to draw on screen.

translate3d() is just a more concise way of translating in two or three directions at once. It accepts three arguments: one each for the X, Y, and Z directions. Translation values for the X and Y direction arguments may be lengths or percentages; however, its Z-direction argument (the third argument) must be a length value. Keep in mind that translateX(50%) translateY(10%) translateZ(100px) is the equivalent of translate3d(50%, 10%, 100px). Use translate3d when you want to translate more than one dimension, but want more concise code.

Scaling the Z-dimension: scaleZ() and scale3d()

We can also scale an object's Z-dimension using the scaleZ() and scale3d() functions. The scaleZ() function transforms points along the Z-axis alone, while scale3d() lets us scale all three dimensions at once. Scaling the Z-dimension changes the depth of an object, but in some combinations can also be used to create zoom effects. Experiment with them and see.

The `scaleZ()` function accepts a number as its argument. As with `scaleX()` and `scaleY()`, positive values greater than 1 increase the size of the element's Z-dimension. Values between 0 and 1 decrease its size. Negative values between 0 and -1 decrease the element's size along the Z-dimension, while values less than -1 increase it. Because these values are negative, however, the element and its children will be inverted. In Figure 6.35, the left die shows an element group with `transform: scaleZ(0.5)` applied. The box on the right has a transformation of `scaleZ(-0.5)` applied. Notice that positions of the six-dot face and single-dot face have been swapped in the example with a negative scale.

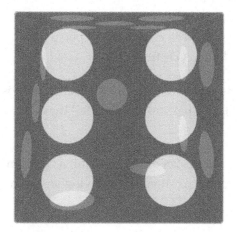 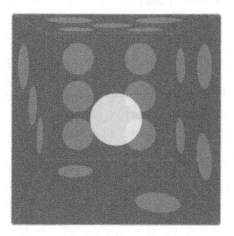

Figure 6.35. Element groups with `transform: scaleZ(0.5)` and `transform: scaleZ(-0.5)` styles

The `scale3d()` function accepts three arguments, and all three arguments are required in order for this function to work. The first argument scales the X dimension. The second argument scales its Y dimension, and the third argument scales the Z dimension. As with `translate3d()`, the `scale3d()` function is just a more concise way to write transforms that scale in multiple dimensions. Rather than using `scaleX(1.2) scaleY(5) scaleZ(2)`, for example, you could use `scale3d(1.2, 5, 2)`.

Transform functions are only part of what you need to create 3D transforms. You'll also require a few more CSS properties. These properties manage how objects are drawn in a simulated three-dimensional space. Using them will make your 3D transforms more realistic.

Creating Depth with the `perspective` Property

In order to make a 3D-transformed object look like it's actually sitting in a three-dimensional space, we must use the `perspective` property. The `perspective` property adjusts the distance between the drawing plane and the viewer. We're still talking about a screen and the projection of three-dimensional coordinates into a two-dimensional space. But adding `perspective` to a containing element causes *its children* to have the appearance of sitting in a 3D space. Yes, you must apply `perspective` to a containing element.

As with `transform`, `perspective` creates both a new containing block and a new stacking context when the value is something other than `none`. Along with the `perspective-origin` property, `perspective` is used to calculate the perspective matrix. We'll cover `perspective-origin` in the next section.[11]

Aside from the `none` keyword, `perspective` also accepts a length as its value. Values must be positive (for example, 200px or 10em), and percentages will fail to work, as will negative values such as -20px.

Smaller values for `perspective` increase the visual size of the element, as seen in Figure 6.36, which has a `perspective` value of 500px. Items that are higher on the Z-axis appear larger than those farther away.

---

[11] Use a `-webkit-` prefix for `perspective` and `perspective-origin` to support users of Safari ≤ 8 and UC Browser (`-webkit-perspective` and `-webkit-perspective-origin`).

Figure 6.36. A group of transformed elements nested within a container with `perspective: 500px`

Larger values, on the other hand, make elements appear smaller. The container element in Figure 6.37 has a `perspective` value of 2000px. This is similar to how your eye perceives objects of varying distances.

Figure 6.37. A group of transformed elements nested within a container with perspective: 2000px

Modifying the Point of View with perspective-origin

If you've studied how to draw in perspective, the perspective-origin property will feel like old hat. To draw in perspective, you first make a point on your page or canvas. This point is known as the **vanishing point**. It's the point in your drawing at which items will theoretically disappear from view.

Next, draw a shape of your choosing. We're going to keep this example simple, and use a rectangle.

Step three is to draw a series of lines towards the vanishing point, as shown in Figure 6.38. These lines, also known as **convergence lines**, serve as guides for drawing shapes that are sized appropriately given their perceived distance from the viewer.

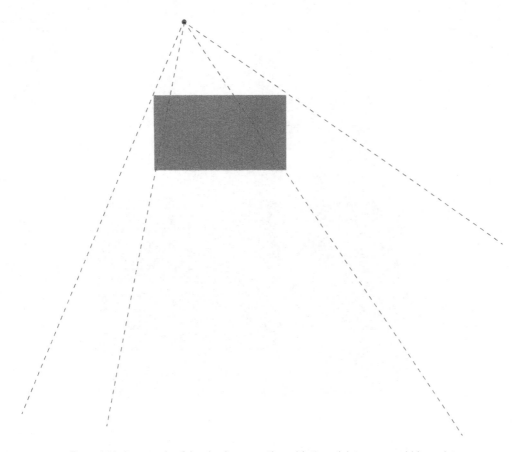

Figure 6.38. An example of drawing in perspective, with the red dot as our vanishing point

As you can see in Figure 6.39, the rectangles that appear closer to the viewer are larger. Those that appear further away are smaller.

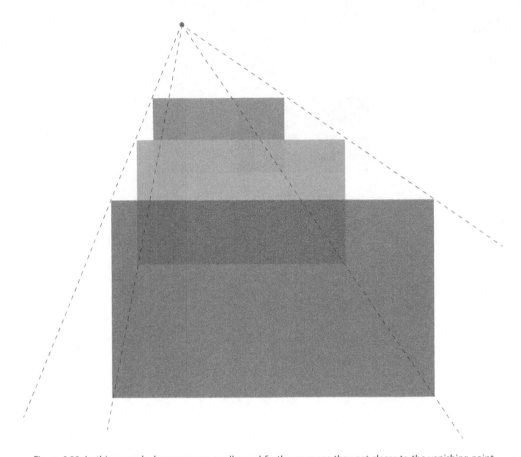

Figure 6.39. In this example, boxes appear smaller and further away as they get closer to the vanishing point

This is essentially how the `perspective-origin` property works. It sets the coordinates of the vanishing point for the stage. Negative Y values give the impression that the viewer is looking down at the stage, while positive ones imply looking up from below it. Negative X values mimic the effect of looking from the right of the stage. Positive X values mimic looking from its left. Figure 6.40 shows a containing element with a perspective-origin of -50% -50%.

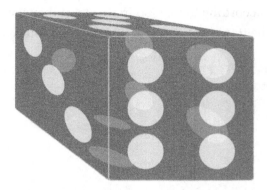

Figure 6.40. A containing element with `perspective-origin: -50% -50%`

As with `transform-origin`, the initial value of `perspective-origin` is 50% 50%—the center point of the containing element. Values for `perspective-origin` may be lengths or percentages.

Positioning keywords—`left`, `right`, `top`, `bottom`, and `center`—are also valid. The `center` keyword is the same as 50% 50%. Both `bottom` and `right` compute to positions of 100% along the vertical and horizontal positions respectively. The `top` and `left` keywords compute to vertical and horizontal positions of 0%. In all cases, `perspective-origin` is an offset from the top-left corner of the container.

Preserving Three Dimensions with `transform-style`

As you work with 3D transforms, you may stumble across a scenario in which your transforms fail to work—or they work, but only for one element. This is caused by grouping property values.[12] Some combinations of CSS properties and values require the browser to flatten the representation of child elements before the property is applied. These include `opacity` when the value is less than 1 and `overflow` when the value is something other than `visible`.

---

[12] http://dev.w3.org/csswg/css-transforms-1/#grouping-property-values

Here's the counterintuitive part: transform and perspective also trigger this flat-tening when their value is something other than none. In effect, this means that child elements stack according to their source order if they have the same Z-index value, regardless of the transform applied. Consider the following source:

```
<div class="wrapper">
    <figure>a</figure>
    <figure>f</figure>
</div>
```

And the following CSS:

```
.wrapper {
    perspective: 2000px;
    perspective-origin: 50% -200px;
}
.wrapper figure {
    position: absolute;
    top: 0;
    width: 200px;
    height: 200px;
}
.wrapper figure:first-child {
    transform: rotateY(60deg) translateZ(191px);
    background: #3f51b5;
}
.wrapper figure:nth-child(2) {
    transform: rotateY(120deg) translateZ(191px);
    background: #8bc34a;
}
```

In this example, since we've applied perspective: 1000px to .wrapper, our figure elements will be flattened. Since both elements also have the same calculated z-index, .wrapper figure:nth-child(2) will be the topmost element in the stack, as witnessed in Figure 6.41. Note that .wrapper figure:first-child is still visible. It's just not the topmost element. Here the computed value of transform-style will be flat.

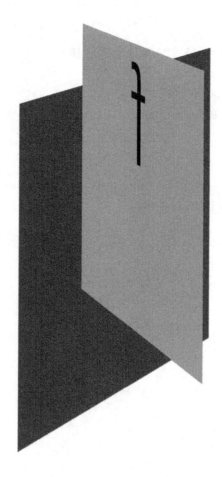

Figure 6.41. Elements with a `transform-style` value of `flat`

To work around this, we set the value of `transform-style` to `preserve-3d`. Let's update our CSS:

```
.wrapper {
    perspective: 2000px;
    perspective-origin: 50% -200px;
    transform-style: preserve-3d;
}
.wrapper figure {
    position: absolute;
    top: 0;
    width: 200px;
```

```
    height: 200px;
}
.wrapper figure:first-child {
    transform: rotateY(60deg) translateZ(191px);
    background: #3f51b5;
}
.wrapper figure:nth-child(2) {
    transform: rotateY(120deg) translateZ(191px);
    background: #8bc34a;
}
```

Now `.wrapper figure:first-child` becomes the topmost element, as our `rotateY` functions suggest it should be in Figure 6.42.

Figure 6.42. Elements with a `transform-style` value of `preserve-3d`

In the vast majority of cases, you should use `transform-style: preserve-3d`. Use `transform-style: flat` only when you want to collapse child elements into the same layer as their parent.[13]

---

[13] The WebKit team's demo Transform Style
[http://www.webkit.org/blog-files/3d-transforms/transform-style.html] shows the effect of `transform-style: flat`. It's an old demo, and created for WebKit browsers, so you'll need to use Safari, Chrome, or Opera 15+ to view it.

Showing Both Faces with the `backface-visibility` Property

By default, the back face of an element is a mirror image of its front face. With stacked or overlapping elements, the reverse side is always visible to the viewer, regardless of which side sits at the top of the stack.

Sometimes, however, we don't want this back side to be visible. Let's return to the card metaphor mentioned in the introduction to this chapter. This time we'll use a playing card, seen in Figure 6.43. With any card, we only want one side to be visible to the user at a time. To manage the visibility of an object's back side, we can use the `backface-visibility` property.

Figure 6.43. With cards, we only want to see one side at a time

The initial value of `backface-visibility` is `visible`. Rear faces will always be shown. But if we want to hide a visible back face, we can use `backface-visibility: hidden` instead.

Let's create our playing card. First our HTML:

```
                              06-transforms/backface-visibility-card.html (excerpt)
<div class="card">
    <div class="side front">
        <div class="suit">&clubs;</div>
    </div>
    <div class="side back"></div>
</div>
```

In this markup, we've set up front and back sides for a `card` container. Here's our card CSS:[14]

```
                                           css/chapter6/backface-vis.css (excerpt)
.card {
    border: 1px solid #ccc;
    height: 300px;
    position: relative;
    transition: transform 1s linear;
    transform-style: preserve-3d;
    width: 240px;
}
```

The important part to notice here is `transform-style: preserve-3d`. Again, we'll need this property to prevent the flattening that occurs by default when we use the `transform` property. Now let's set up the CSS for the front and back sides of our cards:

```
                                           css/chapter6/backface-vis.css (excerpt)
/* Applies to both child div elements */
.side {
    height: inherit;
    left: 0;
    position: absolute;
    top: 0;
    width: inherit;
}

.front {
```

---

[14] For broadest browser compatibility, make sure that you include prefixed versions of `transition` and `transform-style`.

```
    transform: rotateY(180deg);
}

.back {
    background: rgba(204, 204, 204, 0.8);
}

.suit {
    line-height: 1;
    text-align: center;
    font-size: 300px;
}
```

Both sides are absolutely positioned, so they'll stack according to their source order. We've also flipped the `.front` sides around the Y-axis by 180°. When it's all put together, your card should look a bit like the image in Figure 6.44.

Figure 6.44. A see-through card with `backface-visibility: visible` (its intial value)

Both sides of the card are visible at the same time. Let's revise our CSS slightly. We'll add `backface-visibility: hidden` to our `.side` rule set:

```
.side {
    backface-visibility: hidden;
    height: inherit;
    left: 0;
    position: absolute;
    top: 0;
    width: inherit;
}
```

Now, `div.front` is hidden. If you see a gray box and no club symbol, it's working as expected.

The utility of `backface-visibility: hidden` becomes a little clearer when we flip `div.card`. Let's add a `.flipped` class to our CSS:

```
.flipped {
    transform: rotateY(180deg);
}
```

Now when we flip our card over (in Figure 6.45), we see `div.front`, and only `div.front`.

Figure 6.45. Flipping our card

Figure 6.46 shows two cards before being flipped. The card on the left has a `back-face-visibility` value of `hidden`, while the one on the right has a value of `visible`.

Figure 6.46. Two cards prior to flipping

And in Figure 6.47, we can see these same cards after the `flipped` class is added; that is, `<div class="card flipped">`.

Figure 6.47. The same cards after being rotated 180 degrees

Conclusion

Whew! That was a lot to take in. I hope after reading this chapter, you've learned how to:

- effect page layout and stacking order with transforms
- calculate the current transform matrix
- apply 2D transform functions that rotate, translate, and skew objects
- use 3D transforms to create the illusion of depth and dimension

In our next chapter, we'll look at conditional CSS, including `@supports`, newer `@media` features, and related JavaScript APIs.

Chapter **7**

Applying CSS Conditionally

As its name suggests, **conditional CSS** refers to CSS rules that are applied when a condition is met. Conditional CSS consists of **conditional grouping rules**, and the rule sets nested within. A condition in this context may be a CSS property and value combination, as with the `@supports` rule. A condition may test for a browser window condition such as width, as with the `@media` rule. Or a condition may be a device feature such as hover state or pointer input, also as with `@media`. We'll discuss all this in the chapter.

Both `@media` and `@supports` are described by the CSS Conditional Rules Module, Level 3 specification.[1] The `@media` rule—which you probably know as *media queries*—is fully defined by the Media Queries specification.[2]

Of the two kinds of grouping rules, `@media` enjoys the broadest support. Every major browser supports the feature queries defined in the Level 3 version of the Media Queries specification.[3] Most currently used browsers also support its related JavaScript API, `matchMedia()`. Support for Level 4 feature queries, however, is less

---

[1] http://dev.w3.org/csswg/css-conditional-3/
[2] http://dev.w3.org/csswg/mediaqueries-4/
[3] http://www.w3.org/TR/css3-mediaqueries/

widespread. Browser support for `@supports` (and the `CSS.supports` JavaScript API) is a little patchier, but it's still supported widely enough to be discussed here.

Media Queries and `@media`

The `@media` rule and its basic syntax was originally defined by the CSS 2.1 specification.[4] Building on the ten media types defined by HTML4,[5] the intent of `@media` was to enable developers to serve different styles to different media types and devices. Using the `@media` rule, or `media` HTML attribute, we could specify distinct styles for `print` or `screen`.

The Media Queries Level 3 specification[6] extended the `@media` rule, adding support for media features in addition to media types. Media features include conditions such as window width, screen orientation, and resolution. If you've ever practiced responsive web design, you're probably familiar with these feature tests and techniques.

Most of the media types defined by HTML4 are deprecated in Media Queries Level 4 specification,[7] the latest version of the specification. Four media types are defined in the Level 4 specification: `all`, `screen`, `print`, and `speech`. Of those, only the first three have widespread browser support.

Media Queries Level 4 does, however, add a few more features to query, such as `pointer` and `light-level`. Again, most of these are yet to be supported by browsers. We'll briefly discuss some of these in the examples that follow.

 Succession Planning

There's a good chance these remaining media types will also become deprecated in favor of feature tests in a future media queries specification.

Media queries enjoy a wide range of support, as shown in Table 7.1. Internet Explorer 9, however, does not support `matchMedia`, the DOM scripting interface for testing

---

[4] http://www.w3.org/TR/CSS21/media.html#media-sheets
[5] http://www.w3.org/TR/html4/types.html#h-6.13
[6] http://dev.w3.org/csswg/css3-mediaqueries/
[7] http://dev.w3.org/csswg/mediaqueries-4/

media query conditions. That interface is defined by the CSSOM-View Module,[8] covered in the "Using media queries with JavaScript" section later.

Table 7.1. Support for @media (Source CanIUse.com[9])

Internet Explorer	Firefox	Chrome	Safari	Opera
9+[a]	3.5+	4+[b]	3.1+[c]	10.1+

[a] No support for matchMedia API.

[b] Versions 4-29 support the non-standard `min/max-device-pixel-ratio` rather than `min/max-resolution`.

[c] Supports the non-standard `min/max-device-pixel-ratio` rather than `min/max-resolution`.

Media Query Syntax: The Basics

Media query syntax seems simple on the surface, but sometimes it's a bit counterintuitive. In its simplest form, a media query consists of a media type, used alone or in combination with a media condition, such as `width` or `orientation`. Media types, as we discussed earlier, may be one or more of `all`, `screen`, `print`, and `speech`.[10] A simple, type-based media query for screens looks like this:

```
@media screen {
    /* Styles go here */
}
```

CSS style rules are nested within this `@media` rule set. Any styles contained within will only be applied when the document is displayed on a screen (as opposed to being printed).

```
@media screen {
    body {
        font-size: 20px;
    }
}
```

In this example, the base text size for this document will be 20px when it's viewed on a desktop, laptop, tablet, mobile phone, or television.

---

[8] http://dev.w3.org/csswg/cssom-view/

[9] http://caniuse.com/#search=media%20queries

[10] `@media`, with no media type specified, is equivalent to `@media all`.

We can also create a list of media queries to which our styles will apply by separating each query with a comma. Commas in the media query list function similarly to an OR operator. If the browser or device meets any condition in the list, the styles will be applied. For example, we could limit styles to screen or print using the following:

```
@media screen, print {
    body {
        font-size: 16px;
    }
}
```

The real power of media queries, however, comes when you add a media feature query. **Media feature** queries interrogate the capabilities of the device or conditions of the viewport. A media feature query consists of a property and a value, separated by a colon. The entire query *must* be wrapped in parentheses. Here's an example:

```
@media (width: 30em) {
    nav li {
        display: block;
    }
}
```

What we're doing is applying a new style to nav li only when the width of the viewport is equal to 30em;. Since em units are relative, using them for width makes the most sense on screens. Let's use the and keyword to make a more specific media query:s

```
@media screen and (width: 30em) {
    nav li {
        display: block;
    }
}
```

These styles will be applied only when the output device is a screen and its width is 30em. Notice here that the media type is not enclosed by parentheses, unlike our media feature (width: 30em).

The query above has a small problem, however. If the viewport is wider than 30em or narrower than 30em—and not *exactly* 30em—these styles won't be applied. What we need instead is a *range*.

Range Media Feature Queries and `min-` and `max-` Prefixes

A more flexible media query tests for a minimum or maximum viewport width. We can apply styles when the viewport is *at least* this wide, or *more than* that wide. Luckily for us, the Media Queries Level 3 specification defined the `min-` and `max-` prefixes for this purpose. These prefixes establish the lower or upper boundaries of a feature range (see Table 7.2).

Let's update our previous code:

```
@media (max-width: 30em) {
    nav li {
        display: block;
    }
}
```

In this example, `nav li` would have a `display:` property value of `block` from a viewport width of `0`, *up to and including* a maximum viewport width of `30em`.

We can also define a media query range using `min-` and `max-`, along with the `and` keyword. For example, if we wanted to switch from `display: block` to `display: flex` between `30em` and `100em`, we might do the following:

```
@media (min-width: 30em) and (max-width: 100em) {
    nav li {
        display: flex;
    }
}
```

If both conditions are true—that is, the viewport width is at least `30em`, but not greater than `100em`—our styles will apply.

Now, there are other ways to express a range, and here's where the story of media queries becomes more complicated. The latest version of the specification defines a *range* media feature type. This range type includes properties such as `width` and `height`, and allows for comparison operators such as `>` and `<=`. We could, for example, rewrite the query like so:

```
@media (width >= 30em) and  (width <= 100em) {
    nav li {
        display: block;
    }
}
```

That's a little clearer than @media (min-width: 30em) and (max-width: 100em). This more compact syntax, however, is yet to make its way to most browsers—in fact, *it may not*. So stick with min- and max- for now.

Table 7.2. Range media feature types that can be used with the `min-` and `max-` prefixes.

Property	Description	Value type
`aspect-ratio`	The ratio of `width` to `height`	ratio (such as 1024/768 or 16:9)
`device-aspect-ratio`[a]	The ratio of the `device-width` to `device-height`	ratio (such as 1024/768 or 16:9)
`color`	Number of bits per color component of the device; 0 when the device is not a color device	integer
`color-index`	Minimum number of colors available on the device	integer
`height`	Height of the viewport or page box	length
`device-height`[b]	Height of the screen, or page sheet size in the case of printed media	length
`monochrome`	Number of bits per pixel in a monochrome frame buffer	integer
`resolution`[c]	Describes the pixel density of a device	resolution (`dpi`, `dpcm`, and `dppx`) units[d]
`width`	Width of the viewport or page box	length
`device-width`	Width of the screen, or page sheet size in the case of printed media	length

[a] This is deprecated in the Media Queries Level 4 specification. Though widely supported by browsers, these properties are subject to removal. Avoid using them in new stylesheets, and consider updating them in old ones.

[b] Deprecated in the Media Queries Level 4 specification. Though widely supported by browsers, these properties are subject to removal. Avoid using them in new stylesheets, and consider updating them in old ones.

[c] Safari ≤ 9, Android ≤ 4.3, UC Browser ≤ 9, and BlackBerry Browser ≤ 10 use the non-standard, vendor-prefixed `-webkit-device-pixel-ratio` instead of `resolution`

[d] Internet Explorer ≤ 11 only supports dpi units. Microsoft Edge only supports dpi and dppx units.

Not all media feature properties support ranges with min- and max-. Table 7.2 lists those that do, along with the type of value permitted for each. There is a second type of media feature, however: the discrete type.

Discrete Media Feature Queries

Discrete media features are properties that accept one of a set, or a predefined list of values. In some cases, the set of values is a Boolean: either true or false.

Discrete media features are properties for which a quantity makes little sense. Here's an example using the orientation property. The example adjusts the proportional height of a logo when in portrait mode:

```
@media screen and (orientation: portrait) {
    #logo {
        height: 10vh;
        width: auto;
    }
}
```

 (Remember to Use Parentheses)

Here's your gentle reminder that feature queries such as (orientation:portrait) need to be wrapped in parentheses.

The orientation feature is an example of a discrete media feature. It has two supported values, portrait and landscape. With discrete media features, minimum and maximum values don't make much sense for these properties, as you can see in Table 7.3.

Table 7.3. Discrete media feature types, descriptions, and legitimate values for each

Property	Description	Acceptable values
`grid`	Whether the device is grid (such as a teletype terminal or phone with a single fixed font) or bitmap.	Boolean (test using (`grid`))
`hover`	Ability of the primary input mechanism to have a hover state as determined by the user agent	`none` | `on-demand` | `hover`
`any-hover`	Ability of any connected input mechanism to have a hover state as determined by the user agent	`none` | `on-demand` | `hover`
`inverted-colors`	Whether the colors have been inverted by the user agent or operating system	`none` | `inverted`
`light-level`	Queries the ambient light level of the environment around the device	`dim` | `normal` | `washed`
`overflow-block`	Describes the behavior of the device or browser when content overflows the initial containing block or viewport along the block-axis	`none` | `scroll` | `optional-paged` | `paged`
`overflow-inline`	Describes the behavior of the device or browser when content overflows the initial containing block or viewport in the inline-axis	`none` | `scroll`
`orientation`	Describes behavior for whatever is larger out of width or height. When the width is greater than height, the orientation is `landscape`. When the inverse is true, the orientation is `portrait`	`portrait` | `landscape`

Property	Description	Acceptable values
`pointer`	Presence and accuracy of the primary pointing device as determined by the user agent	`none	coarse	fine`
`any-pointer`	Presence and accuracy of *any* pointing device available to the user	`none	coarse	fine`
`scan`	Which scanning process is used by the output display	`interlace	progressive`
`scripting`	Whether scripting languages are supported for the current document	`none	initial-only	enabled`
`update-frequency`	Whether the content can be modified after output (think paper versus screens)	`none	slow	normal`

One discrete feature query that we can use now is `hover` (along with `any-hover`). As you may have guessed by the name, the `hover` media feature query allows us to set different styles based on whether the primary input mechanism supports the `:hover` state. The `any-hover` feature works much the same way, but applies to any input mechanism, not just the primary one. Since this is a discrete feature type, this property has just three possible values:

- `none`: device has no hover state

- `on-demand`: device sometimes has a hover state; for example, after a long press (most browsers and devices)

- `hover`: device has a hover state

Consider the case of radio buttons and checkbox form controls on touch screens. Touch screens typically have an on-demand hover state, but may lack one completely. Adult-sized fingers are also fatter than the pointers of most mouse or trackpad inputs. For those devices, we might want to add more padding around the label, making it easier to tap:

```
@media screen and (hover: on-demand) {
    input[type=checkbox] + label {
        padding: .5em;
    }
}
```

The other media feature that's making its way into browsers is the `pointer` media feature (and `any-pointer`). With `pointer`, we can query the presence and accuracy of a pointing device for the primary input mechanism. The `any-pointer` property, of course, tests the presence and accuracy of any pointer available as an input mechanism. Both properties accept one of the following values:

- `none`: device's primary input mechanism is not a pointing device

- `coarse`: the primary input mechanism is a pointing device with limited accuracy

- `fine`: device's primary input mechanism includes an accurate pointing device

Devices with pointing inputs include stylus-based screens or pads, touch screens, mice, and trackpads. Of those, touch screens are generally less accurate. Stylus inputs, on the other hand, are very accurate; but like touch screens, they lack a hover state. With that in mind, we might update our `hover` query from earlier so that we only add padding when the `pointer` is `coarse`:

```
@media screen and (hover: none) and (pointer: coarse) {
    input[type=checkbox] + label {
        padding: .5em;
    }
}
```

So far, the latest versions of Chrome and Opera support the `hover` and `pointer` media feature queries. Microsoft Edge does as well. Expect support to become more common as new browser versions are released.

Nesting `@media` Rules

It's also possible to nest `@media` rules. Although they're syntactically valid, browser support is a different matter. Fortunately, the latest versions of most browsers handle nested queries just fine, with Internet Explorer 11 being the exception.

Why might nesting media queries be useful? Here's one example:

```css
@media screen {
    @media (min-width: 20em) {
        img {
            display: block;
            width: 100%;
            height: auto;
        }
    }

    @media (min-width: 40em) {
        img {
            display: inline-block;
            max-width: 300px;
        }
    }
}
```

In this example, we've grouped all our `screen` styles together, with subgroupings for particular window widths. Here's another example, using `hover: on-demand`:

```css
@media (hover: on-demand) {
    @media (pointer: coarse) {
        input[type=checkbox] ~ label {
            padding: .5em;
        }
    }
    @media (pointer: fine) {
        input[type=checkbox] ~ label {
            padding: .1em;
        }
    }
}
```

Within this block are two feature queries for `pointer`. When `(pointer: coarse)` is true, we'll add a half-em of padding. When `(pointer: fine)`, is true, we'll use less padding.

Working around Legacy Browser Support with `only`

As mentioned in the beginning of this chapter, `@media` has been around for a while; however, the syntax and grammar of `@media` has changed significantly from its original implementation. As the Media Queries, Level 4 specification explains, the original error-handling behavior:

> [W]ould consume the characters of a media query up to the first non-alphanumeric character, and interpret that as a media type, ignoring the rest. For example, the media query `screen and (color)` would be truncated to just `screen`.

To avoid this, we can use the `only` keyword to hide media queries from browsers that support the older syntax. The `only` keyword must precede a media query, and affects the entire query:

```
@media only screen and (min-resolution: 1.5dppx) {
    /* Styles go here */
}
```

The `only` keyword tells the browser that these styles should be applied only when the following condition is met. The good news is that the older error-handling behavior is mostly an edge-case among browsers in use today. For most current browsers and current web users, using the `only` keyword is unnecessary. I've included it here for completeness.

Negating Media Queries

We can also negate a media query using the `not` keyword. The `not` keyword must come at the beginning of the query, before any media types or features. For example, to hide styles from `print` media, we might use the following:

```
@media not print {
    body {
        background: url('paisley.png');
    }
}
```

If we wanted to specify low-resolution icons for lower-resolution devices instead, we might use this snippet:

```
@media not print and (min-resolution: 1.5dppx) {
    .external {
        background: url('arrow-lowres.png');
    }
}
```

Notice here that not comes before and negates the *entire* media query. You can't insert not after an and clause. Arguments such as @media not print and not (min-resolution: 2dppx) or @media screen and not (min-resolution: 2dppx) violate the rules of media query grammar; however, you can use not at the beginning of each query in a media query list:

```
@media not (hover: hover), not (pointer: coarse) {
    /* Styles go here */
}
```

Styles within this grouping rule would be applied when the device is without a hover state or when the pointing device has low accuracy.

Other Ways to Use Media Queries

Thus far, we've talked about @media blocks within stylesheets, but this isn't the only way to use media types and queries. We can also use them with @import, or the media attribute.

Since CSS2.1 became widely supported, we've been able to use media types with @import rules. For example, to import a stylesheet **typography.css** when the document is viewed on screen or printed to a page, we could use the following CSS:

```
@import url(typography.css) screen, print;
```

We can also, however, add a media feature query to an @import rule. In the following example, we're serving the hi-res-icons.css stylesheet only when the device has a minimum resolution of 1.5dppx or 96dpi:

```
@import url(hi-res-icons.css) (min-resolution: 1.5dppx), (min-
➥resolution: 96dpi);
```

Use @import with Caution

@import has its drawbacks. For browsers and servers using HTTP/1.1, it adds an additional HTTP request and blocks other assets from downloading. Use with care.

We can also use media queries with the media attribute. In fact, this may be one of the instances where media queries are most powerful. The media attribute, as you may already know, can be used with a few HTML elements: style, link, video, and the source element. But we can also set the value of the media attribute to a media query. The example that follows will only apply linked styles if the device width is 480 pixels wide or less:

```
<link rel="stylesheet" href="styles.css" type="text/css" media="
➥screen and (max-width: 480px)">
```

The Stylesheet Will Still Be Downloaded

In every browser tested, the stylesheet will be requested and downloaded, even though the media query doesn't apply; however, linked assets within that stylesheet (for example, background images defined with url()) won't be.

Media Queries in the Linked Stylesheet Take Precedence

If your linked stylesheets also contain media queries, these will take precedence over the value of the media attribute.

It's also possible to use media queries with the media attribute of the style element:

```
<style type="text/css" media="screen and (max-width: 480px)">
    ⋮
</style>
```

As with linked stylesheets, media queries between <style> and </style> will still apply.

Finally, we can use the media attribute with the source element to serve different files for different window widths and device resolutions. What follows is an example using the source element and media attribute with the picture element:

```
<picture>
    <source srcset="image-wide.jpg" media="(min-width: 1024px)">
    <source srcset="image-med.jpg" media="(min-width: 680px)">
    <img src="image-narrow.jpg" alt="Adequate description of the
➥ image contents.">
</picture>
```

picture Element Has Patchy Support

The picture element is yet to be supported in every browser. As of publication, only Firefox and Chrome versions 38+ and Opera versions 25+ support it. To add support for other browsers, use Scott Jehl's Picturefill.[11]

Content-driven Media Queries

A current common practice when using media queries is to set min-width and max-width breakpoints based on popular device sizes. A **breakpoint**, for those unfamiliar, is the width or height that triggers a media query and its resulting layout changes. Raise your hand if you've ever written CSS that resembles this:

```
@media screen and (max-width: 320px) {
    ⋮
}

@media screen (min-width: 320px) and (max-width: 480px) {
    ⋮
}

@media screen (min-width: 481px) and (max-width: 768px) {
    ⋮
}
```

---

[11] https://github.com/scottjehl/picturefill

```
@media screen (min-width: 769px) {
    ⋮
}
```

These are acceptable breakpoints—they work, and work for a large number of users. But mobile device screen widths are more varied than this. Rather than focus on iPhones, iPads, and laptops, consider a content-centric approach.

 Don't Use `device-width` with Media Queries

> Avoid using `device-width` (including `min/max`) altogether for media queries. High DPI devices in particular may have a device width that does not match its actual pixel capability. For instance, the iPhone 6 has a device width of 375 pixels, but its width in renderable pixels is twice that amount.

A content-centric approach to media queries sets breakpoints based on the point at which the layout starts to show its weaknesses. One strategy is to start small, which is also known as a mobile-first approach. As Bryan Reiger puts it,[12] "the absence of support for `@media` queries is in fact the first media query." You can do a lot to create a flexible, responsive layout *before* you need to add media queries. Then as you increase the window width, you can add styles that take advantage of the additional real estate. For example, how wide is the browser window when lines of text become too long to read? That can be the point at which your layout switches from a single-column layout (Figure 7.1) to a two-column layout (Figure 7.2).

---

[12] http://www.slideshare.net/bryanrieger/rethinking-the-mobile-web-by-yiibu

Figure 7.1. A document viewed in a mobile browser width

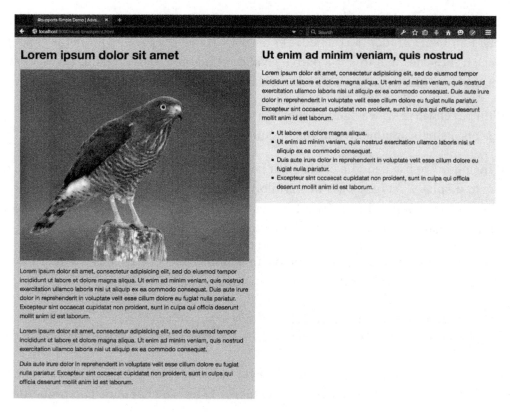

Figure 7.2. A document viewed in a wider laptop-sized browser

There are two advantages to this approach. First: your site will still work on older mobile browsers without support for media queries. This is less of a concern as web users adopt more capable browsers and devices. The second reason is more important: this approach prepares your site for a wider range of screen widths and resolutions.

Using Media Queries with JavaScript

We can also interact with media queries using a JavaScript API, better known as matchMedia(). If you lack any JavaScript know-how, you may get a little lost in this section. We'll keep the examples short, though, so that they're easier to understand. The API for media queries is actually defined by a different specification, the CSSOM View Module.[13] It's not CSS, strictly speaking, but since it's closely related to @media, we'll cover it.

---

[13] http://dev.w3.org/csswg/cssom-view/

The `matchMedia()` method is a property of the `window` object. That means we can refer to it using `window.matchMedia()` or just `matchMedia()`. The former is clearer, since it indicates that this is a native JavaScript method, but the latter saves a few keystrokes. I'm a lazy typist, so I'll use `matchMedia()` in the examples that follow.

With `matchMedia()`, we can test whether a particular media condition is met. It accepts a single argument, and that argument must be a valid media query.

Why might we use a media query with JavaScript, rather than CSS? Perhaps you'd like to display a set of images in a grid on larger screens, but trigger a slide show on small screens. Maybe you want to swap the `src` value of a `video` element based on the screen size or resolution. These are cases for using `matchMedia()`.

Here's a simple example of `matchMedia` in action. This code checks whether the viewport width is greater than or equal to `45em`:

```
var isWideScreen = matchMedia("(min-width: 45em)");
console.log(isWideScreen.matches); // Logs true or false to console
```

Using `matchMedia()` creates a `MediaQueryList` object. Here, that object is stored in the `isWideScreen` variable. Every `MediaQueryList` object contains two properties:

- `media`: returns the media query argument that was passed to `matchMedia()`
- `matches`: returns `true` if the condition is met and `false` otherwise

Since we want to know whether it's true that the browser window is at least `45em` wide, we need to examine the `matches` property.

There are a few cases when `MediaQueryList.matches` might return `false`:

- the condition isn't met at the time `matchMedia()` is invoked
- the syntax of the media query is invalid
- the feature query is without browser support

Otherwise, its value will be `true`.

Here's another example of using `matchMedia`. We'll update the source of a `video` element based on the size of the current viewport and resolution:

```
if(matchMedia("(max-width: 480px) and (max-resolution: 1dppx)") {
    document.querySelector('video').src = 'smallvideo.mp4';
}
```

If the condition doesn't match—or the browser doesn't support the `resolution` feature query—the value for `src` won't be updated.

Error Checking with `not all`

Typically, the value of the `media` property will be the media query we've tested. But maybe you forgot to include the parentheses around your feature query (a syntax error). Or perhaps the query uses a `pointer` feature query, but the browser is yet to support it. In both of those cases, the browser will return a `not all` value. This is media query-speak for "this does not apply to any media condition."

In cases where the media query is a list—that is, when it contains multiple conditions—the value of `matchMedia().media` will also contain multiple values. Should part of that query list be invalid or unsupported, its value will be `not all`. Here's an example:

```
var mq = matchMedia("(hover: none), (max-width: 25em)");
```

In browsers lacking support for the `hover: none` media feature query, the value of `mq.media` will be `not all, (max-width: 25em)`. In browsers that do support it, the value of `mq.media` will be `(hover: none), (max-width: 25em)`. Let's look at another example:

```
var mq = matchMedia("min-resolution: 1.5dppx, (max-width: 25em)");
```

In this example, the value of `mq.media` will also be `not all, (max-width: 25em)`. In this case, however, it's because our first feature query uses the wrong syntax. Remember that media feature queries need to be enclosed in parentheses. The argument should be `matchMedia("(min-resolution: 1.5dppx), (max-width: 25em)");` instead.

Listening for Media Changes

The conditions of our media may not be static. The condition can change when the user resizes the browser, or enters and exits landscape mode. The good news is that we can respond to changes in our document's environment with the `addListener()` method. The `addListener()` method accepts a function as its argument. This function is also known as a *callback function*.

Let's add a class name when our document enters landscape orientation. The first step is to create a `MediaQueryList` object using `matchMedia` and a media query:

```
var isLandscape = matchMedia("(orientation: landscape)");
```

Step two is to define our callback function. Our `MediaQueryList` object will be passed to this callback function at its sole argument:

```
var toggleClass = function (mq) {
    if (mq.matches) {
      document.body.classList.add('widescreen');
    } else {
      document.body.classList.remove('widescreen');
    }
}
```

Media query events are not very smart. They're fired anytime the value of `Media-QueryList.matches` changes, regardless of whether the condition is `true`. This means we'll need to examine the value of `MediaQueryList.matches` or `MediaQueryList.media` for our `MediaQueryList` object. In this case, if the value of `mq.matches` is `true`, we'll add a class name to our body element. Otherwise, we'll remove it.

Finally, let's add this event listener to our `MediaQueryList` object with `addListener`:

```
isLandscape.addListener( toggleClass );
```

To remove a listener, use `removeListener` as shown:

```
isLandscape.removeListener( toggleClass );
```

In early versions of the CSSOM View specification, `addListener` and `removeListener` were supposed to be separate mechanisms, removed from the DOM event queue. This has changed in Level 4. Eventually, we'll be able to use the standard `addEventListener` and `removeEventListener` DOM methods to listen for a `change` event. Our examples from before could then be rewritten like so:

```
isLandscape.addEventListener('change', toggleClass); // Add listener
isLandscape.removeEventListener('change', toggleClass); // Remove
➥ listener
```

Most browsers are yet to implement this change, and still support addListener/re-moveListener exclusively. Chrome and Opera are the exceptions. In those browsers, addListener/removeListener are aliases of addEventListener/ removeEventListen-er. Use addListener and removeListener until other browsers support the newer specification.

Conditional Rules with @supports

Let's move into a more experimental feature of conditional CSS: @supports. The @supports rule lets you add CSS rules based on whether the browser supports a particular property and value. "And value" is key. Some CSS properties and values have been redefined or expanded between CSS2.1 and CSS Level 3. Using @supports lets us test for those changes. Like @media, @supports consists of two parts: the CSS at-rule, and a DOM-based API for use with JavaScript. Unfortunately, @supports enjoys less support than @media, as evident in Table 7.4.

Table 7.4. Support for @supports (Source CanIUse.com[14])

Internet Explorer	Firefox	Chrome	Safari	Opera	Android	UC Browser
No[a]	23+	28+	9+	12.1+[b]	4.4+	No

[a] Microsoft Edge supports @supports.

[b] Version 12.1 uses the older window.supports CSS method. Versions 15+ use CSS.supports.

Why might we use @supports? Here's a scenario: as originally specified,[15] display allowed four possible values—block, inline, list-item, and none. Later the CSS Flexible Box Layout Module Level 1[16] (better known as flexbox) and CSS Display Module Level 3[17] specifications added flex and inline-flex as new values for

---

[14] http://caniuse.com/#feat=css-featurequeries

[15] http://www.w3.org/TR/CSS1/#display

[16] http://dev.w3.org/csswg/css-flexbox/

[17] http://dev.w3.org/csswg/css-text-decor-3/

`display`. With `@supports`, we can define CSS rules that will be applied only when the browser supports `display: flex;`

```
@supports (display: flex) {
    nav ul {
        display: flex;
    }
}
```

To define a condition, wrap the property and value you'd like to test in a set of parentheses as shown. Both portions are required; a condition such as `@supports` (`hyphens`) will not work as a test.

To combine conditions, use the and keyword. For example, if you wanted to apply styles when both the `text-decoration-color` and `text-decoration-style` are supported, you could use the following:

```
@supports (text-decoration-color: #c09) and (text-decoration-style:
➥ double) {
    .title {
        font-style: normal;
        text-decoration: underline double #f60;
    }
}
```

The `@supports` syntax also allows disjunctions using the or keyword. Disjunctions are especially useful for testing vendor-prefixed property support. Let's revisit our `display: flex` example. Some recent versions of WebKit-based browsers such as Safari 8 require a vendor prefix for flexbox support. We can augment our `@supports` condition to take that into account:

```
@supports (display: flex) or (display: -webkit-flex) {
    nav ul {
        display: -webkit-flex;
        display: flex;
    }
}
```

Finally, we can also define a collection of styles if a condition isn't supported by using the not keyword:

```
@supports not (display: flex) {
    nav {
        display: table;
    }
    nav ul {
        display: table-row;
    }
    nav li {
        display: table-cell;
    }
}
```

The not keyword can only be used to negate one condition at a time. In other words, @supports not (text-decoration-color: #c09) and (text-decoration-style: double) will fail to work. But you *can* combine two tests into a single condition. Use an outer set of parentheses; for example, @supports not ((text-decoration-color: #c09) and (text-decoration-style: double)).

CSS.supports DOM API

Along with the @supports rule comes a scriptable API: CSS.supports(). Think of it as a CSS-only version of Modernizr. It's perfect for when you only need to test CSS feature support. CSS.supports() always returns a Boolean true or false value depending on whether the browser supports that property and value combination.

Because CSS.supports() has evolved since it was originally proposed, there are two syntax variations. The first and most widely supported is CSS.supports(_property_, _value_). For example:

```
CSS.supports('text-decoration', 'underline wavy #e91e63');
```

With this syntax, both the property and value must be enclosed in quotes. Arguments must be separated by a comma. The newer syntax is the parenthetical syntax, which accepts an @supports condition as its argument. Similarly to matchMedia, the condition must be wrapped in parentheses:

```
CSS.supports('(text-decoration: underline wavy #e91e63)')
```

This parenthetical syntax is far more robust than the original. With it, we can test multiple conditions using conjunctions (and keyword) or disjunctions (or keyword).

It also supports negation (not keyword). For example, we can test whether a browser supports display: -webkit-flex or display: flex using the following:

```
CSS.supports('(display: -webkit-flex) or (display: flex)');
```

If you forget to include the parentheses when using this syntax, CSS.supports() will return false.

Browser support for CSS.supports() mirrors that of @supports, with one caveat: Opera 12 uses the older window.supportsCSS() method. If you need to support Opera 12, but want to avoid managing different methods, add the following to your JavaScript code:

```
if(!window.CSS && typeof window.supportsCSS === "function"){
    CSS = {};
    CSS.supports = function(property, value) {
        return supportsCSS(property, value)
    }
}
```

There is a drawback to this code, however. The window.supportsCSS() method only accepts arguments in *property, value* form. It can't be used with the newer parenthetical syntax. Attempting to do so will trigger an error.

Understanding the Cascade for @supports and @media

As a general guide, it's smart to place your at-rules blocks later in your code. Using @supports or @media doesn't increase the specificity or importance of a rule. Normal cascade rules apply, meaning that any styles defined after an @supports or @media block will override rules within the block. Consider the following CSS:

```
@supports (text-decoration: underline wavy #c09) {
    .title {
        font-style: normal;
        text-decoration: underline wavy #c09;
    }
}
```

```
.title {
    font-style: italic;
}
```

Here, adding the `title` class to an element will both italicize and underline it. The subsequent `font-style: italic;` line overrides the `font-style: normal;` line. That's not what we want here, however. Instead, we need to flip the order of our rule sets as shown so that `font-style: normal` takes precedence over `font-style: italic;`:

```
.title {
    font-style: italic;
}

@supports (text-decoration: underline wavy #c09) {
    .title {
        font-style: normal;
        text-decoration: underline wavy #c09;
    }
}
```

Not every user will have a browser that supports these features, so be wary of defining mission-critical styles within `@supports` or `@media` rules. Instead, use these features progressively. Define your base styles—the styles that every one of your targeted browsers can handle. Then use `@supports` or `@media` to override and supplement those styles in browsers that can handle newer features.

Conclusion

Now that this chapter is complete, you should know how to use:

- `@media` to create flexible layouts for a range of devices and inputs

- `window.matchMedia()` and the `addListener/removeListener` methods to call JavaScript based on a media query

- `@supports` and the `CSS.supports()` to progressively enhance documents

Both `@media` and `@support` are powerful and flexible ways to progressively enhance your CSS. In the next chapter, we'll look at using CSS with SVG.

Chapter

8

Using CSS with SVG

So far we've talked about using CSS with HTML, but we can also use CSS with SVG, or Scalable Vector Graphics. With CSS, we can change the appearance of SVG based on user interaction. We can use the same SVG document in multiple places, showing or hiding portions of it based on the width of the viewport.

Before we go any further, however, let's talk about what SVG is and why you should use it.

Vector Images versus Raster Images

Most of the images currently used on the Web are **raster** images, also known as **bitmap** images. Raster images are made up of pixels on a fixed grid, with a set number of pixels per inch. JPEG, WebP, GIF, and PNG are all examples of raster image formats.

Raster images are resolution dependent. For example, a 96dpi PNG image will look great on a device with a 96dpi display resolution. When viewed on a 144dpi display, however, a 96dpi image will appear fuzzy or pixelated. Similarly, raster images have fixed dimensions and look best at their original size. Scaling a 150 x 150 pixel image up to 300 x 300 pixels, for example, will distort it.

Vector images, on the other hand, use primitive shapes and mathematical expressions. Rather than pixels on a grid, vector image formats describe the shapes that make up an image and their placement relative to the document's coordinate system. As a result, vector images are resolution *independent*, and retain their quality regardless of display resolution or display dimensions.

Resolution independence is the biggest advantage of SVG. As well as SVG images scaling up or down with no loss of quality, the same image will look great on both high and low DPI (dots-per-inch) devices. That said, SVG is poorly suited to the amount of color data required for photographs. It's best for drawings and shapes. Use it in place of PNG or GIF images for logos, charts, or icons, or as an alternative to custom icon fonts.

Another advantage of SVG is that it was designed to be used with other web languages. We can create, modify, and manipulate them with JavaScript. Or, as we'll see in this chapter, we can style and animate them using CSS.

Associating CSS with SVG Documents

Using CSS with SVG is a lot like using it with HTML. We can apply CSS using the `style` attribute of an SVG element; group CSS within a document using the `style` element; or link to an external stylesheet. The pros and cons of each method are the same as when using CSS with HTML.

Using the `style` Attribute

Here is a simple SVG document where the code creates a black circle, as shown in Figure 8.1s:

```
<svg version="1.1" xmlns="http://www.w3.org/2000/svg" viewBox="0 0
➥ 200 200" enable-background="new 0 0 200 200">
  <circle cx="101.3" cy="96.8" r="79.6"/>
</svg>
```

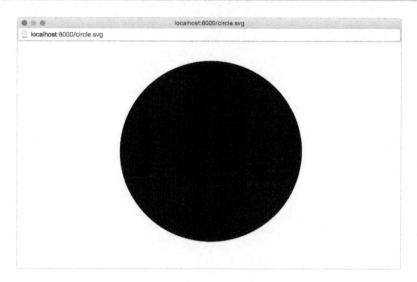

Figure 8.1. A circle in SVG

Let's give our circle a pink fill using CSS and the `style` attribute, the result of which can be seen in Figure 8.2:

```
<svg version="1.1" xmlns="http://www.w3.org/2000/svg" viewBox="0 0
➥ 200 200" enable-background="new 0 0 200 200">
    <circle cx="101.3" cy="96.8" r="79.6" style="fill: #ff99ff" />
</svg>
```

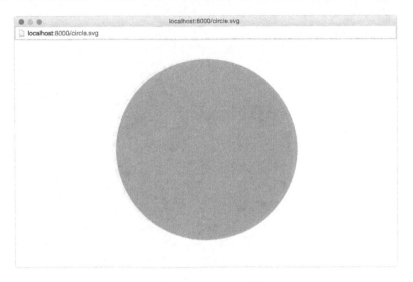

Figure 8.2. Using the `style` attribute to add a fill color

There's one difference between using CSS with HTML and using it with SVG: property names. CSS properties that are available to HTML are generally unavailable to SVG, and vice versa. We'll come back to this point later in the chapter.

Using the `style` attribute isn't the best way to use CSS, of course. Doing so limits the reusability of those styles. Instead we should use embedded or linked CSS.

Embedding CSS in SVG Documents

A better approach to using CSS with SVG is to embed it using the `style` element as shown:

```
<svg version="1.1" xmlns="http://www.w3.org/2000/svg" viewBox="0 0
➥ 200 200" enable-background="new 0 0 200 200">
    <style type="text/css">
    <![CDATA[
        circle {
            fill: #0c0;
        }
```

```
    ]]>
    </style>
    <circle cx="101.3" cy="96.8" r="79.6" />
</svg>
```

Notice here that we've wrapped our CSS in `<![CDATA[` and `]]>` tags (CDATA is short for character data). This tells the SVG parser that this is not SVG content and shouldn't be treated as such. SVG is a form of XML, and XML has stricter parsing requirements for escaping characters. Using these tags ensures that we avoid introducing character escaping errors into our SVG.

Embedding CSS in an SVG document lets us reuse those styles for multiple elements within the same document, but it prevents that CSS from being shared across multiple documents. That's probably acceptable for logos and icons; however, if you're creating a library of chart styles, consider an external CSS file instead.

Linking from SVG to an External CSS File

As with HTML, linking to an external CSS file makes it possible to share styles across several SVG documents. To link an external CSS file, add `<? xml-stylesheet ?>` to the beginning of your SVG file:

```
<?xml version="1.0" encoding="utf-8"?>
<?xml-stylesheet href="style.css" type="text/css"?>
<svg version="1.1" xmlns="http://www.w3.org/2000/svg" viewBox="0 0
➡ 200 200" enable-background="new 0 0 200 200">
    <circle cx="101.3" cy="96.8" r="79.6" />
</svg>
```

Or you can use the XHTML `link` element. Just add the namespace attribute `xmlns=http://www.w3.org/1999/xhtml` to your tag:

```
<defs>
    <link href="style.css" type="text/css" rel="stylesheet"
➡ xmlns="http://www.w3.org/1999/xhtml"/>
</defs>
```

The `link` element is not an SVG element. It belongs to HTML and XHTML. Under the rules of XML, though, we can borrow elements and their behavior from other

XML dialects such as XHTML. To do this, however, we have to add the `xmlns` namespace attribute to the `link` tag.

Unfortunately, linking to external CSS will fail to work if you use the `img` element. Same if you inline your SVG document in HTML. In those cases, you'll need to either:

1. utilize the `style` element within your SVG document

2. link your CSS from the HTML document; for example:

```
<head>
    ⋮
    <link href="svg.css" type="text/css" rel="stylesheet" />
</head>
```

3. use the `object` element to embed your SVG file. Using `object` offers the additional advantage of making the SVG's document tree available to your HTML document's DOM (for example, `document.querySelector('object').contentDocument`).[1]

When using inline SVG within an HTML document, those SVG elements become part of the HTML document tree. While it is still possible to embed CSS within that inline document, you may wish to group the CSS for that SVG document with the CSS of its parent document.

It's also possible to use CSS with SVG documents that were generated by drawing software such as Inkscape or Illustrator. These can be edited using a standard text editor. In most cases, doing so will not affect your ability to modify the image with that drawing application; however, the application may change your markup when you resave the document.

Differences between SVG and HTML

While SVG and HTML are both markup languages, there are two significant differences between them that affect how they work with CSS: SVG does not adhere to the CSS box model, and SVG elements cannot be positioned.

---

[1] Craig Buckler's piece "How to Add Scalable Vector Graphics to Your Web Page" [http://www.sitepoint.com/add-svg-to-web-page/] discusses these methods in detail.

SVG Does Not Adhere to the CSS Box Model

Unlike HTML, SVG shapes are not limited to rectangles and boxes. Most box-model-related properties are inapplicable to SVG elements. You can't, for instance, change the padding or margin of an SVG element. Nor can you use the box-sizing, box-shadow, outline, or border-* properties.

You can, however, use CSS to set or change a range of SVG properties. The full list is outlined in the SVG specification.[2] We'll discuss a few of them in this chapter, within the context of specific techniques.

SVG Elements Cannot be Positioned

Although it's possible to set the X and Y coordinates of an SVG element, SVG does not have the same model of positioning as HTML. Avoid setting the value of the CSS position property as it will have no effect. Related to this, SVG also lacks the idea of a z-index and stacking contexts.[3] SVG elements are stacked according to their source order. Those that fall later in the document sit towards the top of the stack. If you want to reorder SVG elements, you'll need to move them around in the source or with JavaScript.

In fact, most CSS 2.1 properties do not apply to SVG documents. Exceptions include animations and transforms, font-*, display, overflow, visibility, and a few text-related properties. Instead, you'll have to use SVG-specific styling properties with SVG documents.[4]

Styling an SVG Element

Here's a simple example of how to style SVG elements using CSS. First our SVG document. It's a stand-alone file:

```
<?xml version="1.0" encoding="utf-8"?>
<?xml-stylesheet href="s.css" type="text/css" ?>
<svg version="1.1" xmlns="http://www.w3.org/2000/svg" xmlns:xlink=
```

---

[2] http://www.w3.org/TR/SVG/styling.html#SVGStylingProperties

[3] The SVG 2 specification [http://www.w3.org/TR/SVG2/render.html#ZIndexProperty] *does* define behavior for z-index and stacking contexts in SVG documents, but this has yet to make its way into browsers.

[4] http://www.w3.org/TR/SVG/styling.html#SVGStylingProperties

```
➥ "http://www.w3.org/1999/xlink" x="0px" y="0px" viewBox="0 0 497
➥ 184" enable-background="new 0 0 497 184" xml:space="preserve">
    <polygon id="star" points="77,23.7 98.2,66.6 145.5,66.5 111.2,
➥ 106.9,119.3,154 77,131.8 34.7,154 42.8,106.9 8.5,67.5 55.8,
➥ 66.6 "/>
    <circle id="circle" cx="245" cy="88.9" r="67.5"/>
</svg>
```

This markup creates the image shown in Figure 8.3.

Figure 8.3. A star and a circle in SVG

As has been mentioned, we cannot use most CSS properties with SVG documents. But we can change aspects such as an element's color, so let's make our star yellow:

```
#star {
    fill: rgb(255,185,0);
}
```

You'll often see the `fill` attribute used with SVG tags (for example, `<circle fill="#336699" cx="3" cy="10" r="100">`), but it's also a styling property that can be used with CSS.

We can also adjust an element's `stroke`, which is the outline of an SVG shape. It exists, even if no `stroke` properties are set. Let's give our circle a 5px dark-blue dashed border. We'll also make its fill the color of cornflower blue:

```
circle {
    fill: cornflowerblue;
    stroke: darkblue;
    stroke-width: 10;
```

```
    stroke-dasharray: 10, 15;
    stroke-linecap: round;
}
```

Together this gives us the result in Figure 8.4.

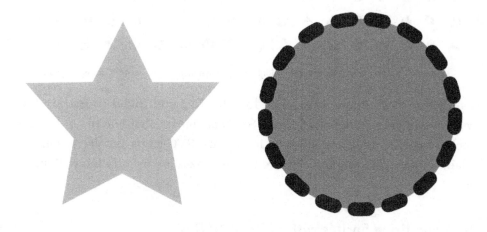

Figure 8.4. Using CSS to style SVG elements

Most SVG attributes are unavailable to CSS; however, text, font, stroke, clipping, filter, gradient, color, and painting properties are available. In other words, it's not possible to change the x or y attributes of an element using CSS (you'd need to use JavaScript), but you can modify appearance-related properties.[5]

Creating SVG Sprites

Image spriting is a technique for reducing the number of HTTP requests by combining several smaller images—typically bitmap icons—into a single file, as shown in Figure 8.5. Reducing the number of network requests typically boosts website performance. Rather than requesting multiple image files, the browser only needs to request one. Displaying a specific icon becomes a matter of shifting the background position of this bitmap file.[6]

---

[5] Just a reminder that the complete list is available in the Styling [http://www.w3.org/TR/SVG/styling.html#SVGStylingProperties] section of the SVG specification.

[6] If you're unfamiliar with CSS sprites, CSS-Tricks has an excellent primer, "CSS Sprites: What They Are, Why They're Cool, and How To Use Them." [https://css-tricks.com/css-sprites/]

Figure 8.5. Multiple icons merged into a single image: Glyphicons from Twitter's Bootstrap 2.3.1

SVG sprites work similarly. Instead of downloading multiple SVG images, the browser downloads a single file. Using SVG also means that you're not limited to monochromatic icons as you are with icon fonts. SVG icons are also easier to maintain, in my opinion, but be aware that file sizes are usually larger than icon fonts.

Avoid Using Sprites with SPDY or HTTP/2

If you are serving assets using the SPDY or HTTP/2 protocols, don't use sprites. As explained in Chapter 2, browsers that support SPDY or HTTP/2 can download multiple assets in parallel; there's no waiting for one request to complete before another begins. With SPDY or HTTP/2, the benefit of reducing the number of requests is outweighed by the cost of sending more bytes than the document needs.

SVG sprites take advantage of document fragment identifiers and the `:target` pseudo-class. They're supported in every major browser that supports SVG except for Safari 7, and UCBrowser ≤ 9.9; however, support for using SVG fragments as background images is currently limited to Firefox and Internet Explorer.[7]

In this document, we have three icons, a star, a hexagon, and a triangle:

```
<?xml version="1.0" encoding="utf-8"?>
<svg version="1.1" xmlns="http://www.w3.org/2000/svg" xmlns:xlink=
➥"http://www.w3.org/1999/xlink" x="0px" y="0px" viewBox="0 0 50 50"
➥ style="enable-background:new 0 0 50 50;" xml:space="preserve">
```

---

[7] Craig Buckler describes this technique in his SitePoint article, "How to Use SVG Image Sprites." [http://www.sitepoint.com/use-svg-image-sprites/]

```
    <style type="text/css">
      .st0{fill:#FF0000;}
      .st1{fill:#92029E;}
      .st2{fill:#007EFC;}
      :not(:target) {
         display: none;
      }
    </style>
    <polygon id="star" class="st0" points="24.4,1.7 31.9,16.8 48.5,
➡19.2 36.5,30.9 39.3,47.4 24.4,39.6 9.6,47.4 12.4,30.9 0.4,19.2
➡ 17,16.8 "/>
    <polygon id="hexagon" class="st1" points="48.9,31.4 31.6,49.2
➡ 7.6,43.1 0.8,19.2 18.1,1.4 42.2,7.5 "/>
    <polygon id="triangle" class="st2" points="0.8,1.5 42.1,25.3 0.8
➡,49.2 "/>
</svg>
```

Each element has an `id` or fragment identifier. We've also embedded our CSS in this SVG document, and used the `:not()` pseudo-class in combination with the `:target` pseudo-class. You'll recall in Chapter 2 that `:target` applies styles to a document fragment as indicated by the document's URL. Here, it's used to hide portions of our SVG document that do not match the target.

Now we can link this SVG from our HTML or CSS. For example, to use our star icon as a background image, we might use the following:

```
.star-bg {
    background: url(../../images/svg-icons.svg#star);
    background-size: 20px 20px;
}
```

And we'll end up with a result such as that seen in Figure 8.6.

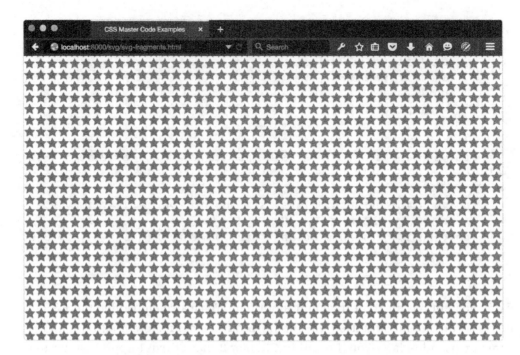

Figure 8.6. Using an SVG document fragment as a background image

Again, using fragments in background images only works in Firefox and Internet Explorer. In WebKit and Blink-based browsers, we're limited to using foreground images:[8]

```
<object type="image/svg+xml" data="../images/svg-icons.svg#triangle"
➥></object>
```

This is not the only SVG icon technique. It is, however, the one that takes the most advantage of CSS, which is why we're discussing it here. For other icon and spriting methods that rely more on the native features of SVG, read "SVG `symbol` a Good Choice for Icons"[9] from CSS-Tricks and Peter Gasston's "Better SVG Sprites with Fragment Identifiers"[10].

---

[8] We're using `object` here for the broadest browser compatibility. Current versions of Safari display buggy behavior when using fragments with the `img` element.

[9] https://css-tricks.com/svg-symbol-good-choice-icons/

[10] http://www.broken-links.com/2012/08/14/better-svg-sprites-with-fragment-identifiers/

Animating and Transitioning SVG CSS Properties

Using CSS with SVG becomes more interesting when we add transitions and animations to the mix. The process is just like animating HTML elements with CSS, but with SVG-specific properties. Let's create a pulsing star effect using the following SVG document:

08-svg/twinkling-star.html *(excerpt)*

```
<svg version="1.1" xmlns="http://www.w3.org/2000/svg" x="0px"
➡ y="0px" viewBox="0 0 497 184" xml:space="preserve">
    <defs>
        <link href="twinkle.css" type="text/css" rel="stylesheet"
➡ xmlns="http://www.w3.org/1999/xhtml"/>
    </defs>
    <polygon class="star" points="77,23.7 98.2,66.6 145.5,66.5 111.2
➡,106.9 119.3,154 77,131.8 34.7,154 42.8,106.9 8.5,67.5
➡ 55.8,66.6 "/>
    <polygon class="star twinkle" points="77,23.7 98.2,66.6 145.5,
➡66.5 111.2,106.9 119.3,154 77,131.8 34.7,154 42.8,106.9
➡ 8.5,67.5 55.8,66.6 "/>
</svg>
```

Our document contains two star-shaped polygon elements, each with a `class` name of `star`. To create the pulsing effect, we'll animate the first one. Here's our CSS:

css/chapter8/svg.css *(excerpt)*

```
@keyframes twinkle {
    from {
        fill-opacity: .4;
    }
    to {
        fill-opacity: 0;
        transform: scale(2);
    }
}
.star {
    fill: rgb(255,195,0);
    transform-origin: 50% 50%;
    -moz-transform-origin: 76px 97.15px;
```

```
}

.twinkle {
    animation:  twinkle 1.5s infinite forwards ease-in;
}
```

Here we've just used the SVG-specific property `fill-opacity`. As with CSS, if the value of an SVG styling property can be interpolated, it can also be animated or transitioned. You can see two different points of the animation in Figure 8.7.

Figure 8.7. Our pulsing star at two different points in the animation

Let's look at another example. This time we'll create a drawing effect by transitioning the `stroke-dasharray` property. Here's our SVG document:

08-svg/svg-wipe-in.html *(excerpt)*

```
<svg version="1.1" xmlns="http://www.w3.org/2000/svg"
➥xmlns:xlink="http://www.w3.org/1999/xlink" x="0px" y="0px"
    viewBox="0 0 200 200" enable-background="new 0 0 200 200">
    <circle fill="transparent" stroke-width="16" cx="101.3"
➥ cy="96.8" r="79.6"/>
</svg>
```

We introduced `stroke-dasharray` without explaining what it does. The `stroke-dasharray` property accepts a comma-separated list of length or percentage values to create a dashed pattern. Odd-numbered values determine the dash length. Even-numbered values determine the gap length. A `stroke-dasharray` value of 5, 10 means that the stroke will be five pixels long with a gap of 10 pixels between each dash. A value of 5, 5, 10 alternates five and 10 pixel dash lengths with five pixel gaps in between.

We can use `stroke-dasharray` to create a drawing effect by starting with a 0 dash length and a large gap, and ending with a large dash length and a dash gap of 0. Then we just transition between the two. Here's what our CSS looks like:

css/chapter8/svg.css (excerpt)

```
circle {
    transition: stroke-dasharray 1s ease-in;
    fill: transparent;
    stroke-dasharray: 0, 500;
}
.animate {
    stroke-dasharray: 500, 0;
}
```

At the beginning of the transition, our stroke is invisible because the dash length is 0 and our gap is 500. But when we add the `animate` class to our circle, we shift the dash length to 500, and eliminate the gap. The effect is a bit like drawing a circle with a pair of compasses, as seen in Figure 8.8. Why 500? It's the smallest value that worked to create this particular effect.

Figure 8.8. Our `stroke-dasharray` transition near its end

Unfortunately, there's a limit to how much we can animate using CSS. For instance, we're unable to use CSS to animate the shape of a path to make a star into a hexagon. For that, we'd need to use a JavaScript animation library , such as Bonsai.js[11], or Synchronized Multimedia Integration Language (SMIL).[12] Unfortunately, SMIL lacks any support in Internet Explorer and is deprecated in Chrome 45+.

Using SVG with Media Queries

With HTML documents, we might show, hide, or rearrange parts of the page based on the conditions of the viewport. If the browser window is 480 pixels wide, for example, we might shift our navigation from a horizontal one to a vertical collapsible list. We can do a similar job with media queries and SVG documents. Consider a logo, such as that of the fictitious Hexagon Web Design & Development in Figure 8.9.

---

[11] https://github.com/uxebu/bonsai
[12] http://www.w3.org/TR/SMIL/

Figure 8.9. A logo and word mark for the fictitious Hexagon Web Design & Development

Without media queries, this SVG logo would simply stretch or shrink to fit the viewport or its container. But with media queries, we can do more clever tasks.

Let's distinguish between the HTML document viewport and the SVG document viewport. When SVG is inline, the HTML viewport and the SVG viewport are one and the same. The SVG document behaves more or less like another HTML element; however, when an SVG document is linked—as with the object or img elements—we're dealing with the SVG document viewport. Media queries work in both cases, but when the SVG document is linked, its viewport is independent of its HTML document. In that case, the size of the browser window does not determine the size of the SVG viewport. Instead, the viewport is determined by the dimensions of the object or img element. Take the (abridged) SVG document that follows as an example:[13]

images/svgmq.svg *(excerpt)*

```
<svg version="1.1" id="HexagonLogo" xmlns="http://www.w3.org/2000/
➡svg" xmlns:xlink="http://www.w3.org/1999/xlink" x="0px" y="0px"
➡ viewBox="0 0 555 174" xml:space="preserve">
   <defs>
      <style type="text/css">
      /* CSS goes here */
      </style>
   </defs>
   <g id="hex">
```

---

[13] A full demonstration of this technique, including the complete source of this SVG document, is available in the code archive.

```
        <polygon id="hexagonbg" points="55.2,162 10,86.5 55.2,11
➡ 145.5,11 190.7,86.5 145.5,162  "/>
        <path id="letterH" fill="#FFFFFF" d="M58,35.5h33v35.2h18.
➡4V35.5 h33.2v103.4h-33.2v-38.3H91v38.3H58V35.5z M77.5,126.5V87.
➡3h45.6v39.2h4V47.9h-4v35.6H77.5V47.9h-4v78.6H77.5z"/>
    </g>

    <g id="word-mark">
        <g id="hexagon-word">
            ...
        </g>
        <g id="web-design-and-dev">
            ...
        </g>
    </g>
</svg>
```

In smaller viewports, let's show just the H in a hexagon symbol:

```
@media (max-width: 20em) {
    [id=word-mark] {
        display: none;
    }
}
```

CSS Must Be Embedded in SVG for IE

This technique only works in Internet Explorer if the CSS is embedded within the SVG file. It will fail to work with an externally linked stylesheet.

Now, whenever our SVG's container is less than or equal to 20em, only the symbol portion of our logo will be visible, as indicated in Figure 8.10. To trigger this view from the HTML document, set the width of the SVG container:

```
<object data="hexlogo.svg" type="image/svg+xml"
↪ style="width: 20em;"></object>
```

Figure 8.10. Showing/hiding elements based on the SVG viewport size

As you may have noticed from looking at Figure 8.10, our SVG image retains its intrinsic dimensions even though part of it has been hidden. This, unfortunately, is a limitation of SVG. To fix it, we need to change the `viewBox` attribute of the SVG document, but only when the viewport is below a certain size. This is a great use-case for `matchMedia`.[14]

The `viewBox` attribute, as its name suggests, determines the viewable area of an SVG element. By adjusting it, we can determine which part of an SVG image fills the viewport.

What follows is an example using `matchMedia` and a media query to update the `viewBox` attribute. Because this JavaScript is embedded within SVG, we must wrap it between `<![CDATA[` and `]]>` escape tags:

```
<defs>
    <script type="text/javascript">
    <![CDATA[
```

---

[14] We discussed `matchMedia` in Chapter 7

```
    var svg, originalViewBox, max20em, mq, updateViewBox;

    svg = document.querySelector('svg');

    /* Store the original value in a variable */
    originalViewBox = svg.getAttribute('viewBox');

    /* Define our media query and media query object */
    mq  = matchMedia("(max-width: 20em)");

    /* Define the handler */
    updateViewBox = function(){
        if (mq.matches) {
            /* Change the viewBox dimensions to show the hexagon */
            svg.setAttribute('viewBox', "0 0 200 174");
        } else {
            svg.setAttribute('viewBox', originalViewBox);
        }
    }

    /* Fire on document load */
    // WebKit/Blink browsers
    svg.onload = updateViewBox;

    // Firefox & IE
    svg.addEventListener('SVGLoad', updateViewBox, true);
    /* Fire if the media condition changes */
    mq.addListener(updateViewBox);
]]>
</script>
</defs>
```

 ## More on Interactive SVG Documents

For a fuller primer on creating interactive SVG documents, read the "Dynamic SVG and JavaScript"[15] chapter of *An SVG Primer for Today's Browsers* from the W3C.

Now, whenever the SVG container is 20em or less, the value of viewBox will be "0 0 200 174". When it exceeds 20em, viewBox will be restored to its initial value as represented in Figure 8.11.

---

[15] http://www.w3.org/Graphics/SVG/IG/resources/svgprimer.html#JavaScript

Figure 8.11. An SVG logo with media queries when the object container is 20em (top) wide and 40em wide

Since this technique uses the the onload event attribute / SVGLoad event, it's a good idea to embed our CSS in the SVG file. When CSS is external, the SVG load event may fire before its associated CSS finishes loading. As we discussed in Chapter 7, Internet Explorer 9 is without support for matchMedia. You can still use CSS media queries to show or hide portions of an SVG image, but you may need to serve additional CSS to IE9 for consistent rendering.

Using Media Queries with background-size

SVG documents and media queries are not limited to foreground images. We can also resize the SVG viewport using the CSS background-size property. The latest major browsers support this technique, but older browser versions do not. Be careful when using this technique in production.[16]

We'll start with this SVG document:

---

[16] Internet Explorer <= 10 lacks support for this technique, as do some older versions of Firefox.

```
<?xml version="1.0" encoding="utf-8"?>
<svg version="1.1" id="Layer_1" xmlns="http://www.w3.org/2000/svg"
➥ xmlns:xlink="http://www.w3.org/1999/xlink" x="0px" y="0px"
➥ viewBox="-20 -20 250 250" xml:space="preserve">
    <defs>
        <style type="text/css">
        <![CDATA[
            circle {
                stroke: #000;
                stroke-width: 30;
                fill: #009688;
            }
            @media (width: 100px) {
                circle {
                    fill: #673ab7;
                }
            }
            @media (width: 300px) {
                circle {
                    fill: #ffc107;
                }
            }
        ]]>
        </style>
    </defs>
    <circle cx="100" cy="100" r="100" />
    <circle cx="100" cy="100" r="50" />
</svg>
```

This is a simple case. Our `circle` elements will get a new `fill` color at specific viewport widths. When the viewport is 20 pixels wide, the fill will be yellow. When it's 300 pixels wide, it will be purple.

To make this work, we have to use our SVG image as a background image and set the selector's `background-size` property. In this case, we'll use our image as a background for the body `element` and for `li` elements. Figure 8.12 shows the results:

```
body, li {
    background: url(../images/circles.svg);
}

 body {
    background-color: #9c27b0;
```

```
        background-size: 300px auto;
}
li {
        background-size: 20px auto;
        background-repeat: no-repeat;
        background-position: left 3px;
        padding-left: 25px;
}
```

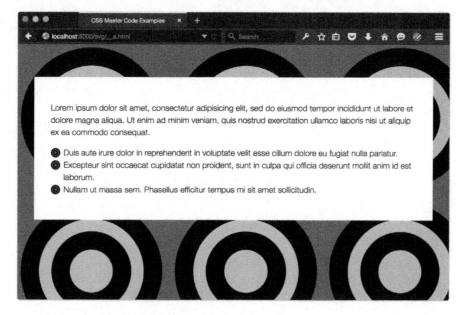

Figure 8.12. Manipulating the SVG viewport with the CSS background-size property

Conclusion

Using SVG with CSS gives us more possibilities for flexible and adaptive documents. Upon completing this chapter, you should now know how to:

- use CSS to style SVG elements

- animate SVG properties

- employ CSS media queries and the matchMedia API to show and hide portions of an SVG document

- utilize the :target pseudo-class with SVG to create a spriting system

Preprocessors

Authoring CSS can be tedious. There's a set of repeated colors and fonts to manage and remember. We need to keep track of vendor prefixes. And sometimes we want to do tasks, such as nesting or grouping rules, that are beyond the native capabilities of CSS.

This is where preprocessors come in handy. **Preprocessors** add syntax capabilities and features that CSS lacks: mixins make it a breeze to manage vendor prefixes; built-in functions save us from unit and color conversions; and the ability to extend a selector lets us consolidate style rules.

As the name suggests, preprocessors take a special syntax and compile it to CSS. They are tools for *writing* CSS, although some tools also handle minification and concatenation.

In this chapter, we'll look at two of the leading CSS preprocessor tools: Less[1] and Sass.[2] These are not the only preprocessors in existence, but they are by far the most

---

[1] http://lesscss.org/

[2] http://sass-lang.com/

popular. While not a comprehensive look at either tool, it will be enough to get you started.

Which preprocessor to choose depends on which syntax, tools, environment, and workflow you prefer. Aside from installation and compilation, the basic features of Less and Sass are similar enough that we'll discuss them in parallel. For a more detailed exploration of Less and Sass, consult the documentation for each.

Installing Less

Less is available as:

- a Node.js-based tool, installable from its package manager npm
- a tool for Rhino[3], Mozilla's Java-based JavaScript engine
- a browser-based tool
- part of GUI-based tools such as Koala[4], Harp[5], and CodeKit[6]
- a client-side JavaScript application

Instructions for how to use the first three are covered on the Less website.[7] We'll focus on the Node.js-based tool. I trust you've installed Node and NPM after reading Chapter 2. Installing Less works the same way as installing other NPM-distributed packages:

```
npm install -g less
```

Linux and OS X users may need to use sudo. If the command line scares you, using a GUI-based tool is perfectly fine. You can safely skip ahead to the *Ruleset Nesting* section.

Using Less from the Command Line

To use the command line version of Less, run lessc in a terminal window:

---

[3] https://developer.mozilla.org/en-US/docs/Mozilla/Projects/Rhino
[4] http://koala-app.com
[5] http://harpjs.com/
[6] https://incident57.com/codekit/
[7] http://lesscss.org/

```
lessc /path/to/lessstylesheet.less
```

You'll need to run `lessc` every time you wish to compile your Less files to CSS. One way around this limitation is to use an application such as Koala, Harp, or CodeKit, instead of the Node.js version. These applications will "watch" your Less files or directories for changes, rewriting CSS files with every save. If you're building a Grunt or Gulp workflow, you can also use the `grunt-less` or `gulp-less` plugins to run the `lessc` command whenever you save a file.

Running `lessc` will print CSS to the terminal window by default; however, you can redirect that output to a file:

```
lessc /path/to/lessstylesheet.less > /path/to/output.css
```

If you wish to minify your CSS output, use the `-x` flag:

```
lessc -x /path/to/lessstylesheet.less > /path/to/output.css
```

When using the command line tool, Less files don't require a **.less** extension. You could use **.css** or **.lcss** instead; however, third-party applications and client-side Less require it. For the broadest compatibility, use **.less**.

Installing Sass

Sass was originally written as a Ruby gem. In recent years, though, it's been ported to a C/C++ library known as LibSass. As a result, Sass tools are also available for Python, Node.js, and other platforms.

If the command line makes you skittish, there are several open-source and paid applications that include Sass support. These include the aforementioned Koala, Harp, and CodeKit. Another option is Scout.[8]

We'll focus on the Ruby-based version of Sass in this chapter, as it's the definitive implementation of Sass. You'll need to install Ruby if you're yet to do so; however, setting up a server or knowing anything about programming with Ruby is not required in order use Sass. To install Sass, use the following command:

---

[8] http://mhs.github.io/scout-app/

```
gem install sass
```

OS X and Linux users may need to use sudo.

Using Sass from the Command Line

As with Less, you can use Sass from the command line to compile your files to CSS. Sass files should be saved with an *.scss* extension:

```
sass sassfile.scss output.css
```

 Sass Syntaxes

Sass has two syntaxes: original Sass syntax and SCSS (or Sassy CSS). **Original Sass syntax** uses indentation rather than curly braces to delineate rule sets. **SCSS** is more like a superset of plain CSS, and uses curly braces. We'll be focusing on SCSS. Files that employ original Sass syntax should use a *.sass* extension.

Sass also supports basic minification. Just add `--style=compressed` to your `sass` command:

```
sass sassfile.scss output.css --style=compressed
```

With the `--watch` flag, Sass can also update CSS output after every saved change:

```
sass --watch sassfile.scss:output.css
```

Additionally, Sass can watch and output entire directories of files:

```
sass --watch /path/to/scss/:/path/to/css/
```

Each Sass file in a watched directory will be compiled to a corresponding CSS one.

Now that we've looked at how to install and use Less and Sass, let's dig into the common features of both.

Ruleset Nesting

Ruleset nesting can improve the organizing of your CSS by grouping related styles. It also saves some keystrokes.

Consider the following CSS rulesets:

```
article {
    margin: 2em auto;
}
article p {
    margin: 0 0 1em;
    font-family: 'Droid Serif','Liberation Serif',serif;
}
```

In both Less and Sass, we can rewrite this to take advantage of nesting:

```
article {
    margin: 2em auto;

    p {
        margin: 0 0 1em;
        font-family: 'Droid Serif','Liberation Serif',serif;
    }
}
```

This gives us a descendant selector, and the output will match the standard CSS above.

Sass and Less also allow you to reference the parent selector from within a nested ruleset. This is especially useful when dealing with child selectors (>), pseudo-elements, and pseudo-classes. To incorporate a parent selector, use an ampersand (&). Take a look at the following example:

```
p {
    font-family: 'Droid Serif','Liberation Serif',serif;

    .error & {
        font: bold 11px / 1.5 sans-serif;
    }
}
```

```
a {
    text-decoration: none;
    border-bottom: 2px solid #000;

    &:link{
        border-bottom-color: #fc0;
    }
    &:hover {
        border-bottom-color: #f30;
    }
}
```

Compiling the preceding code results in the following output from both Less and Sass:

```
p {
    font-family: 'Droid Serif', 'Liberation Serif', serif;
}

.error p {
    font: bold 11px / 1.5 sans-serif;
}

a {
    text-decoration: none;
    border-bottom: 2px solid #000;
}

a:link {
    border-bottom-color: #fc0;
}

a:hover {
    border-bottom-color: #f30;
}
```

It's also possible to nest a ruleset inside a nested ruleset. Take a look at the example below:

```
nav {
    > ul {
        height: 1em;
        overflow: hidden;
```

```
        position: relative;

        &::after {
            content: ' ';
            display: block;
            clear: both;
        }
    }
}
```

Here we've nested styles for `::after` inside a declaration block for ul, which itself is nested inside a nav declaration block. When compiled, we end up with the following CSS:

```
nav > ul {
    height: 1em;
    overflow: hidden;
    position: relative;
}
nav > ul::after {
    content: ' ';
    display: block;
    clear: both;
}
```

Let's look at a slightly more complex example of nesting:

```
article {
    color: #222;
    margin: 1em auto;
    width: 80%;

    &.news {
        h1 {
            color: #369;
            font-size: 2em;

            [lang]{
                font-style: italic;
            }
```

```
            }
        }
    }
```

This isn't too egregious, right? Our [lang] selector is only four levels deep, but let's look at our compiled CSS output:

```
article {
    color: #222;
    margin: 1em auto;
    width: 80%;
}
article.news h1 {
    color: #369;
    font-size: 2em;
}
article.news h1 [lang] {
    font-style: italic;
}
```

Now we have a couple of high-specificity selectors: `article.news h1` and `article.news h1[lang]`. As discussed in Chapter 2, high-specificity selectors increase the size of your CSS files. They use more characters than necessary, and require even higher high-specificity selectors to override them.

Neither Less nor Sass has a hard limit on how deeply rulesets can be nested. But a smaller amount of nesting results in lower specificity and CSS that's easier to maintain. If you've nested more than three levels, there's a good chance you need to refactor your code.

@import and Partials

The CSS `@import` rule allows developers to add rules from one stylesheet to another stylesheet document. Unfortunately, `@import` often has a negative impact on website load times. As Steve Souders explains in his blog,[9] using `@import` from within a linked stylesheet will cause the browser to *download each file sequentially*, increas-

---

[9] http://www.stevesouders.com/blog/2009/04/09/dont-use-import/

ing total page load time. More generally, the greater amount of HTTP requests you have, the more time it takes a page to download all of your assets.[10]

For this reason, the current best practice is to avoid using @import in CSS files; however, in Less and Sass, @import is a fantastic way to organize and manage your CSS.

Less and Sass support what are known as **partials** or partial source files. These files are smaller chunks of CSS, often organized by functionality. You might, for example, have separate partials for forms, tables, and typography styles.

We can include the contents of a partial in our CSS output using the @import command. This way we can split our CSS across multiple files for development, but still generate a single file for production.

Let's look at a super simple example using Less. We'll create a file named **errors.less** that contains styles for error and warning messages:

```
.error {
    border-radius: 3px;
    border: 1px solid #000;
    font-size: .9rem;
    margin: 10px 0;
    padding: 10px;
}

.critical {
    background: rgb(255,232,232);
    border-color: red;
    color: red;
}

.warning {
    background: rgb(255,255,204);
    border-color: rgb(255,153,0);
    color: rgb(255,153,0);
}
```

Now in our main .less file—we'll name it **styles.less**—we can import the styles of errors.less:

---

[10] This is not accurate for sites served over SPDY or HTTP/2.

```
body {
    background: #FFFDFB;
    color: #222;
    font: 100 16px / 1.5 sans-serif;
}
@import "errors";
```

Notice that @import "errors"; comes at the end of our CSS file. With standard CSS, @import statements must be listed at the beginning of the stylesheet. With preprocessors, it can appear at any position.

We can also omit the file extension when we import a file this way. Including it won't cause problems, but it's unnecessary.

Let's compile our Less files to CSS. Running lessc styles.less > styles.css creates this output:

```
body {
    font: 100 24px / 1.5 sans-serif;
}
.error {
    border: 1px solid #000;
    border-radius: 3px;
    font-size: .9rem;
    padding: 10px;
    margin: 10px 0;
}
.critical {
    background: #ffe8e8;
    border-color: red;
    color: red;
}
.warning {
    background: #ffffcc;
    color: #ff9900;
    border-color: #ff9900;
}
```

Sass works similarly, but in the case of Sass partials, filenames:

- should begin with an underscore character

- must use an .scss extension instead of a .less extension.

Variables

Another feature of preprocessors are **variables**. Variables allow us to store a value—say, a font size or color—in one place and reuse it in another. Later, if we change that value globally, we only need to update a single line.

Variables are an oft-requested feature for CSS. For a few years, it looked like they would become a reality with the CSS variables specification.[11] Unfortunately, Firefox is the only browser that supports standard CSS variables currently. Chrome and Opera paused development (although recently restarted it), while Internet Explorer is still weighing it up. Preprocessors give us this capability now.

Variables are one area where the syntax of Less and Sass differ. Less variables must begin with an @ symbol:

```
@brand-color: #0e79c4;
```

For Sass, prefix variable names with a dollar sign (the $ character):

```
$brand-color: #0e79c4;
```

In both cases, variables are defined much like CSS property values, using a colon rather than an equals sign. We can then use them as values in our rule sets:

```
h1 {
    color: @brand-color; // or $brand-color if using Sass.
}
```

Variables are especially useful for managing colors and font styles. For example, you might store a project's color values in a `variables.less` or `_vars.scss` partial:

```
$brand-color-a: #ff3b00; // Tomato red
$brand-color-b: #f8f8ff; // Cool white
$img-border: #708090     // Cool gray
```

Then we can use `@import` to pull these values into our CSS.

---

[11] http://dev.w3.org/csswg/css-variables/

Variable Interpolation

Less and Sass have a feature called **variable interpolation**. Variable interpolation lets you use variable values in ways other than as property values. Think of interpolation as a template system for building selector and value strings. Wrap the variable name in a special syntax: #{} for Sass and @{} for Less; the tool replaces them with the variable's values during compilation.

You may, for example, want to define part of a selector name using a variable. Here's an example using Sass:

```
$prefix: sports;
```

To build the selector name, you'd use the following syntax (again, for Sass). Notice here that we're using the entire variable name, including the $ prefix inside the curly braces:

```
.#{$prefix}-section {
    background-color: #0000ca;
}
```

And here's the same example using Less. With Less, we only need the variable name:

```
@prefix: sports;

.@{prefix}-section {
    background-color: #0000ca;
}
```

When compiled, both examples create this output:

```
.sports-section {
    background-color: #0000ca;
}
```

You can use interpolation for all your variables, not just for selector names. In fact, you'll find it absolutely necessary when your CSS syntax is ambiguous for the compiler. Let's look at another example of code ambiguity that affects the Sass compiler. Consider this SCSS:

```
$base-font-size: 16px;
$base-line-height: 1.5;

body {
    font: 100 $base-font-size / $base-line-height sans-serif;

}
```

You might expect this to compile to the following CSS:

```
body {
    font: 100 16px / 1.5 sans-serif;
}
```

Less handles this as you.d expect. With SCSS, though, what you end up with is this:

```
body {
    font: 100 10.66667px sans-serif;
}
```

Sass permits mathematical expressions as property values. In this case, the / character is treated like a division operator instead of valid CSS syntax. To get around this, we use interpolation:

```
body {
    font: 100 #{$base-font-size} / #{$base-line-height} sans-serif;
}
```

Now the previous SCSS when compiled gives us the output we expect:

```
body {
    font: 100 16px / 1.5 sans-serif;
}
```

Both Less and Sass have more advanced variable capabilities than what we've covered here. Consult each tool's documentation for more.

Mixins

Another advantage of using preprocessors is the ability to create reusable snippets of code in the form of **mixins**. Mixins are great for managing vendor prefixes, or reusing particular styles in multiple places. The syntax differs quite a bit between Less and Sass, but the concept is largely the same.

Mixins in Less

With Less, mixins look a lot like CSS selectors. In fact, they're mostly the same. For example, you can create a class that adds `display: inline-block` to an element:

```
.dib {
    display: inline-block;
}
```

You could add the following class to your markup: `<p class="dib">`. But if you'd rather keep your markup simple and highly semantic, you might instead turn this `.dib` class into a mixin:

```
.dib {
    display: inline-block;
}

p {
    .dib;
    font-size: 16px;
}
```

When compiled, Less will include both our `.dib` class and `display: inline-block` as part of our p rule set:

```
.dib {
    display: inline-block;
}

p {
```

```
    display: inline-block;
    font-size: 16 px;
}
```

It's also possible to create a mixin rule set without it being included in the output. To do so, add parentheses to the selector. In this example, `.dib` would become `.dib()` instead.

Mixins can also accept parameters, making them perfect for managing vendor prefixes. Let's look at an example using the CSS3 `transition` property. First, we'll define our mixin:

```
.transition(@props) {
    -webkit-transition: @props;
    transition: @props;
}
```

Now we can use it within our rule sets:

```
.fade {
    .transition(opacity 100ms linear);
}

.open {
    .transition(height 500ms linear);
}
```

When compiled, Less replaces the value of `@props` with the argument passed, and outputs the prefixed CSS we've prescribed:

```
.fade {
    -webkit-transition: opacity 100ms linear;
    -moz-transition: opacity 100ms linear;
    transition: opacity 100ms linear;
}

.open {
    -webkit-transition: height 500ms linear;
```

```
    -moz-transition: height 500ms linear;
    transition: height 500ms linear;
}
```

The advantage of using a mixin here is twofold: it saves us some typing, and it's easier to maintain. We can just remove the prefixed properties once they're no longer necessary.

Mixins in Sass

Sass mixins use a syntax that's slightly more complicated that the Less equivalent. The advantage is that it's clear at a glance what is and isn't a mixin. Sass mixins also differ from Less in that they're *never* included in the compiled CSS output. Our transition mixin would look like this in Sass:

```
@mixin transition($props) {
    -webkit-transition: $props;
    -moz-transition: $props;
    transition: $props;
}
```

Add mixins to your SCSS using the @include directive:

```
.fade {
    @include transition(opacity 100ms linear);
}

.open {
    @include transition(height 500ms linear);
}
```

The compiled output looks like this CSS:

```
.fade {
    -webkit-transition: opacity 100ms linear;
    -moz-transition: opacity 100ms linear;
    transition: opacity 100ms linear;
}

.open {
    -webkit-transition: height 500ms linear;
```

```
    -moz-transition: height 500ms linear;
    transition: height 500ms linear;
}
```

Sass mixins don't have to accept parameters, however. Let's use our `.dib` example from the previous section:

```
@mixin .dib {
    display: inline-block;
}

p {
    @include dib;
    font-size: 16px;
}
```

This produces the following output:

```
p {
    display: inline-block;
}
```

Again, Sass *never* includes the mixin in the compiled CSS. If you did wish to include it, use the `@extend` directive instead. It's discussed in the next section.

Extending Selectors

Finally, let's talk about extending CSS selectors. The syntax of Less and Sass diverge here as well, but the concept is very similar. **Extending** is a way to combine multiple selectors in a single rule set.

Extending in Less

To extend a selector in Less, use the Less-only `:extend` pseudo-class, which doesn't exist in CSS. The `:extend` pseudo-class requires one argument: the selector of the rule set you wish to merge with the current rule set. You must use `:extend` within a rule set, and it must be prefixed with a parent selector ampersand (**&**). Here's a simple example:

```less
.message {
    border: 1px solid #000;
    font: 11px / 1.5 sans-serif;
}

.error {
    &:extend(.message);
    background: #ffd1d1;
    border-color: #f00;
}

.warning {
    &:extend(.message);
    background: #ffc;
    border-color: #fc0;
}
```

Here we've decided to extend the `.message` class styles to `.error` and `.warning`. After compiling, we get the following CSS output:

```css
.message,
.error,
.warning {
    border: 1px solid #000;
    font: 11px / 1.5 sans-serif;
}
.error {
    background: #ffd1d1;
    border-color: #f00;
}
.warning {
    background: #ffc;
    border-color: #fc0;
}
```

Unlike a mixin, extending a class means that the extended selector will be combined with the extendee into a comma-separated group. Here `.message`, `.error`, and `.warning` share a rule set. Mixins, on the other hand, copy declarations across rule sets.

With Less, we're not just limited to extending class names. We can extend ID selectors such as `#display`, child selectors such as `nav > ul`, and even pseudo-class selectors such as `nth-child()`.

Extending in Sass

Conceptually, extending in Sass is the same as extending in Less. Extending in Sass also combines selectors into a single rule set. Syntactically, however, there are a couple of differences.

To extend a class with Sass, use the `@extend` directive followed by the selector you wish to extend. Let's rewrite our example from the previous section to use Sass syntax:

```
.message {
    border: 1px solid #000;
    font: 11px / 1.5 sans-serif;
}

.error {
    @extend .message;
    background: #ffd1d1;
    border-color: #f00;
}

.warning {
    @extend .message;
    background: #ffc;
    border-color: #fc0;
}
```

This creates the following CSS output:

```
.message, .error, .warning {
    border: 1px solid #000;
    font: 11px / 1.5 sans-serif; }

.error {
    background: #ffd1d1;
    border-color: #f00; }
```

```
.warning {
    background: #ffc;
    border-color: #fc0; }
```

Here, too, our extended and extendee selectors are grouped together in a single rule set. Sass also supports extending ID selectors. To date, however, there's no support for extending more complex selectors such as #sidebar > h3 or p span.

We can also extend pseudo-classes, although Sass's handling is a little bit counter-intuitive. Consider the following Sass code:

```
tr:nth-child(even) {
    background: #eee;
}

th {
    @extend tr;
    border: 1px solid #000;
    font: 11px / 1.5 sans-serif;
}
```

You might expect the CSS output to look like this example with selectors combined in one line:

```
tr:nth-child(even),
th {
    background: #eee;
}
```

What follows is the actual output:

```
tr:nth-child(even), th:nth-child(even) {
    background: #eee;
}
```

When extending a selector that consists of a class or element and a pseudo-class, Sass will also add the pseudo-class to the extended selector's parent.

Conclusion

Less and Sass are powerful tools for writing and organizing CSS; however, be mindful that it's easy to add bloat to your CSS by overusing nesting and mixins. Examine your CSS output files periodically and refactor your Sass or Less input, if necessary. A good question to ask yourself is: "Would I have written this CSS without a preprocessor?" This is also where the code quality tools we discussed in Chapter 2 can come in handy.

Chapter 10

Conclusion

In this book, we've covered some of the finer points and broad strokes of CSS. In some ways, we've only scratched the surface. There's quite a bit of CSS to cover, especially on the leading edge. With the CSS Working Group's switch to modularized specifications and shorter browser release cycles, new CSS features are created and implemented quite quickly these days. Attempting to keep up and stay ahead of the curve can leave your head spinning. Indeed, there are a few specifications and features that we've barely mentioned in this book.

So what's on the horizon? Document layout is one area of CSS in which there's been a lot of activity. Both the Multi-column and Flexible Box modules have largely stabilized. They're ready to use in projects targeting newer browsers, though older ones still require fallbacks. Soon, however, we'll be able to use the Grid Layout Module.[1]

---

[1] http://www.w3.org/TR/css3-grid-layout/

Grid Layout

With grid layout, we'll be able to create document layouts such as the one in Figure 10.1 without rows of div elements.

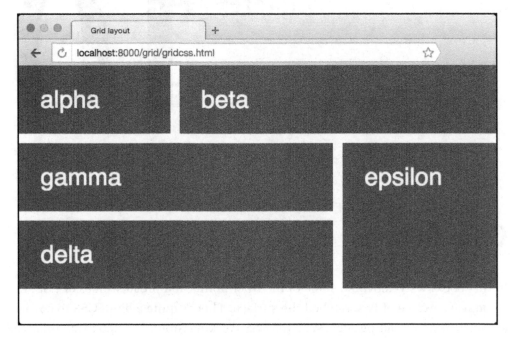

Figure 10.1. Grid layout enables complex page layouts

It uses the following markup:

```
<div class="grid">
    <div class="alpha">alpha</div>
    <div class="beta">beta</div>
    <div class="gamma">gamma</div>
    <div class="delta">delta</div>
    <div class="epsilon">epsilon</div>
</div>
```

There's one wrapping div element with a class name of grid, and five child elements. Compare that to the markup we'd need to use today:

```
<div class="grid-row">
    <div class="alpha">alpha</div>
    <div class="beta">beta</div>
```

```
    </div>
<div class="grid-row">
    <div class="grid-row-span-2">
        <div class="gamma">gamma</div>
        <div class="delta">delta</div>
    </div>
    <div class="epsilon">epsilon</div>
</div>
```

Grid syntax takes some fiddling and practice to understand. First, we trigger a grid layout with display: grid. Next, we define our column, row, and gutter (the space between columns and rows) widths. This is all done on the grid container element:

```
.grid {
    display: grid;
    grid-template-columns: 210px 20px 1fr 20px;
➥   /* column size, gutter size, column, gutter, column */
    grid-template-rows: auto 20px auto 20px auto 20px;
➥ /* row size, gutter size, row, gutter, row */
}
```

 Limited Browser Support

> Browser support for grid layout is very much in flux. The examples here work in Chrome and Microsoft Edge with vendor prefixes. However, the latest version of the specification includes properties and units that may make this syntax obsolete.

Then we can define the column and/or row spans for each child element of the grid:

```
.alpha {
    grid-column: 1 / 2;
}
.beta {
    grid-column: 3 / 6;
}
.gamma {
    grid-column: 1 / 4;
    grid-row: 3 / 5;
}
.delta {
    grid-column: 1 / 4;
    grid-row: 7 / 10;
```

```
    }

    .epsilon {
        grid-column: 5 / 6;
        grid-row: 3 / 10;
    }
```

Each `grid-column` value is a shorthand for the `grid-column-start` and `grid-column-end` properties. Each `grid-row` value is a shorthand for `grid-row-start` and `grid-row-end`. They indicate which rows or columns a grid item element should span. For example, `grid-column: 3 / 6` indicates to "start this element's span at column three of the grid, and end it at column six."

Grid layouts, when used with the `fr` unit, are designed to be flexible and responsive. With media queries, we can also change the layout of the grid—or drop it entirely—at different breakpoints. Here, for example, we could change `display: grid` to `display: block` for narrower viewports.

Think of grid layout as complementary to flexbox. Flexbox lets us arrange items either horizontally (`flex-direction: row`) or vertically (`flex-direction: column`). With grid layouts, however, a single element can stretch horizontally across columns and vertically across rows—flexbox is one-dimensional, while grid layout is two-dimensional. As a result, grid layout is the better choice for entire documents, but flexbox is better for document components such as media objects and search forms. To learn more about grid layout, see Rachel Andrews' Grid by Example site.[2]

Internet Explorer 10 and 11 and Microsoft Edge have experimental support for an older vesrion of the grid layout spec; properties require a vendor prefix. Chrome and Opera also support grid layout; it is unprefixed, but disabled by default. Webkit has support, but prefixed. Yandex browser,[3] which uses Chromium/Blink as its base, does enable grid layout by default. With Yandex browser, grid layout properties can skip the prefix.

---

[2] http://gridbyexample.com/

[3] https://browser.yandex.com/

CSS Shapes

Grid layout isn't the only layout-related specification that's coming soon to browsers. CSS Shapes[4] will enable developers to flow content into and around complex, non-rectangular shapes.

Let's look at a simple example using a floated element and some accompanying text. First, our markup.

```
<div shape="shape"></div>
<p class="content">Integer venenatis, nisi sed congue ...</p>
```

And we'll use the following CSS:

```
.content {
    width: 600px;
}
.shape {
    background: purple;
    shape-outside: polygon(0 0, 100% 40%, 100% 100%, 80% 100%);
    clip-path: polygon(0 0, 100% 40%, 100% 100%, 80% 100%);
    float: left;
    width: 300px;
    height: 300px;
    margin: 20px;
}
```

The shape-outside property determines how other elements in the document will flow around .shape. In order to make elements to actually flow, we've added float: left, as shown in Figure 10.2.

---

[4] http://www.w3.org/TR/css-shapes/

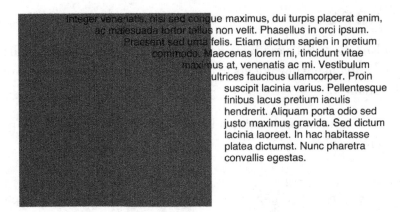

Figure 10.2. Using `shape-outside` without a `clip-path`

However, the background color of `.shape` doesn't follow the edges of the polygon created with `shape-outside`. For that, we need to set a `clip-path` value equal to that of `shape-outside`. That gives us the layout shown in Figure 10.3.

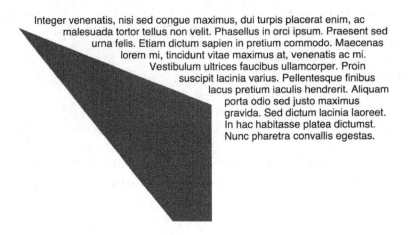

Figure 10.3. An example of the kinds of layouts made possible with CSS Shapes

Support for CSS Shapes is currently limited to Webkit and Blink-based browsers. Chrome 37+ and Opera 24+ support CSS Shapes without a vendor prefix. Safari 7.1+ also supports CSS Shapes, but with a `-webkit-` prefix. Microsoft and Mozilla are still considering whether to implement shapes in their browsers.

Perhaps surprisingly, the `clip-path` property is not defined by the CSS Shapes specification. Instead, it's outlined in CSS Masking Module Level 1[5]. Chrome 24+, Safari 7+ and Opera 15+ support the property with a `-webkit-` vendor prefix. Firefox also supports `clip-path` with a `-moz-` prefix, but doesn't support CSS shapes.

Despite its relative lack of browser support, it's safe to use CSS Shapes in projects. Just ensure that you also use a fallback for browsers that lack support.

Scroll Snap Points

As the web platform grows, it has also gained features that mimic native applications. One such feature is the CSS Scroll Snap Points Module.[6] **Scroll snap points** let developers define the distance an interface should scroll in one instance. You might use it to build slide shows (as in Figure 10.4) or paged interfaces—features that currently require JavaScript and expensive DOM operations.

Figure 10.4. Scroll Snap Points make for great touch-based slide shows

Here's an example using markup and CSS adapted from David Storey's piece "Setting native-like scrolling offsets in CSS with Scrolling Snap Points"[7]:

---

[5] ttp://www.w3.org/TR/css-masking/

[6] http://drafts.csswg.org/css-snappoints/

[7] http://generatedcontent.org/post/66817675443/setting-native-like-scrolling-offsets-in-css-with

```
<div class="slideshow">
    <img src="images/beach.jpg" alt="beach">
    <img src="images/bird.jpg" alt="bird">
    <img src="images/crater-lake.jpg" alt="lake">
    <img src="images/hollywood.jpg" alt="hollywood">
    <img src="images/london.jpg" alt="london">
    <img src="images/snail.jpg" alt="snail">
</div>
```

Now for our CSS:

```
* {
    box-sizing: border-box;
}
html, body {
    padding: 0;
    margin: 0;
}
.slideshow {
    overflow: auto;
    overflow-y: hidden;
    height: 100vh;
    width: 100vw;
    white-space: nowrap;

    /* Internet Explorer 10 and 11 support */
    -ms-scroll-snap-type: mandatory;
    -ms-scroll-snap-points-x: snapInterval(0%, 100%);

    /* Webkit browsers */
    -webkit-scroll-snap-type: mandatory;
    -webkit-scroll-snap-points-x: repeat(100%);

    /* Standardized syntax */
    scroll-snap-type: mandatory;
    snap-points-x: repeat(100%);
}

img {
    width: 100%;
```

```
    height: 100%;
    display: inline-block;
}
```

Internet Explorer 11 supports an older version of the specification, which uses the `snapInterval` function. The latest version of the specification uses `repeat`, but with a slightly different syntax. In both cases, the argument passed determines the distance the scrolling element should move when scrolled.

As a specification, Scroll Snap Points is still in flux. Chromium and the browsers that build on its code base are working to add support; however, we can—and should—start experimenting with implementations now.

Partial support for Scroll Snap Points is available in Internet Explorer 10+ and Microsoft Edge (with the `-ms-` vendor prefix). Firefox 39+ supports Scroll Snap Points, but it must be enabled; properties do not require a prefix. From the `about:config` menu, search for `layout.css.vertical-text.enabled` and toggle its value to true. Scroll Snap Points will also be available in Safari 9 (with a `-webkit-` prefix), a beta version of which is available now. The final version of Safari 9 may or may not be released by the time this book is published.

Blend Modes and CSS Filters

Visual effects is another area of CSS with some interesting activity. Aside from transforms, there are two specifications to keep an eye on: Compositing and Blending Level 1[8] and Filter Effects Module Level 1.[9]

Blend modes make it possible to blend background colors and images using effects commonly found in graphics software such as Photoshop. Defined modes include `multiply`, `screen`, `overlay`, and `color-dodge`. We can use these blend modes to combine layered elements and backgrounds, as shown in Figure 10.5.

---

[8] https://drafts.fxtf.org/compositing-1/
[9] http://www.w3.org/TR/filter-effects/

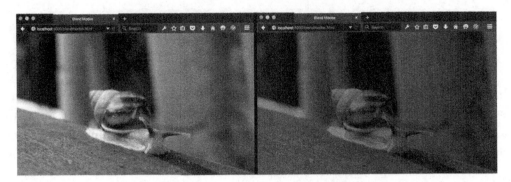

Figure 10.5. The original background image (left) is modified (right) using `background-blend-mode: multiply`

Here we've used the `background-blend-mode` property to give the background photograph a purplish tint. For `background-blend-mode` to work, you'll have to set one or more background images *or* a background image and a background color. To create the background effect in Figure 10.5, you'd use the following CSS:

```
.blend {
    background: orchid url(images/snail.jpg);
    background-blend-mode: multiply;
}
```

Current versions of Chrome, Firefox, Safari, and Opera support the `background-blend-mode` as well as the `mix-blend-mode` property. Safari, however, lacks support for the `hue`, `saturation`, `luminosity`, and `color` filters.

Blend modes affect how the layers within a stacking context may be visually combined. **CSS Filters**, on the other hand, alter the rendering of layers *without* combining them. With CSS Filters, we can blur objects, change them from color to grayscale or sepia tone, modify their hue, or invert their colors. Each CSS filter is a function, and we can use them alone or in a filter list, as shown in Figure 10.6.

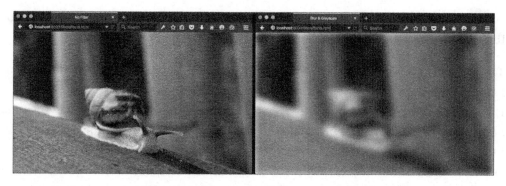

Figure 10.6. The effect of `filter: blur(10px) grayscale(1)`

If we wanted to blur an image and make it grayscale as in Figure 10.6, we can use the following CSS:

```
img {
    filter: blur(10px) grayscale(1);
}
```

Full support for filters are available without a prefix in Firefox 35+. Firefox versions 3.6-34 only support the `url()` function for filters. Chrome 18+, Opera 15+, and Safari 6+ also support filters with a `-webkit-` prefix. Microsoft Edge supports filters, but is without support for the `url()` function. Filter effects can also be animated, unlike blend modes.

Keeping track of all of this can be overwhelming. Just when you think you're up to date on everything, you find a new spec that you didn't know existed, or an existing spec changes in a significant way. Because specifications and implementations are often in flux, keeping up with changes to CSS can be quite tough, but it is possible.

How to Follow Changes and Additions to CSS

The World Wide Web Consortium manages a list of current specifications and their status.[10] If you don't mind getting in the weeds, the CSS Working Group mailing list is a great—though overwhelming—way to track discussions and contribute to the development of CSS specifications. The CSS Working Group also has a Twitter

---

[10] http://www.w3.org/Style/CSS/

account[11] if you'd just like to keep up with developments, rather than wade through the entire list.

There are also several resources for tracking browser support for CSS features. Can I Use[12] is perhaps the leader in this space. It tracks support for a range of CSS, HTML, SVG, and JavaScript features in every major browser across several versions. Some browser vendors also provide their own feature-tracking dashboards. Chrome Status[13] and Platform Status[14] are great ways to keep up with what CSS features are supported in Chrome and Microsoft Edge. Most browser vendors also contribute support data to the robust documentation of the Mozilla Developer Network.[15]

For general CSS tricks, tips, and techniques, CSS-Tricks[16] is an excellent resource. Codrops also has a top-notch CSS Reference[17] that details selectors, properties, and at-rules.

Of course, SitePoint, too, has a treasure trove of CSS-related material. SitePoint.com's HTML and CSS channel has how-to's for getting the most out of Sass and Less, including a Sass Reference.[18] You'll also find introductory articles to CSS frameworks such as Pure, Foundation, and Bootstrap. If you need help, you can always ask a question in the SitePoint Forums.[19]

My hope is that you've come away with a better understanding of a range of CSS topics, including selectors, preprocessors, and project architecture. This, in addition to newer areas of CSS such as media queries, animation, and transforms. These topics will help you on your journey to mastering CSS.

---

[11] https://twitter.com/csswg

[12] http://caniuse.com/

[13] https://www.chromestatus.com/features

[14] http://dev.modern.ie/platform/status/

[15] https://developer.mozilla.org/

[16] https://css-tricks.com

[17] http://tympanus.net/codrops/css_reference/

[18] http://www.sitepoint.com/sass-reference/

[19] http://community.sitepoint.com/c/html-css

CPSIA information can be obtained at www.ICGtesting.com
Printed in the USA
LVOW03s1747220915

455256LV00015B/39/P